Microsoft® Public Cloud Services

Setting up your business in the cloud

Blain Barton

GREG THANKS FOR BEING SO LOYAL TO THE I.T. COMMUNITY.

B-

PUBLISHED BY
Microsoft Press
A division of Microsoft Corporation
One Microsoft Way
Redmond, Washington 98052-6399

Library of Congress Control Number: 2014951856
ISBN: 978-0-7356-9705-8

Printed and bound in the United States of America.

First Printing

Microsoft Press books are available through booksellers and distributors worldwide. If you need support related to this book, email Microsoft Press Support at mspinput@microsoft.com. Please tell us what you think of this book at http://aka.ms/tellpress.

Acquisitions and Developmental Editor: Karen Szall
Editorial Production: Online Training Solutions, Inc. (OTSI)
Technical Reviewer: Randall Galloway; Technical Review services provided by Content Master, a member of CM Group, Ltd.
Copyeditor: Kathy Krause (OTSI)
Indexer: Susie Carr (OTSI)
Cover: Twist Creative • Seattle

Contents at a glance

Contents

What do you think of this book? We want to hear from you!

Microsoft is interested in hearing your feedback so we can improve our books and learning resources for you. To participate in a brief survey, please visit:

http://aka.ms/tellpress

Chapter 6   Build and run servers without using hardware   129

Chapter 7   Understand Server Manager   175

Chapter 8   Run Windows apps remotely   189

Chapter 9   Give users access to third-party apps   205

Chapter 10   Build a website for your business   221

Chapter 11   Build a Windows app by using Windows App Studio   241

What do you think of this book? We want to hear from you!

Microsoft is interested in hearing your feedback so we can improve our books and learning resources for you. To participate in a brief survey, please visit:

http://aka.ms/tellpress

Foreword

Blain Barton has a passion for technology as well as a very deep passion for education. Throughout our years of working together, it has always been apparent that he values the engagement and participation of students as he delivers highly technical topics in a manner that they can enjoy and from which they can glean the technical knowledge he provides to further their education and success. He is both educational and entertaining with his classroom delivery!

I work very closely with local high schools, in addition to the National Center for Women and Information Technology (NCWIT), to provide opportunities for young women to engage in technology activities and further their education in technological topics. Blain has always provided great support for these initiatives and acknowledges the need for more women in technology careers. His support and understanding of these initiatives are greatly valued and have provided some awesome opportunities to our local young women.

Blain has shown great support for education at every level. I have worked with him on many projects, and his determination and excitement for making these platforms available to all individuals is unsurpassed by anyone else I know. He supports many of the initiatives that Hodges University implements to educate a highly diverse population that is inclusive of all who want to learn technology.

In this book, Blain orchestrates the blending of all of the various aspects of Microsoft public cloud services into a comprehensive guide for using these services to their maximum capacity. In doing so, he delivers an informative how-to platform that gives the reader step-by-step instructions to ensure a successful transition to taking full advantage of cloud services and the benefits that they provide. His hard work and dedication to educational platforms is evident from beginning to end. He is truly an educator at heart.

After reading this book, you will possess a greater understanding of the Microsoft Azure platform and the robust business support that it provides, and you will have the knowledge to properly implement the targeted functionality that a business necessitates. Leveraging technology to best suit specific business and financial needs can be difficult, but this book makes it understandable and attainable by providing you with the specific tools and the knowledge you need to properly implement them.

I wish you much success in all of your future endeavors!

—Professor Tracey Lanham

Program Chair of the Computer Information Technology Programs
Hodges University, Fisher School of Technology
https://www.linkedin.com/in/professorlanham

Introduction

Public cloud services give business owners a fantastic opportunity to use the latest technology without investing in hardware and an IT department. More and more businesses are turning to cloud deployments as an efficient way of doing business. Whether you're a student, an entrepreneur, a startup, a small business owner, or a cloud computing professional, this book is for you if you are thinking about a public cloud deployment for your business.

This book steps you through the process of setting up your business in the cloud. It includes instructions and links to demos that will get you started, in addition to some advanced topics. The instructions take advantage of the trial versions of products from Microsoft so you can get up and running quickly and find the right tools for your business.

This "how-to" book assumes you have no working knowledge of Microsoft public cloud services and administration. That's okay; the book will educate you about all the public cloud services that will help you make your business thrive.

Over the last 22 years with Microsoft, I've personally seen a revolutionary technical transformation from "traditional" on-premises infrastructures consisting of the procurement of physical hardware, the provisioning of physical operating system software from physical media, the testing of hubs, the configuring of switches, and the planning and implementation of network topologies. With today's technology, you have the ability to manage all practical aspects of your business without major investments in hardware and software, and without being an experienced IT administrator or hiring a staff to maintain that infrastructure.

As I reflect back to 1988 when I started in Microsoft Manufacturing and Distribution, the company was leading the list of the "top" software companies. At that time, they were listed in order by revenue: Microsoft #1, Lotus #2, and Ashton-Tate #3. New products from Microsoft then included Basic Professional Development System (PDS), QuickBasic 1.0 for the Mac, and three new CD-ROM titles: Microsoft Small Business Consultant, Microsoft Stat Pack, and the Microsoft Programmers Library. The company established subsidiaries in Spain and Korea, and announced plans for a software center in India. Windows 286/386 was introduced, and the company shipped OS/2 with Presentation Manager. Mike Maples joined Microsoft to head the applications division. The Microsoft company meeting was held at the new Washington State Convention Center. The meeting's theme was "Making It All Make Sense," and the gift to attendees was a portable stereo/tape player. Boy, how times have changed.

In a relatively short time, we've moved from assembling "package software" to providing the devices and services available in the world today. The days of putting a CD-ROM or DVD into your computer tray and "locking and loading" the physical software from media are really coming to an end. Now you can pay only for services that you use, as you use them, and often it is just a matter of downloading the software to get started or subscribing to the services. For example, within the Microsoft public cloud, software services such as Microsoft Office 365, Microsoft Azure, and Microsoft Intune are provisioned right from within a Microsoft datacenter. (In the tech world, *provisioning* means providing everything you need related to a service.) When running these services, you don't have to worry about hardware failures and electrical costs.

Over my career, I've personally seen this new technical transformation from physical packaged software to software and services that are accessed from an online portal. What motivates me is making sure we build great experiences that expand your digital lifestyles and work for your businesses, whether you are an individual user, an owner of a small business startup, a student, or one of the IT pros and developers in this world of cloud computing. I was inspired to write this book by a group of students, so I assume my homework assignment is completed.

Prerequisites for setting up your subscriptions

To complete the exercises in this book, you need an Internet browser and a connection to the Internet. You will be downloading free trial versions of various products.

> **IMPORTANT** When you access a free trial version and set up your subscription, the clock starts ticking. You will have access to the product for a limited time. It is important that you do not set up your trial subscription until you need it for the chapter you are reading. If you set up your subscription ahead of time, the subscription might expire before you use it in the exercises in the book.

- **Office 365** To get your trial version of Office 365, go to *http://aka.ms /office365plan*. Scroll down the column under Office 365 Business, and click Free Trial.
- **Microsoft Azure** To get your free 30-day trial of Azure, go to *http://aka.ms/try-azure*.
- **Microsoft Intune** To get your free trial of Microsoft Intune, go to *http://aka.ms/go-intune*.

About the companion content

In addition to the links to demos, articles, and free courses referenced in the book, companion content for this book can be downloaded from the following page:

http://aka.ms/pcs/files

Acknowledgments

I'd like to thank the following people for their contributions to this book: Adnan Cartwright, Yung Chou, Jennelle Crothers, Joe Homnick, Alex Melching, Jeff Mitchell, Dan Stolts, Ed Wilson, Tommy Patterson, James Quick, and Kevin Remde. I also appreciate all the reviewers who generously contributed their time and provided feedback on the drafts of this book. A very special thanks to the folks on the editing team and to Karen Szall for her help in encouraging me to finish this project. Kathy Krause was the steady presence behind the scenes, managing all the pieces in motion. Randall Galloway jumped in with technical reviews, and extra help and advice on how to approach a constantly changing set of products. My thanks to everyone who helped bring this all together.

Free ebooks from Microsoft Press

From technical overviews to in-depth information on special topics, the free ebooks from Microsoft Press cover a wide range of topics. These ebooks are available in PDF, EPUB, and Mobi for Kindle formats, ready for you to download at:

http://aka.ms/mspressfree

Check back often to see what is new!

Microsoft Virtual Academy

Build your knowledge of Microsoft technologies with free expert-led online training from Microsoft Virtual Academy (MVA). MVA offers a comprehensive library of videos, live events, and more to help you learn the latest technologies and prepare for certification exams. You'll find what you need here:

http://www.microsoftvirtualacademy.com

Errata, updates, & book support

We've made every effort to ensure the accuracy of this book and its companion content. You can access updates to this book—in the form of a list of submitted errata and their related corrections—at:

http://aka.ms/pcs/errata

If you discover an error that is not already listed, please submit it to us at the same page.

If you need additional support, email Microsoft Press Book Support at:

mspinput@microsoft.com

Please note that product support for Microsoft software and hardware is not offered through the previous addresses. For help with Microsoft software or hardware, go to:

http://support.microsoft.com

We want to hear from you

At Microsoft Press, your satisfaction is our top priority, and your feedback our most valuable asset. Please tell us what you think of this book at:

http://aka.ms/tellpress

The survey is short, and we read every one of your comments and ideas. Thanks in advance for your input!

Stay in touch

Let's keep the conversation going! We're on Twitter:

http://twitter.com/MicrosoftPress

CHAPTER 1

What the cloud can do for your business

- What is the cloud? **1**

- What kinds of Microsoft public cloud services are available? **2**

- What can Microsoft public cloud services do for your business? **3**

- Putting it all together **4**

What is the cloud?

The cloud: no doubt you've heard that term. But if you're like a lot of people, you might not know what it means—or how it could help your business.

Simply put, *the cloud* refers to software and services that run on the Internet. This is in contrast to the software and services that run locally, on your computer. The cloud is also used to store data. When you store data or use a cloud service, you can access the data from anywhere, using any device that connects to the Internet—not just from your computer's hard drive or your company's network server.

Although people talk about the cloud like it's a single entity, it is in fact made up of massive datacenters all over the world. These centers store the programs and services that people access online, in addition to any data that users upload to the cloud.

There's more than one cloud, and many different types, too. These types include the following:

- **Private cloud**   A cloud that is used solely by a single organization. In a private cloud, the datacenters that support the cloud are on the premises of the organization. The only people who can access the software and services in the cloud, or store data there, are people authorized by the organization to do so. Building and maintaining a private cloud can be a costly endeavor, and might be suitable only for very large organizations. Often, businesses use private datacenters because they need to support older physical computers that have been powering their organizations for years.

- **Public cloud**   Technically, in terms of architecture, there is little difference between a private cloud and a public cloud. But a public cloud is accessible by anyone who wants to use it. Anyone can access software and services on a public cloud, or store data there. Usually, software and services on a public cloud are offered on a "pay-as-you-go" basis, although some are free.

- **Hybrid cloud**   A hybrid cloud is what you might expect—a combination of a private cloud and a public cloud. An organization might take the hybrid cloud approach if, for example, it wanted to store sensitive data on a private cloud, but be able to access that data by using a program on a public cloud.

- **Community cloud**   In this model, a group of organizations with similar needs, interests, or concerns might share a private cloud in order to share resources.

The focus of this book is Microsoft public cloud services.

What kinds of Microsoft public cloud services are available?

Microsoft offers more than 200 public cloud services. These services are divided into three main categories:

- **Software as a service (SaaS)**   SaaS describes a way of licensing and delivering software by using a subscription model. Subscriptions can be paid on a monthly or yearly basis, or through special licensing programs. With SaaS, the software is located in the cloud, and users access it through the Internet. It is not installed on the user's computer. Examples of SaaS are Microsoft Office 365, Xbox Live, and Microsoft Intune.

- **Infrastructure as a service (IaaS)**   With IaaS, users can rent compute, storage, and networking resources by using datacenter hardware to deploy virtual machines. (A *virtual machine* is a virtual computer within a physical computer, implemented in software. It emulates a complete hardware system, from processor to network card.) Users pay for these resources as they would a utility, like power or water, with the cost reflecting the actual amount of resources consumed. Examples of IaaS are virtual machines within Microsoft Azure.

- **Platform as a service (PaaS)**   With PaaS, users can develop, run, and manage web apps in a ready-made, cloud-based environment. Examples of using PaaS include building an app, an SQL database, or a website.

What can Microsoft public cloud services do for your business?

Microsoft public cloud services can help your business in lots of ways. Most notably, they can save you money. For one thing, by using Microsoft public cloud services, you can avoid purchasing expensive servers. With cloud services, you can run your business by using devices like smartphones, laptops, tablets, and printers. You can also scale back your IT staffing. After all, less hardware to support means a smaller in-house staff to support it. But there are other, less obvious savings. For example, if your business uses cloud services, your staff might be able to work from home on a permanent basis. That will help you save on your lease, utility bills, garbage services, and office supplies.

Using Microsoft public cloud services can also help you grow your business. You can use the money you save to invest in other areas of your business, like people and marketing. As your business grows, you can scale up your use of these services.

Perhaps most importantly, with Microsoft public cloud services, you can focus on your business, not on the technology needed to run it. These services are always on and always connected. You pay only for what you consume, by using a transparent infrastructure that runs 24 hours a day, 7 days a week, and 365 days a year to meet the needs of your business. Unlike your staff, Microsoft public cloud services never take a vacation. Moreover, these services are constantly evolving, bringing more uptime, elasticity, scale, on-demand networking, computing, and storage.

Throughout the rest of this book, you'll explore using several Microsoft public cloud-based tools to run your business. These include the following:

- **Microsoft Azure**   Azure is the Microsoft cloud platform, offering a collection of compute, storage, data, networking, and app services. It is both an IaaS and a PaaS and is used to build, deploy, and manage apps and websites.

- **Azure Site Recovery**   With Azure Site Recovery, employees can back up or replicate and recover important data.

- **Azure RemoteApp**   With RemoteApp, employees can access desktop programs on their local computers from any Internet-connected laptop, tablet, or smartphone.

- **Office 365**   Office 365 makes all the Office programs that office workers know so well (Microsoft Word, Excel, PowerPoint, Outlook, OneNote, Access, and Publisher) available online on a subscription basis.

- **Microsoft Intune**   With Microsoft Intune, employees can gain protected access to corporate programs, data, and resources from virtually anywhere, using almost any device.

- **Microsoft Skype for Business**   With this cloud service, employees can easily place audio and video calls and exchange instant messages.

- **Microsoft Dynamics CRM Online**   Drive sales and marketing with this online customer relationship management (CRM) solution.

- **Yammer Services**   With this private social network tool, employees can quickly self-organize, collaborate, and make decisions.

- **Office 365 Video**   Use this video-streaming service to bring world-class video streaming to your organization.

- **Server Manager**   With this tool, you can view and manage your server's productivity both in the cloud and on-premises.

- **OneDrive for Business**   With OneDrive for Business, you can securely store all your files and share them with coworkers. Files can be synchronized across all your devices, so that you can access them anywhere, anytime, whether you're online or not.

- **Windows App Studio**   Want to create an app? Then App Studio is for you. With App Studio, you can quickly build, test, and share Windows and Windows Phone apps.

> ### Preparing your plan
>
> How do you know which Microsoft public cloud services are for you? To answer that, you'll need a strong business plan. This book does not cover building a business plan, but I encourage you to seek out information about building one. (There are some great sample business plans in Office 365.) Building a business plan will help you identify the needs of your business. When you know these, you can determine what services you will need.

Putting it all together

Each Microsoft public cloud-based service is a formidable tool in its own right. But it's when you put them all together, creating an ecosystem of services and devices, that they really shine. Just imagine a scenario in which features like Office 365, Microsoft Intune, and Azure work with services like Windows Server, Microsoft Dynamics CRM Online, Yammer, and Skype for Business, all connected to your various devices. No matter where you travel, these services and your data travel with you. Even better, you leave all the hardware and maintenance to Microsoft, freeing you to focus on running your business (see Figure 1-1).

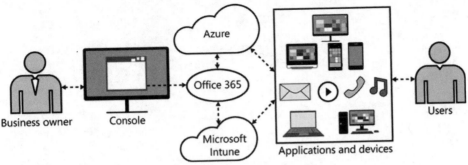

FIGURE 1-1 Microsoft public cloud services leave you free to focus on running your business.

Summary

- *The cloud* refers to software and services that run on the Internet. The cloud is also used to store data and build business intelligence.

- When you store data or use a service in the cloud, you can access it from anywhere, with any device that connects to the Internet, including Windows, iOS, and Android devices.

- The cloud is made up of massive datacenters all over the world. There is more than one cloud, and many different types. These include private clouds, public clouds, hybrid clouds, and community clouds.

- Microsoft offers more than 200 public cloud services. These are divided into three main categories: software as a service (SaaS), infrastructure as a service (IaaS), and platform as a service (PaaS).

- Using Microsoft public cloud services for your business can help you save money, grow your business, and focus on your business rather than on the hardware support needed to run it.

- Although each public cloud-based service is a formidable tool in its own right, it's when you put them all together, creating an ecosystem of services and devices, that they really shine.

CHAPTER 2

Get started with Office 365

Introduction to Office 365

Microsoft Office has long offered a range of applications to boost productivity. These include the following:

- **Word**   Microsoft Word is a word-processor program. It's ideal for generating documents of all kinds.

- **Excel**   Microsoft Excel is a program for handling spreadsheets. You can use spreadsheets to store and analyze data in tabular form, which makes them ideal for handling accounting and bookkeeping tasks.

- **PowerPoint**   If your business requires you to create slideshows or presentations, you'll appreciate the many robust and built-in features of Microsoft PowerPoint.

- **Outlook**   Microsoft Outlook serves as a full-featured email client, calendar, task manager, and address book.

- **OneNote**   With Microsoft OneNote, you can gather notes—even ones that are handwritten—drawings, screen clips, and audio files into one easy-to-access place. It's great for brainstorming or just keeping track of ideas.

- **Access**   Microsoft Access is a database management system. If you need to track data for your business, you can use Access to do it.
- **Publisher**   With the Microsoft Publisher desktop-publishing application, users can quickly and easily design marketing materials like brochures, business cards, newsletters, calendars, and more.

Office 365 is like Office, except it expands its domain from the personal computer to the cloud. Office 365, one of the public cloud-based services offered by Microsoft, is a software as a service (SaaS) suite that includes not only the personal computer versions of Office, but also mobile versions and the server services needed to connect them. With Office 365, you can use the familiar applications you've probably run on your PC for years—Word, Excel, and PowerPoint, and in some cases, depending on which subscription option you choose, Outlook, OneNote, Access, and Publisher—to save, edit, and modify documents in the cloud. In addition, you can store the files you create in Microsoft OneDrive for Business, which is included with the bundle. (You'll learn more about OneDrive for Business in Chapter 3, "Store your files in the cloud with OneDrive for Business.")

MICROSOFT VIRTUAL ACADEMY   Get more information about Office 365 fundamentals at *aka.ms/go-mva/o365fund.*

Some subscription models of Office 365 also include the following:

- **Yammer**   Yammer collaboration software is like a private social network. You can use Yammer to get connected to the right people, share information across teams, and organize around projects so you can go further, faster. With Yammer, collaboration just happens—even on the go. Yammer helps your company work like a network so you can listen, adapt, and grow in new ways.
- **Office 365 Video**   Office 365 Video is a website portal where people in your organization can post and view videos. Essentially, it's a streaming video service for your organization. Videos can be organized by channel. For example, you might have one channel for a specific group or department and another for a particular subject.

Of course, individual users can optimize their productivity by using the top-notch applications that Office 365 offers. But the power of Office 365 really lies in its support for collaboration and the sharing of information. With Office 365, teams can work together, tracking tasks, project timelines, documents, and emails all from one centralized place. If you're ready to learn more about Office 365—what it's good for and how to set it up—read on!

IMPORTANT   A detailed overview of the ins and outs of the various Office 365 applications—for example, Word and Excel—is beyond the scope of this book. Instead, this chapter will focus on getting you set up to use Office 365.

Skype for Business

Another program, Skype for Business, has recently been updated to work seamlessly with Office 365. With Skype for Business, previously known as Microsoft Lync, users can make calls online—including international calls—by using almost any device. Instant messaging is also supported. For more information, go to *www.skype.com/en/business.*

Under the hood of Office 365

There are three main functions inside Office 365 that support the collaboration and sharing of information, providing a singular experience:

- **Exchange Online**   Microsoft Exchange Online facilitates email management and administration. With Exchange, you can synchronize email, calendars, and contacts across all your devices.

- **SharePoint**   Every business has a repository of files used to conduct day-to-day business. Microsoft SharePoint provides a place to store and manage all those files, and to manage access to them. SharePoint also helps with keeping track of multiple versions of a file and setting up notifications when a new version is ready. SharePoint can even help with building workflows for business processes.

- **Skype for Business**   Skype for Business, previously known as Lync, integrates with Exchange and SharePoint to facilitate real-time communications like instant messages, video and audio meetings, and screen sharing, across all devices. This makes collaboration a breeze. You can also use Skype for Business to determine each user's status—for example, "Available" or "In a Meeting," with color coding to help convey information at a glance—thanks to a feature called presence. For example, if you have a meeting scheduled on your calendar, Skype for Business automatically sets your presence to "In a Meeting" and sets your color to red to indicate that you are busy.

All this happens behind the curtain. There's no need for you to manage these operations. Instead, you can focus on running your business!

IMPORTANT   If you are using or are going to use Office 365, set up your tenant for Office 365 first, then Microsoft Intune, followed by Microsoft Azure Directory integration. You'll find more information about tenants in Chapter 9, "Give users access to third-party applications.

Find the right subscription

Office 365 is an SaaS suite. As such, it is subscription-based (also known as license-based). Microsoft offers various subscription plans to fit your needs. All Office 365 plans are billed monthly for the total number of users.

To determine which subscription option is right for your business, you must first identify your business needs. Then it's a matter of determining which Office 365 features will help you meet those needs. With your subscription, you pay for only those features you need and that will deliver the most for your business right now. You can always upgrade (or downgrade) your subscription if needed.

All Office 365 subscriptions offer the following:

- **A 99.9-percent financially backed uptime guarantee**   That is, the servers on which the Office 365 services are hosted are guaranteed to be up and running 99.9 percent of the time.

- **Phone and web support**   Get help with critical issues 24 hours a day, seven days a week, not just during regular business hours.

- **A community forum**   Use this to look up information and work with other users to find quick answers.

There are two primary subscription groups:

- **Office 365 Business**   The options in this group are meant for organizations that have fewer than 300 users.

- **Office 365 Enterprise**   Office 365 Enterprise does not have a user limit.

> **TIP**   Don't be afraid if you're on the edge of 300 users. You can easily upgrade your subscription from Office 365 Business to Enterprise.

Office 365 Business subscription options for small and medium organizations

The Office 365 Business subscription group offers the following options:

- Office 365 Business Essentials
- Office 365 Business
- Office 365 Business Premium

> **NOTE**   Because the pricing of each of these subscription options is subject to change, no pricing information is included here. For up-to-date information on pricing and features, go to *products.office.com/en-us/business/compare-more-office-365-for-business-plans*. When you are ready to choose a plan, go to *aka.ms/office365plan*.

Table 2-1 presents all the Office 365 Business subscription options and their corresponding features.

TABLE 2-1 Office 365 Business subscription options

Feature	Office 365 Business Essentials	Office 365 Business	Office 365 Business Premium
Full, installed Office applications (Word, Excel, PowerPoint, Outlook, Publisher, and OneNote) on up to five PCs or Macs per user		X	X
Office Mobile apps on up to five Windows Phone, Android, or iOS (Apple) tablets and phones per user		X	X
Online versions of Office, including Word, Excel, and PowerPoint	X	X	X
File storage and sharing on OneDrive for Business with 1 terabyte (TB) of storage per user	X	X	X
Business class email, calendar, and contacts with a 50-gigabyte (GB) inbox	X	X	X
Unlimited online meetings, instant messaging (IM), and video conferencing	X		X
An intranet site for your teams, with customizable security settings	X		X
A corporate social network (Yammer) to help employees collaborate across departments	X		X
Personalized search and discovery	X		X

Office Online web apps

As shown here, some Office 365 subscription options include desktop versions of the suite's various applications—such as Word and Excel. In addition to these versions, there are also Office Online versions of these applications. These online versions are Internet based. That is, you access and use them through your Internet browser—for example, Internet Explorer, Safari, Firefox, or Chrome. These applications have less functionality than the desktop versions but are great if you need to use them on devices that don't have the desktop versions installed.

Using the 30-day trial

Not ready to make a decision about which subscription option is right for you? Don't worry. Microsoft offers a free 30-day trial for some subscription options. To use it, go to *aka.ms/office365plan*, click the appropriate Free Trial link near the bottom of the page, and follow the directions in this book's introduction to set everything up.

MICROSOFT VIRTUAL ACADEMY Get more information about how to get the most out of your Office 365 trial at *aka.ms/go-mva/office365trial*.

Sign in for the first time

As soon as you've decided which subscription model you want to use and have set everything up, your next step is to configure the service and get started with some management tasks. First, however, you'll need to sign in. When you access Office 365 for the first time, a Welcome page appears. Follow these steps to complete the first-time sign-in process:

1. Enter the requested basic information about who you are and where you're located (see Figure 2-1). Click Next to continue.

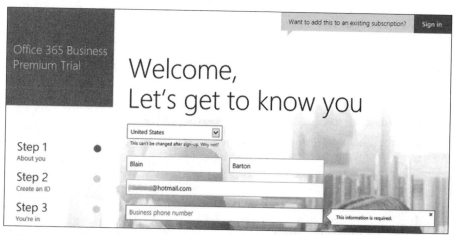

FIGURE 2-1 The first step in creating your new ID is to provide some basic information.

2. Create your user ID and password (see Figure 2-2), which you'll use to access the service. Enter a user name (such as **admin**) and the domain name. Then create your password. Enter your password a second time for confirmation, and click Next.

FIGURE 2-2 Create your user name and password.

IMPORTANT Make sure you establish a strong password policy for all users. Strong passwords use a mix of uppercase and lowercase letters, numbers, and special characters such as the asterisk or dollar sign. Learn more about creating strong passwords at *aka.ms/secure-password*.

Notice the box to the right of the User ID box. It contains a blank space followed by the text *.onmicrosoft.com*. This text is part of a domain name that Microsoft automatically creates when you sign in to Office 365 for the first time. You provide the rest of the domain name by typing it into the blank space in the box. For example, suppose your company is called Trawbridge. In that case, you might enter **trawbridge** in the blank space. The domain name would then be *trawbridge.onmicrosoft.com*.

NOTE A *domain name* is a string of text that appears in a URL or email address. For example, for the URL *www.microsoft.com*, the domain name is *microsoft.com*. Similarly, *trawbridge.com* is the domain name in the email address gchan@trawbridge.com.

NOTE Don't worry—if you already have a domain name for your company, you can associate it with Office 365. For example, if you already own the domain name *trawbridge.com*, you'll have the chance to set that as your domain name, omitting the *onmicrosoft*, in a moment.

3. On the next page (see Figure 2-3), select either Send Text Message or Call Me. Depending on what you choose, you will receive either a text message or a phone call to confirm that you are who you say you are and to create a valid account. Enter your phone number. Then, depending on which option you chose, click Text Me (as shown here) or Call Me.

FIGURE 2-3 Complete the security verification to finish creating an ID.

After you enter the required information, you will receive a verification message via a text message on your phone. When you do, click Create My Account on the verification page.

Explore the Office 365 Admin Center

You use the Office 365 Admin Center to set up your organization in the cloud. The Office 365 Admin Center opens to a Dashboard page. On the left is a navigation pane, which you use to access different areas of the Admin Center. Click the app launcher in the upper-left corner of the title bar to activate the app tiles, as shown in Figure 2-4. These tiles give you access to the settings for Exchange, Skype for Business, SharePoint, and any other apps you have installed. If you are the administrator, an Admin tile also appears.

FIGURE 2-4 The Admin Center provides quick access to various apps, so that you can set up new user accounts and manage your subscription.

Configure a custom domain

> **IMPORTANT** If you do not have a custom domain name at this time, use the default domain name created for you. You can always go back and change it after you have purchased a custom domain from a provider.

If your organization already has a custom domain name, configure it as follows:

1. In the Office 365 Admin Center, click the Domains link in the navigation pane on the left side of the page, as shown in Figure 2-5.

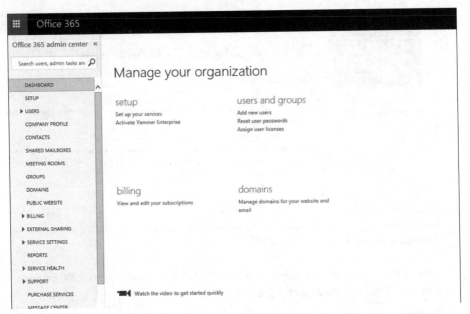

FIGURE 2-5 Click Domains to configure your new domain settings.

2. On the Manage Domains page, shown in Figure 2-6, click Add Domain. This starts a wizard that walks you through adding your domain to Office 365.

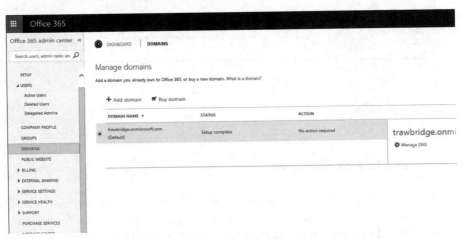

FIGURE 2-6 Click Add Domain to add a domain you already own.

3. The Add A New Domain In Office 365 Wizard opens, showing a brief description of the three-step process of adding a domain (see Figure 2-7). Click Let's Get Started.

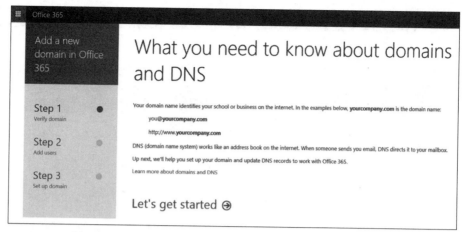

FIGURE 2-7 Add a domain to Office 365.

4. Enter the name of the domain that you own—in this example, **trawbridge.com**, as shown in Figure 2-8—and click Next.

FIGURE 2-8 Enter the custom domain name.

5. In the next step of the wizard, you will confirm ownership of the domain. How you do this depends on what Domain Name System (DNS) hosting provider, or registrar, you use. To find out what steps you must take, click the drop-down list and click your hosting provider.

6. After you complete the steps required by your hosting provider, you'll be prompted to sign in to your account with that provider, as shown in Figure 2-9.

> **NOTE** The remaining steps vary based on your setup and provider.

FIGURE 2-9 Confirm that you own the domain.

7. Enter the user name and password for your hosting account, as shown in Figure 2-10, and click Secure Login. The wizard checks to make sure that you own the domain name you have entered. (Note that this check can take up to 72 hours.)

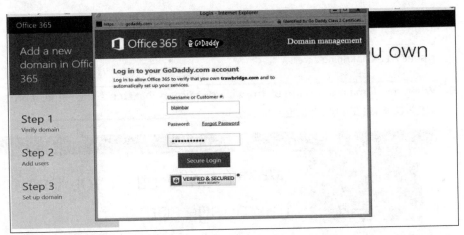

FIGURE 2-10 When prompted, enter the user name and password for your account with the hosting provider.

IMPORTANT You will sign in after the end of the subscription process, and the subscription process will sign you out. You then must sign in as the new account, which in my case is *admin@trawbridge.com*, with the same password that I had for the previous domain.onmicrosoft.com.

8. When prompted, confirm that you want to make a change to the domain by clicking Accept on the page shown in Figure 2-11.

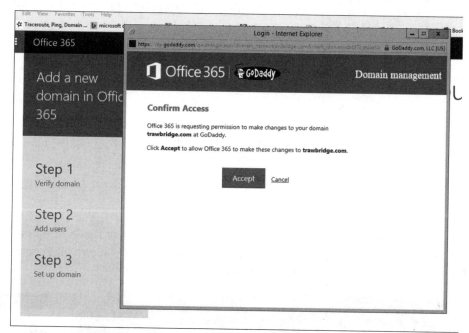

FIGURE 2-11 Confirming access.

9. When the domain is confirmed, the wizard indicates that step 1, the verification process, is complete (see Figure 2-12). Click Next.

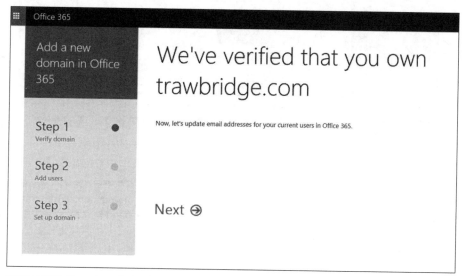

FIGURE 2-12 Your domain has been verified.

10. The Let's Update Your Current Office 365 Users page appears (see Figure 2-13). For now, click Skip This Step. (You will learn how to add users in the next section.)

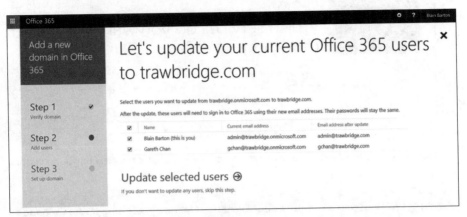

FIGURE 2-13 Skip step 2 for now.

11. The Get Ready To Update DNS Records To Work With Office 365 page appears (see Figure 2-14). Click Next.

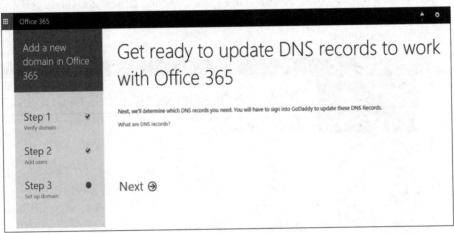

FIGURE 2-14 Begin step 3, updating DNS records to work with Office 365.

12. The wizard asks you which services you want to use with your domain (see Figure 2-15). Select the Outlook For Email, Calendar, And Contacts check box. Also select the Lync For Instant Messaging And Online Meetings check box. Then click Next.

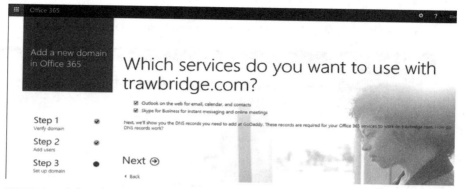

FIGURE 2-15 Select the Outlook and Lync check boxes and click the Next button to continue.

NOTE You can find out more about Exchange Online by referring to the Exchange Guides at *aka.ms/exchangeguides*.

13. If your domain is registered with GoDaddy, you can add your DNS records automatically. Click Add Records, as shown in Figure 2-16, and Office 365 will do the rest. If your domain is registered with another provider, click Add These Records Yourself and follow the prompts.

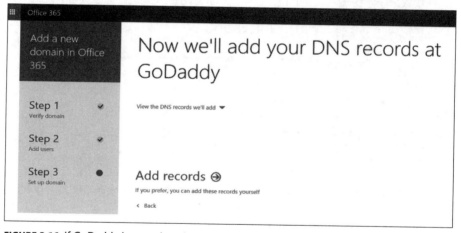

FIGURE 2-16 If GoDaddy is your domain provider, click Add Records to set up the DNS records automatically.

14. After Office 365 validates that the records are configured correctly, you are redirected to the Manage Domains section of the Office 365 Admin Center, shown in Figure 2-17. Notice that the domain you added appears.

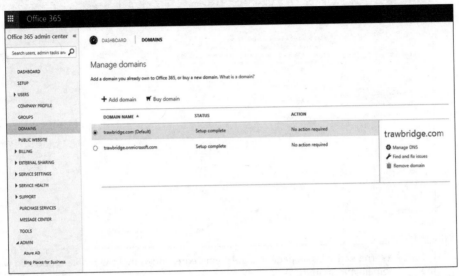

FIGURE 2-17 The domain you added appears on the Manage Domains page in the Admin Center.

15. Sign out from your Office 365 account. Then sign back in with the new account (in this case, **admin@trawbridge.com**) with the same password that you had for the previous domain.onmicrosoft.com (see Figure 2-18).

FIGURE 2-18 Sign out and sign back in using the new account.

16. The profile is updated with the new domain information and will be available when you sign in (see Figure 2-19).

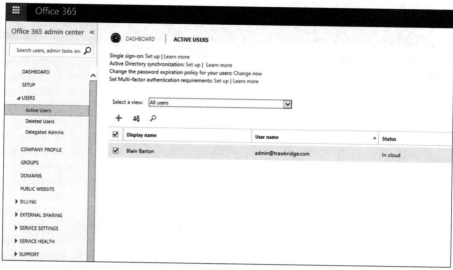

FIGURE 2-19 The Active Users page in the Admin Center shows that the profile is updated with the new domain information.

Add, edit, and delete user accounts

Unless you run a one-person operation, you'll likely need to add other users to your Office 365 subscription. When you do, they can use all the programs and features that Office 365 provides.

To add a user to Office 365, sign in to your Office 365 account and open the Admin Center. Then follow these steps:

1. Click Users and then Active Users in the pane on the left.

2. Click the Add User button (the plus sign). The Create New User Account page opens (see Figure 2-20).

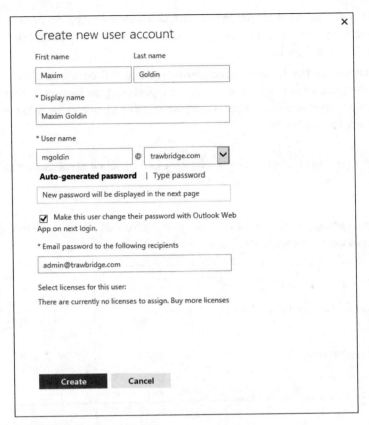

FIGURE 2-20 Create a new user.

3. Enter the following information. When you're finished, click Create.

- **First name**   This is the user's first name.
- **Last name**   This is the user's last name.
- **Display name**   When you enter the user's first and last names, they are automatically concatenated for the display name. If you want to change the display name to a nickname or some other type of shorthand, go ahead and do it now.
- **User name**   This is the name your new user will use to sign in to his or her account when accessing Office 365. Be sure to click your new custom domain in the drop-down list on the right.
- **Password**   If you leave the default Auto-Generated Password, a random password will be chosen and emailed to the user. Alternatively, you can set a password for the user. To do so, click Type Password and enter the password you want to use.

NOTE   The initial password is temporary. The user will need to change it within 90 days.

- **Make this user change their password with Outlook Web App on next login** Select this check box if you want the user to change the password the next time he or she signs in.

- **Email password to the following recipients** After you choose a password option, enter the user's email address so that the password can be sent to that user. Also enter your own email address so that you, the administrator, also get the password, for safekeeping.

> **NOTE** This email address should be one to which the user currently has access. Don't send it to his or her new Office 365 email address.

4. A confirmation message similar to the one shown in Figure 2-21 informs you that the user account has been created. Click Close.

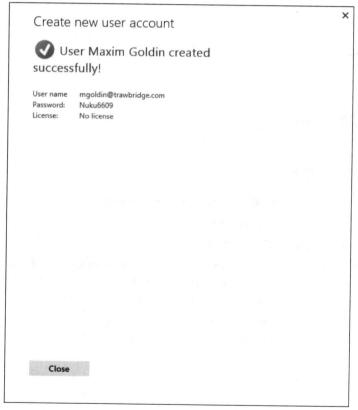

FIGURE 2-21 You'll receive a notification that the account has been successfully created.

If you prefer, you can add multiple users at the same time.

TIP Before you begin this process, make sure you have enough licenses for everyone you want to add. To find out how many subscriptions you have available, click the Billing option in the left pane of the Admin Center and click Subscriptions. If you need to purchase more licenses, click the Change License Quantity link and follow the prompts.

To add multiple users, follow these steps:

1. In Excel, create a spreadsheet with the following column headings:
   - User Name
   - First Name
   - Last Name
   - Display Name
   - Job Title
   - Department
   - Office Number
   - Office Phone
   - Mobile Phone
   - Fax
   - Address
   - City
   - State or Province
   - Postal Code
   - Country or Region

2. Populate the spreadsheet with the information for each person you want to add. The User Name and Display Name fields are required for each user. To leave other fields blank, enter a space followed by a comma. When you're finished, save the spreadsheet.

3. In the Office 365 Admin Center, click Users and then Active Users in the pane on the left. Then click the Add Users button (the button with two people and a plus sign).

4. The Bulk Add Users Wizard starts. On the Select A CSV File page, click the Browse button and locate and select the spreadsheet you created in steps 1 and 2. Then click Next.

5. The wizard verifies that the entries in the spreadsheet are formatted correctly. If there are no errors, click Next. (If there are errors, view the verification log, and then correct the errors in your spreadsheet.)

6. On the Settings page, click Allowed. Then click the Select A Location drop-down list and click the country or region where these users are located. Finally, click Next.

7. On the Assign Licenses page, click the licenses you want to apply for the individuals listed in your spreadsheet. Then click Next.

8. On the Send Results In Email page, enter the email address of anyone who should receive a list of these new users, along with their temporary passwords, via email. Then click Create. The list is emailed to the address you specified.

9. The Results page lists the users whose accounts were created and their temporary passwords. Click Close to close the wizard.

10. Notify each user that his or her account has been created and supply each user with his or her temporary password.

Sometimes a user's information changes. For example, a user might get married and change his or her name. Fortunately, editing a user account to reflect this and other changes is simple. To edit a user account, sign in to your Office 365 account and open the Admin Center. Then follow these steps:

1. In the Office 365 Admin Center, click Users and then Active Users in the pane on the left.

2. On the page that appears, click the user whose account you want to edit. Then click Edit.

3. The Details page appears. If the information on this page is OK as is, click Save. If you need to change any information on this page, do so before you click Save.

4. Click Settings. Follow the same procedure as with the Details page.

5. On the Licenses page, retain, replace, or add licenses as needed. Then click Save.

If a user leaves your organization, you should delete his or her account. Not only will this prevent the departed employee from accessing the account, it will free up the associated license for a new user. To delete a user account, sign in to your Office 365 account and open the Admin Center. Then follow these steps:

1. In the Office 365 Admin Center, click Users and then Active Users in the pane on the left.

2. On the page that appears (see Figure 2-22), click the user whose account you want to delete. Then click Delete.

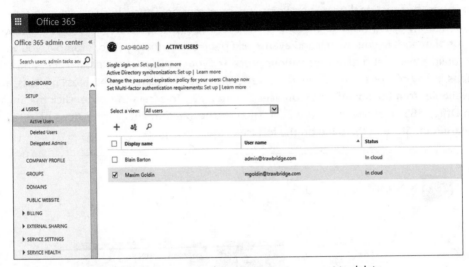

FIGURE 2-22 Select the check box next to the user account you want to delete.

3. In the confirmation message that appears, click Yes.

Work with files

Your Office 365 subscription includes SharePoint. SharePoint offers the following built-in tools:

- **Team sites**   With SharePoint, a team site is created automatically. You can create additional team sites as needed. These SharePoint team sites are used for collaboration within teams, such as for managing shared content, tracking tasks, posting announcements, and managing workflow.

- **Document libraries**   You can use SharePoint document libraries to store, organize, sync, and share documents. Because all your documents are in one place, everybody can access the latest versions whenever they need them. You can also use document libraries to sync your documents to your local computer for offline access. You can create document libraries for each project you're working on or for specific types of documents, such as reports, presentations, or proposals.

- **Custom lists**   With the Custom List app, you can build and share custom lists.

- **Task lists**   You can use the built-in Tasks app to build and share task lists. That way, you can delegate to team members as needed.

- **Site Mailbox**   The Site Mailbox app helps you keep emails and documents close together by connecting your site to an Exchange mailbox. You can then view your email on SharePoint and view site documents in Outlook.

In addition to these built-in apps, there are several other apps that you can add to your SharePoint team sites. Some are free, whereas others must be purchased. Adding apps really expands the functionality of SharePoint and, by extension, Office 365. For example, you can add a forms library (used to create and store forms), a picture library (great if you deal with a lot of images in your work), and even a wiki page library (handy if, for example, you want to build a wiki that outlines the various processes you use in your business). These and other apps, many of which are designed for a specific type of business or business process, are available from the SharePoint Store (see Figure 2-23). To access this page, click the Sites tile in Office 365, as shown in Figure 2-24. Then, in the Site Contents > Your Apps page, click SharePoint Store in the pane on the left (see Figure 2-25).

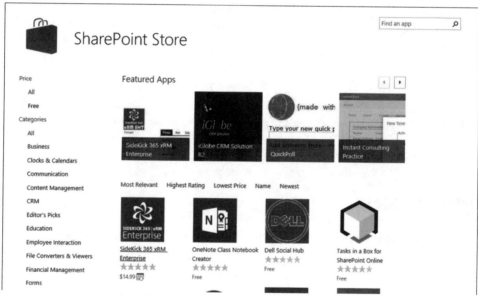

FIGURE 2-23 You can buy many types of SharePoint apps in the SharePoint Store.

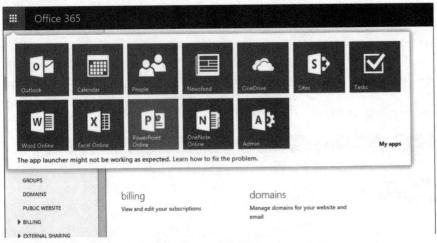

FIGURE 2-24 Choose Sites from the main Office 365 tiles.

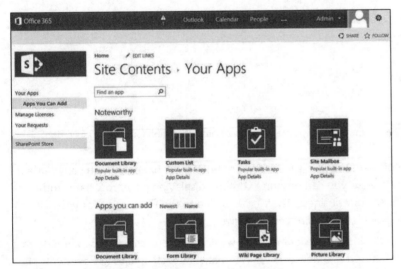

FIGURE 2-25 Open the SharePoint Store from this screen.

To explore your SharePoint tools and settings, sign in to your Office 365 account and open the Admin Center. Then follow these steps:

1. Click the Admin menu and choose SharePoint. Your main SharePoint page opens. Here the SharePoint team sites of which you are a member are displayed.

2. Click a team site to view the content created and shared by that team.

3. Click Documents in the navigation pane on the left to display a list of documents available on that team site—that is, the contents of the team site's document library.

4. Click a document to open it. Alternatively, you can click the ellipsis (…) to the right of the document to open a preview of the document, as shown in Figure 2-26. You can click Edit to open and edit the document without checking it out and locking it so others cannot edit it while you are in the file. Also, you can click the ellipsis on the lower right to view a list of menu choices, and click Check Out to lock the file and check it out to you for edit. Figure 2-26 shows a SharePoint team site with the Office Online version of Excel and its menu displayed.

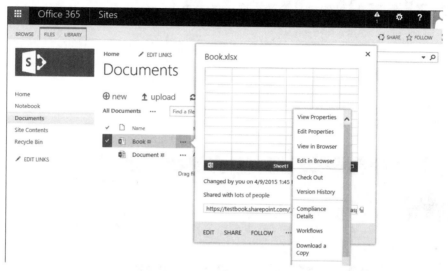

FIGURE 2-26 A SharePoint team site represents a centralized location for your organization's documents.

To make it easier for team members to find your files in a list or library, you can create a view. When you create a view, you can organize content, displaying it by type, date, author, or a custom value specific to your business. The view is added to the View menu for your list or library. For help adding views, see *aka.ms/addingviews*.

SharePoint supports document versioning. With versioning, you can have each update to a document saved and recorded as a new version. Alternatively, each update will overwrite the previous version of the file.

> **TIP** Checking out a file is the safest way to edit a document. It ensures that there aren't two people editing the document at the same time.

Use Office Mobile on all your devices

Your business can benefit by having Office available on all your mobile devices—including your Windows Phone, Android, or iOS (Apple) smartphone or tablet. As you discovered earlier in this chapter, in the section "Find the right subscription," many subscription options allow for as many as five devices per user, including mobile devices.

You can use the following Office applications while you're on the go:

- Word
- Excel
- PowerPoint
- OneNote
- Outlook
- Yammer

Figure 2-27 shows a device with Office installed. In addition, you can set up your mobile device to use OneDrive for Business and Skype for Business (Lync).

FIGURE 2-27 You can install Microsoft Office for iPad on your iPad.

How you set up your device depends on what type of device you have—Windows Phone, Android, or iOS. The following lists provide more information:

- **Windows Phone**

    - For help setting up Office Mobile on your Windows Phone, go to *aka.ms/win-phone-setup-office.*

    - For help setting up email on your Windows Phone, go to *aka.ms/android-phone-setup-email.*

- **Android**

    - For help setting up Office Mobile on your Android device, go to *aka.ms/win-phone-setup-email.*

    - For help setting up email on your Android device, go to *aka.ms/android-setup-email.*

- **iOS**

    - For help setting up Office Mobile on your iPhone, go to *aka.ms/iphone-setup-office.*

    - For help setting up Office Mobile on your iPad, go to *aka.ms/ipad-setup-office.*

    - For help setting up email on your iPhone or iPad, go to *aka.ms/iphone-ipad-setup-email.*

Summary

- Office has long offered a range of applications to boost productivity. Office 365 is like Office, but it expands its domain from the personal computer to the cloud.

- Office 365 is a software as a service (SaaS) suite that includes not only the personal computer versions of Office, but also mobile versions and the server services needed to connect them.

- With Office 365, you can use the familiar applications you've probably run on your PC for years—Word, Excel, and PowerPoint, and in some cases, depending on which subscription option you choose, Outlook, OneNote, Access, and Publisher—to save, edit, and modify documents in the cloud. Some subscription models also offer Yammer and Office 365 Video.

- Exchange facilitates email management and administration and can be used to synchronize mail, calendars, and contacts across all your devices.

- Every business has a repository of files used to conduct day-to-day business. SharePoint provides a place to store and manage all those files, and to manage access to them. SharePoint also helps with keeping track of multiple versions of a file and setting up notifications when a new version is ready. SharePoint can even help with building workflows for business processes.

- Skype for Business integrates with Exchange and SharePoint to facilitate real-time communications like international calling options, instant messages, video and audio meetings, and screen sharing, across all devices. This makes collaboration a breeze. With Skype for Business, you can also view each user's status—for example, "Available" or "In a Meeting," with color coding to help convey information at a glance—thanks to a feature called *presence*. For example, if you have a meeting scheduled on your calendar, Your presence is automatically set to "In a Meeting" and your color is set to red to indicate that you are busy.

- Some Office 365 subscription offerings include the full Office desktop software version in addition to hosted versions of Exchange, SharePoint, Skype for Business, and OneDrive for Business, all of which can be accessed via Microsoft public cloud services. Office web apps offer more limited features but are free.

- The first time you access Office 365, you will create a user account.

- The Office 365 Admin Center lists links for your services and includes an Admin drop-down menu along the top of the page. This menu gives you access to Office 365 settings, in addition to settings for Exchange, Skype for Business, and SharePoint. On the left is a navigation pane, which you use to access different areas of the Admin Center.

- If your organization has a custom domain, such as trawbridge.com, you can configure Office 365 to use it.

- Unless you run a one-person operation, you'll likely need to add other users to your Office 365 subscription. When you do, they can use all the programs and features that Office 365 provides. Doing so is easy.

- Your Office 365 subscription includes SharePoint. SharePoint offers several built-in tools, including team sites, document libraries, custom lists, task lists, and a site mailbox. In addition to these built-in apps, there are several other apps that you can add to your SharePoint team sites.

- Your business can benefit by having Office available on all your mobile devices— including your Windows Phone, Android, or iOS (Apple) smartphone or tablet. Many subscription options allow for as many as five devices per user, including mobile devices. Although not all Office 365 applications are available for Office Mobile, you can use Word, Excel, PowerPoint, OneNote, Outlook, and Yammer while on the go. In addition, you can set up your mobile device to use OneDrive for Business and Skype for Business.

CHAPTER 3

Store your files in the cloud by using OneDrive for Business

Introduction to OneDrive for Business

Employees in your organization no doubt work with data, video, and audio, so where should these files be stored?

Of course, you could purchase expensive hardware to handle the storage of these files, but that would require a significant outlay of capital, not to mention the workload involved in managing them. A better option is to store this data in the cloud. That way, your users can access it anytime, anywhere, and with just about any device (as long as they have an Internet connection).

Microsoft offers a product with which you can do just that: Microsoft OneDrive for Business. OneDrive for Business is a cloud-based file storage service that helps with security for your files. With OneDrive for Business, you can store and access your files online.

NOTE OneDrive for Business is also different from the Microsoft SharePoint team sites and document libraries discussed in Chapter 2, "Get started with Office 365." These tools are designed for storing team-related or project-related documents.

Find the right subscription

If you have subscribed to Microsoft Office 365, you already have OneDrive for Business. Each Office 365 user has unlimited storage space. (Note that this chapter assumes you have an Office 365 subscription.)

If you don't have an Office 365 subscription, you can subscribe to OneDrive for Business as a standalone application. Different subscription plans offer varying amounts of storage space. For details, go to *https://onedrive.live.com/about/en-us/plans/.* If you've already created a user ID and password for Microsoft products, click the Sign In button to add the OneDrive for Business subscription to any existing subscriptions you might have.

If you want to try the service before committing to a subscription, Microsoft offers a free 30-day trial. (This trial also includes Office Online.) For more information, go to *aka.ms/onedrive4biztrial.*

MICROSOFT VIRTUAL ACADEMY Watch demos to learn about the fundamentals of OneDrive for Business at *aka.ms/go-mva/onedrivesync.*

Explore OneDrive for Business

To get started using OneDrive for Business, first sign in to Office 365. Then, on the Office 365 Home page, click the OneDrive tile, shown in Figure 3-1.

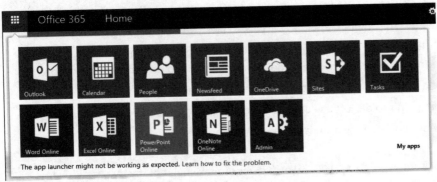

FIGURE 3-1 Click the OneDrive tile on the Office 365 Home page.

The Documents page opens, as shown in Figure 3-2. This page shows the contents of your OneDrive for Business library.

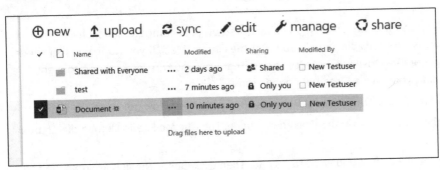

FIGURE 3-2 The Documents page lists what is in your library.

Notice that there are several actions you can initiate on this page:

- **New**   Click this button to create new Office 365 documents or to create new files and folders in OneDrive for Business.
- **Upload**   If you need to upload files from File Explorer (Windows) or the Finder (Mac) to OneDrive for Business, click this button.
- **Sync**   Click this button to sync OneDrive for Business with your local computer.
- **Edit**   Click this button to select a document from the list to edit.
- **Manage**   Click this button to manage activities with documents or folders.
- **Share**   Click this button to share a file or folder with others.

In addition, the left pane offers several options:

- **Documents**   This folder acts as a repository for all your files. To keep things organized, it's a good practice to create subfolders within this folder. For example, you might create a subfolder for each project you are working on.
- **Shared with Me**   Files that others have shared with you will appear in this folder.
- **Followed**   This folder allows easy access to files you have followed.
- **Site Folders**   This link takes you directly to your document libraries within OneDrive for Business, where you can manage all your files and folders from one location.
- **Recycle Bin**   Files that have been deleted will be stored here.
- **Recent**   This folder offers easy access to files you have worked on recently.

To learn more about many of these options, read on.

MICROSOFT VIRTUAL ACADEMY   Watch demos for examples of the functionality of OneDrive for Business at *aka.ms/go-mva/onedrive4biz*.

Copy files to OneDrive for Business

Like most users, you probably have many files stored on your computer's local hard drive, which you access via File Explorer (Windows) or the Finder (Mac). If you want, you can copy these files to your OneDrive for Business library. That way, you can access them from anywhere, assuming you have an Internet connection.

To copy a file to your OneDrive for Business library, do the following:

1. Click the Upload link on the Documents page. The Choose File To Upload dialog box opens.
2. Select the file or files you want to upload. Then click Open. The files are uploaded to your Documents library.

TIP   An even faster way to copy a file to OneDrive for Business is to drag it from File Explorer or the Finder to the target folder on the OneDrive for Business Documents page.

NOTE   By default, any files you upload will be private. However, you can choose to share your files if you want. You'll learn how to share your files later in this chapter.

Save and open files within OneDrive for Business

OneDrive for Business is integrated into Office 365. This means that when you save a file from within an Office 365 application such as Microsoft Word, Excel, or PowerPoint, you have the option to save it to OneDrive for Business. Here's how:

1. In the Office application, click File, Save As, OneDrive *Your Company Name*.

2. Select a folder location, enter a name for the file, and click Save.

You can also open files stored on your OneDrive for Business from within an Office 365 application. In this case, you choose File, Open, OneDrive *Your Company Name*. Then locate and select the file you want to open and click Open.

Manage files

In OneDrive for Business, you can copy, move, download a copy, and delete your files just as you can in File Explorer (Windows) or the Finder (Mac).

■ To move a file within OneDrive for Business, click the ellipsis to the right of the file name, as shown in Figure 3-3. In the pop-up window, click the ellipsis on the lower right, select Move Or Copy from the menu (similar to the menu in Figure 3-4), select the folder into which you want to move the file, and click Move.

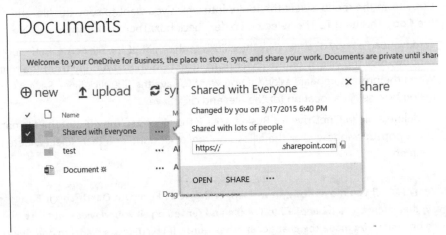

FIGURE 3-3 Click the ellipsis to the right of the file or folder you want to manage.

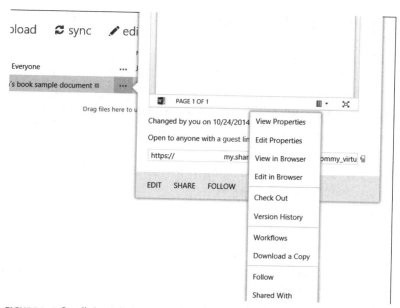

FIGURE 3-4 Scroll through the menu items to find the action you want to perform.

- To copy a file within OneDrive for Business, click the ellipsis to the right of the file name. In the pop-up window, click the ellipsis on the lower right, select Move Or Copy from the menu, select the folder into which you want to copy the file, and select the Copy This Item To The Selected Folder check box. Then click Copy.

- To download a copy of a file, click the ellipsis to the right of the file name. In the pop-up window, click the ellipsis on the lower right, select Download A Copy from the menu. When the prompt appears asking if you want to save the file, click Save, Save As. In the dialog box, select a location for the file, and click Save.

- To delete a file in OneDrive for Business, click the ellipsis to the right of the file name. In the pop-up window, click the ellipsis on the lower right, and then select Delete from the menu.

> **IMPORTANT** If you move, copy, download, or delete a file in your OneDrive for Business library, that change will be applied to the file and synced on all your devices, not just the device on which you made the change. In other words, if you delete a file from one device, it will be deleted from all your devices.

> **TIP** If someone inadvertently deletes a file that is vital to your organization, you can retrieve it from the Recycle Bin.

Create a new file or folder

Most computer users organize their files by placing them in separate folders. For example, a user might have one folder for each project at work. In OneDrive for Business, you can create files and folders as needed.

To create a file or folder, follow these steps:

1. Click the New button on the OneDrive for Business Documents page.

2. From the menu that appears, choose a file type to create a new file or click New Folder (see Figure 3-5).

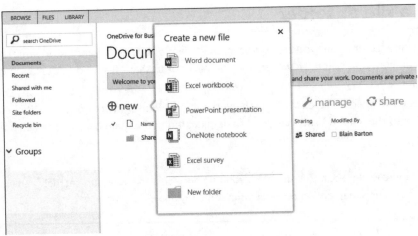

FIGURE 3-5 Click New to create a new file or folder in your library.

3. The Create A Folder dialog box opens (see Figure 3-6). Enter a name for the new folder and click Create, and the folder is created.

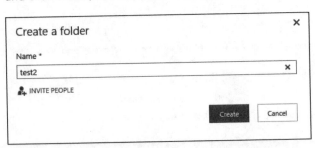

FIGURE 3-6 Enter a name in the Create A Folder dialog box.

After you create a new folder, you can add files to it as usual. You can also add a folder within this folder by following the same procedure. You can also apply permissions to the folder, allowing others to access it if you want. (You'll learn how to share files and folders later in this chapter.)

Share a file or folder

By default, any file or folder you store in your OneDrive for Business library is private. That is, only you can view and edit it. However, you can also opt to share files and folders with one or more people. That way, you can more easily collaborate on projects.

If you want to share a file or folder with every Office 365 user in your organization, copy or move it into the Shared With Everyone folder, located in the main pane of the Documents page.

NOTE If you're signed in to Office 365, you might be able to share with partners outside your organization, depending on what your company allows.

To share a file or folder with individual users in your organization, follow these steps:

1. On the Documents page, locate the file you want to share, click the ellipsis to the right of the file or folder name, and click Share in the pop-up window (see Figure 3-7).

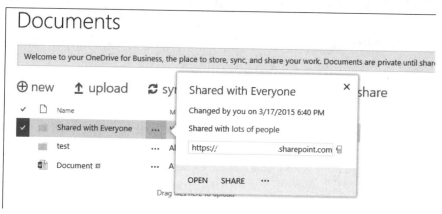

FIGURE 3-7 Click Share to share your file or folder with others.

2. In the Share dialog box, shown in Figure 3-8, enter the email address of the person you want to share the file or folder with.

FIGURE 3-8 Share your document with others.

3. Click the drop-down list to the right of this text box to indicate what type of permissions you are granting to this individual. You can give permission to view the file or to edit the file.

4. If you want, enter a message in the text box below the email text box. When you share the file, this message will be sent to the person whose email address you just entered. This gives you the opportunity to send a message stating that you are sharing the file or folder and why. This is particularly helpful if you are sharing the file or folder with a group of people—you only enter the message once and it gets sent to everyone you are sharing with!

5. To require the user to sign in to Office 365 in order to access the document, select the Require Sign-In check box (This requirement is for access to files, not to folders.)

6. If you want the user to receive an invitation to share the file or folder via email, click Options below the text boxes and select the Send An Email Invitation check box.

7. Click Share.

TIP You can also share a file or folder from within an Office application. To do so, choose File, Share, Invite People. A dialog box similar to the one you just saw opens; fill it out as described in the preceding steps.

Of course, just as you can share your files (and folders), others can share their files with you. When someone shares with you, you will likely receive an email invitation to access the file. In addition, the file will appear in the Shared With Me folder, which is in the left pane of the OneDrive for Business page.

Follow shared files

If you're invited to share a number of files but are particularly interested in only a few, you can opt to *follow* them. When you follow a document, it appears in your Followed folder in the left pane of the OneDrive for Business page, so that you can find it easily.

To follow a file, click the Follow link that appears in the email invitation you received for the file. Alternatively, locate the file in OneDrive for Business, click the ellipsis to the right of the file's name, and click Follow in the dialog box that appears.

If you no longer want to follow a file, you can stop following it. To do so, open the Followed folder, locate the document, and click the Stop Following link that appears below it.

Work on shared files

If you share a file that you generated by using an Office 365 application in OneDrive for Business, multiple users can edit it at the same time. As you edit the file, the application will indicate whether others are working on it, too.

Check out a file

Sometimes you might prefer to work on a document by yourself. In that case, you can check out the file. When you check out a file, you essentially place a lock on it. Others can open and view it in read-only mode, but only you can edit it. To check out a file, follow these steps:

1. In OneDrive for Business, locate the file you want to check out.
2. Click the ellipsis to the right of the file name. A window containing information and options pertaining to the document opens. Click the ellipsis on the lower right of the window to view a menu of options, as shown in Figure 3-9.

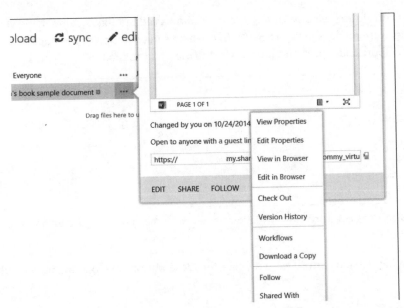

FIGURE 3-9 Click Check Out from the menu that appears when you click the ellipsis next to the name of the file you want to edit.

3. Click Check Out. The file shows the checked-out status with a green arrow, and only you will be permitted to edit that file. If other people try to edit the file, they will receive a message that the file is checked out for edit. Others can view the file in read-only view. They can also download a copy, which they can edit.

4. When you are finished editing the file, save it and close it. You will be prompted to check in the file so that your edits will be stored in the library and the file will be available to others for edit.

View a file's version history

If you need to find out who has edited a file (and when), you can use the Version History feature. With this feature in OneDrive for Business, you can review a list of people who have edited a file and when those edits were performed. You can also use the feature to revisit an older version of the document. This is handy if edits were made in error.

To view a file's Version History, follow these steps:

1. In OneDrive for Business, locate the file whose version history you want to view.

2. Click the ellipsis to the right of the file name and click Version History on the menu that appears (see Figure 3-9, shown earlier).

3. The Version History window opens, showing who has edited the document and when the edits were made (see Figure 3-10). To open an earlier version of the document, click the appropriate date and time link in the Modified column.

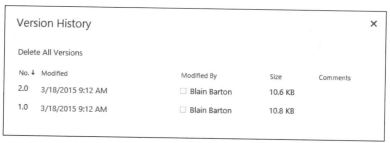

FIGURE 3-10 Use the Version History window to view when changes were made to the file and by whom.

4. To close the Version History window, click the Close button (the X) in the upper-right corner.

Sync OneDrive for Business to your computer

You can set up OneDrive for Business to sync your files to your local computer. You can then access the files directly from File Explorer (Windows) or the Finder (Mac), bypassing the Office 365 Home page altogether.

With OneDrive for Business, your files are synchronized automatically (as long as your local computer is connected to the Internet). However, for all this to work, you must first run a special application to set things up.

IMPORTANT The aforementioned sync application is available by default if your Office 365 subscription includes the Office desktop programs. The first time you use the Sync feature, you'll be directed to a website to download the program.

To set up OneDrive for Business to sync with your computer, follow these steps:

1. Click the Sync button on the OneDrive for Business Documents page.

2. Click Sync Now. The files and folders in your OneDrive for Business library are synchronized with your local computer.

3. To open the synced OneDrive for Business folder in File Explorer (Windows) or the Finder (Mac), click Show My Files. The folder appears in the Favorites list, as shown in Figure 3-11.

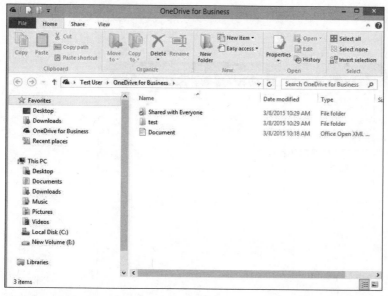

FIGURE 3-11 On your local computer, you can view your OneDrive for Business library.

Use OneDrive for Business on the go

The beauty of OneDrive for Business—or just about any application available from the cloud—is that you can access it anywhere, on any device.

You can access OneDrive for Business in one of two ways:

- From your Internet browser
- Via the OneDrive for Business app, which you can install on your mobile device

Access OneDrive for Business on an Internet browser

To access OneDrive for Business from an Internet browser—which is handy if you are on a public computer, such as one found in an Internet café or library—follow these steps:

1. Open the Internet browser on your computer, smartphone, tablet, or other Internet-connected device.

2. In the address bar of the Internet browser, enter **onedrive.com**. Then sign in to the site by using your user ID and password.

3. Click the OneDrive link at the top of the page. The OneDrive web interface opens.

As shown in Figure 3-12, the interface looks a little different from the one you're used to.

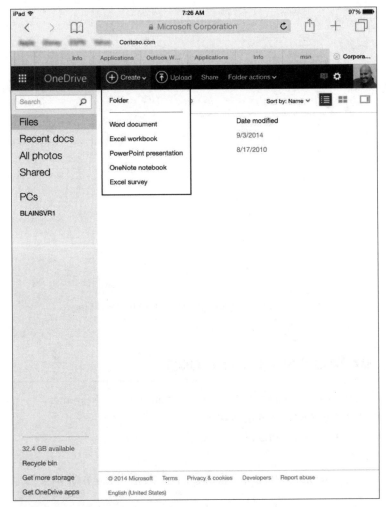

FIGURE 3-12 You can access OneDrive from your Internet browser, even if you are on a mobile device such as an iPad (shown here).

It offers the following links at the top of the page:

- **Create** This button is the same as the New button on the regular OneDrive home page. Click it to create new Office 365 documents or to create new folders in OneDrive.

- **Upload** Select a file you want to upload from your device to OneDrive, and then click the Upload button.

- **Share** Click this button to share a file or folder with others. When you do, you'll be prompted to invite others to use the document, as shown in Figure 3-13. This process is similar to the one you explored in the "Share a file or folder" section earlier in this chapter.

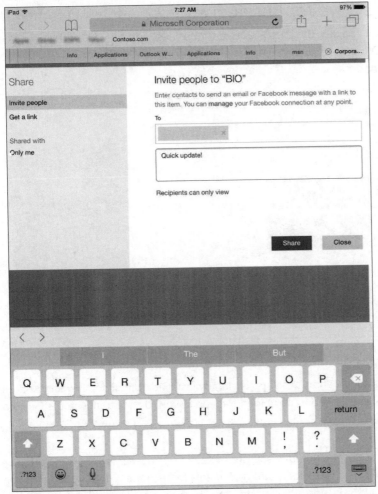

FIGURE 3-13 When you click Share, you are prompted to invite others to share the selected document.

In addition, the left pane of the browser (see Figure 3-12, shown earlier) offers several options:

- **Files**   This folder acts like your Documents folder, storing all your files.

- **Recent docs**   This folder offers easy access to files you have worked on recently.

- **All Photos**   Interestingly, the OneDrive interface has no corresponding Photos folder. Here, however, you can store all your photos in one easy-to-access folder.

- **Shared**   As you might guess, all shared files appear here. These are both files you share and files shared with you.

- **PCs**   This folder shows all the computers that have the local app installed, the computers you have shared files with, and the computers you have signed in to with your Microsoft account. It includes an option to add the machine.

Use the OneDrive for Business app

As mentioned, you can also use the OneDrive for Business app on your mobile device to access your OneDrive for Business library, as shown in Figure 3-14. This app is available for Windows Phone, Android, and iOS (Apple) devices.

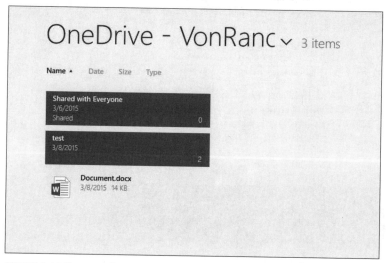

FIGURE 3-14 You can view your documents by using the mobile OneDrive for Business app.

If you have a Windows Phone, the app is already installed on it. If you have an Android or iOS (Apple) device, you'll need to download the app to your device from Google Play Store or the App Store, respectively. When you have the app on your phone, you sign in to it using your user ID and password.

The OneDrive for Business mobile app operates in much the same way as the other versions of the software. You tap folders and documents to open them; tap Upload to upload files to the OneDrive for Business library; and tap Share to share files with others. The primary difference is that in the mobile app, you can only view documents. If you want to edit a document by using your phone or tablet, you must have Office 365 installed on the device.

> **NOTE** You can find more information about OneDrive for iOS at *aka.ms/onedriveios-faq*.

Summary

- OneDrive for Business is a cloud-based file storage service that provides protected access to files. With OneDrive for Business, you can store and access your files online.

- Microsoft also offers a consumer-level solution called *OneDrive*. This personal solution is completely separate from OneDrive for Business, which is considerably more robust and secure.

- If you have subscribed to Office 365, you already have OneDrive for Business. Each Office 365 user has 1 terabyte (TB) of storage space. If you don't have an Office 365 subscription, you can subscribe to OneDrive for Business as a stand-alone application. Different subscription plans offer varying amounts of storage space.

- Like most users, you probably have many files stored on your computer's local hard drive, which you access via File Explorer (Windows) or the Finder (Mac). If you want, you can copy these files to your OneDrive for Business. That way, you can access them from anywhere, assuming you have an Internet connection.

- When you save a file from within an Office 365 application such as Word, Excel, or PowerPoint, you have the option to save it to OneDrive for Business. You can also open files stored on your OneDrive for Business from within an Office 365 application.

- In OneDrive for Business, you can copy, move, rename, and delete your files just as you can in File Explorer (Windows) or the Finder (Mac).

- You can create new folders and new files in Office 365 applications from within OneDrive for Business.

- By default, any file you store in OneDrive for Business is private. That is, only you can view and edit it. However, you can also opt to share files with one or more people, so that you can more easily collaborate on projects. In addition, others can choose to share their files with you.

- If you share a file that you generated by using an Office 365 application in OneDrive for Business, multiple users can edit it at the same time. As you edit the file, the application will indicate whether others are working on it, too. Sometimes, however, you might prefer to work on a document alone. In that case, you can check out the file. When you check out a file, you essentially place a lock on it. Others can open and view it in read-only mode, but only you can edit it.

- If you need to find out who has edited a file (and when), you can use the Version History feature in OneDrive for Business. With this feature, you can review a list of people who have edited a file and when those edits were performed. You can also revisit an older version of the document. This is handy if edits were made in error.

- You can set up OneDrive for Business to sync your files to your local computer. You can then access the files directly from File Explorer (Windows) or the Finder (Mac), bypassing the OneDrive for Business interface altogether.

- The beauty of OneDrive for Business is that you can access it anywhere, on any device, either from the device's Internet browser or via the OneDrive for Business app, which you can install on your device.

CHAPTER 4

Keep track of customers by using Microsoft Dynamics CRM Online

> **IMPORTANT** The version of Microsoft Dynamics CRM Online that is best for you depends on the size of your organization. This chapter assumes you have 5 to 25 users and are using Microsoft Dynamics CRM Online without Microsoft Office 365 integration.

What is Microsoft Dynamics CRM Online?

What's the most important part of your business? If you're like most people, your answer is the customer. Indeed, businesses devote considerable energy to acquiring—and keeping—customers.

That's where customer relationship management (CRM) software comes in. With CRM software, companies can reduce the costs associated with acquiring new customers by organizing and automating certain business processes. Companies can also use CRM software to improve their customers' experience with sales, marketing, and customer service. Perhaps most importantly, CRM software offers one central, organized, easy-to-access place to store data about all your customers and prospects.

Microsoft Dynamics CRM Online is such a program. With Microsoft Dynamics CRM Online, businesses can drive sales productivity and marketing effectiveness through social insights, business intelligence, and campaign management—all from the Microsoft public cloud. Microsoft even offers mobile versions of this software, with which employees can manage these functions while on the go.

> **TIP** You can integrate Microsoft Dynamics CRM Online with Microsoft Office 365 for an even more efficient CRM approach. For more information, go to "Office 365 + Microsoft Dynamics CRM" at *www.microsoft.com/en-us/dynamics/crm-office-365.aspx*.

In addition to Microsoft Dynamics CRM, which is designed for use by sales representatives, sales managers, customer service agents, and customer service managers, Microsoft offers two other tools to aid in your CRM efforts. These work in tandem with Microsoft Dynamics CRM Online.

- **Microsoft Dynamics Marketing** This software includes a full suite of tools for data segmentation, behavior tracking, digital asset management, and brand management. It's geared for brand managers and campaign managers. Sales teams can also use this software for more insights into campaigns and targeting.

- **Microsoft Social Listening** This tool provides volume and sentiment analysis of social networking data. It's ideal for those members of your staff who handle your business's social media efforts, in addition to those employees in sales, marketing, and customer service who want to get a sense of your products, competitors, and industry.

Read on to learn about all these tools.

Find the right subscription

Like many tools in the Microsoft public cloud, Microsoft Dynamics CRM Online is a software as a service (SaaS) suite and is subscription-based. Microsoft offers the following subscription levels. You can mix and match these levels to accommodate the needs of your employees:

- **Professional** Choose the Professional plan for access to the full range of Microsoft Dynamics CRM capabilities, plus Microsoft Social Listening.
- **Sales Productivity** This option is designed for sales staff. It offers everything in the Professional plan, plus access to Office 365 and Microsoft Power BI. (Power BI is a tool that you can use to organize your data.)
- **Enterprise** This plan offers the same tools as the Professional plan, plus access to Microsoft Dynamics Marketing, Unified Service Desk, and Parature Enterprise. Unified Service Desk is a framework that gives you a unified view of customer data stored in Microsoft Dynamics CRM. Parature provides solutions for customer engagement.

> **NOTE** Because the pricing of each of these subscription options is subject to change, no pricing information is included here. For up-to-date information on pricing and features, visit *aka.ms/crm-office365*.

> **TIP** If you're not sure which option is right for you, you can obtain a 30-day free trial. For details, visit *aka.ms/crm-freetrial*.

Explore the Microsoft Dynamics CRM Online work areas and dashboards

To start Microsoft Dynamics CRM Online, sign in at *https://<yourcompanyname>.crm.dynamics.com* with the user name and password you created during the trial setup of Microsoft Dynamics CRM Online. A page like the one shown in Figure 4-1 is displayed.

FIGURE 4-1 Sign in to the free trial of Microsoft Dynamics CRM Online.

Microsoft Dynamics CRM Online offers three work areas: Sales (see Figure 4-2), Service (see Figure 4-3), and Marketing (see Figure 4-4). Each work area has its own dashboard, offering a quick view of various details. You'll also find tools tailored for that aspect of the business.

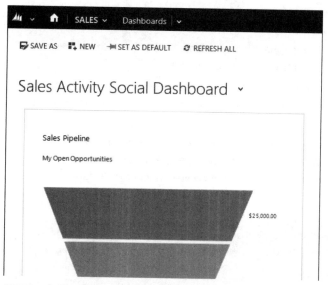

FIGURE 4-2 The Sales work area gives you a visual overview of the sales pipeline.

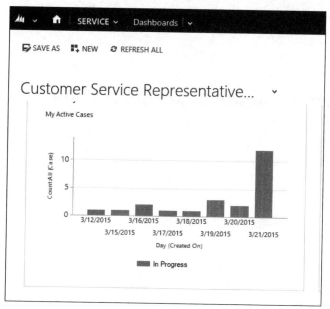

FIGURE 4-3 The Customer Service work area gives you details in a visual format.

FIGURE 4-4 The Marketing work area is tailored to your business.

To choose a work area, click the Microsoft Dynamics CRM list and then click the tile for the work area you want to view (see Figure 4-1, shown earlier). The work area opens.

NOTE Microsoft Dynamics CRM Online can work in tandem with Office 365. That means if you run Office 365 and have already created user accounts for it, you can set those user accounts up to work with Microsoft Dynamics CRM Online (assuming you've obtained the necessary licenses). For more information, go to "Office 365 + Microsoft Dynamics CRM" at *http://aka.ms/crm-Office365.*

Work with contacts, accounts, leads, and opportunities

With Microsoft Dynamics CRM Online, you can work with four main types of data:

- **Contacts**   This is data about people you know and work with.
- **Accounts**   This is data about companies with whom you do business. Typically, an account will have contacts associated with it.
- **Leads**   A lead represents a potential sale.
- **Opportunities**   Leads that you nurture might become opportunities.

You can set up this information within each of the work areas for sales, marketing, and customer service; you can also share information between work areas.

> **NOTE**   In addition to these, you can also work with cases. A case contains data about a customer question or complaint. You'll learn more about cases later in this chapter.

Work with contacts

As mentioned, a contact is a data record about a person you know and work with. If you maintain a list of contacts in your email program, you can import that list into Microsoft Dynamics CRM Online. In addition, you can create new contacts. After you have entered or imported your contacts into Microsoft Dynamics CRM Online, you can easily view and sort them, and you can email or call them directly from the program.

Import contacts

Before you can import your contacts from an email program, you must export them from that program. The resulting file must be in one of the following formats:

- Comma-separated values (.csv)
- Text (.txt)
- Compressed (.zip)
- Microsoft Excel spreadsheet (.xls or .xlsx)

To find out how to export your contacts, search your email program's Help file for the word "export." As you review the search results, look for articles that pertain to exporting contacts or exporting your address book.

After you export your contacts, it's time to import them into Microsoft Dynamics CRM Online. Here's how:

1. On the Microsoft Dynamics CRM Online navigation bar, click Microsoft Dynamics CRM, and then click Settings.

2. The Settings option appears on the navigation bar. Click Settings, and then select Data Management. Click Imports, and then on the My Imports page, click Import Data.

3. The Upload Data File page of the Import Data Wizard opens (see Figure 4-5). Click Browse. Then locate and select the folder where you saved the file containing your contacts, and click Open. Finally, click Next.

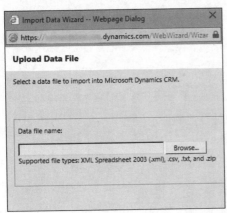

FIGURE 4-5 Enter the name of the file that contains the contact information you want to import.

4. On the Review File Upload Summary page (see Figure 4-6), review the file name, format, and data delimiters. Then click Next.

NOTE Delimiters are the characters that separate fields. For example, in a comma-separated file, also known as a CSV file, fields are separated by a comma.

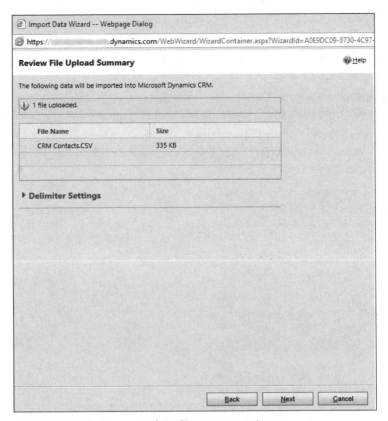

FIGURE 4-6 Verify the name of the file you want to import.

5. On the Select Data Map page, click Default (Automatic Mapping), and then click Next.

6. On the Map Record Types page, in the drop-down list, under Record Types, click Contact. Then click Next.

7. On the Map Fields page, if you notice an alert icon next to any record type, map the column from your contacts file to the corresponding field in Microsoft Dynamics CRM (see Figure 4-7). Then click OK and Next.

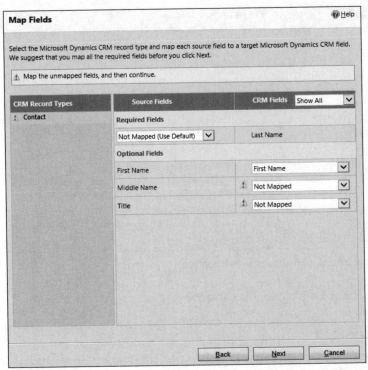

FIGURE 4-7 Use the Map Fields dialog box to map the names and titles of the contacts you are importing.

8. On the Review Mapping Summary page, review the summary and click Next.

9. On the Review Settings And Import Data page, click Submit.

10. On the Data Submitted For Import page, to verify that the wizard was successful, click Imports and review the report.

11. Click Finish to complete the operation.

Create a contact

Entering a new contact is a simple matter. Here's how it's done:

1. On the Microsoft Dynamics CRM Online navigation bar, click Create (the plus sign). Then click Contact.

2. The Contact page opens (see Figure 4-8). Enter as much data as you can about the contact. (Only a last name is required.)

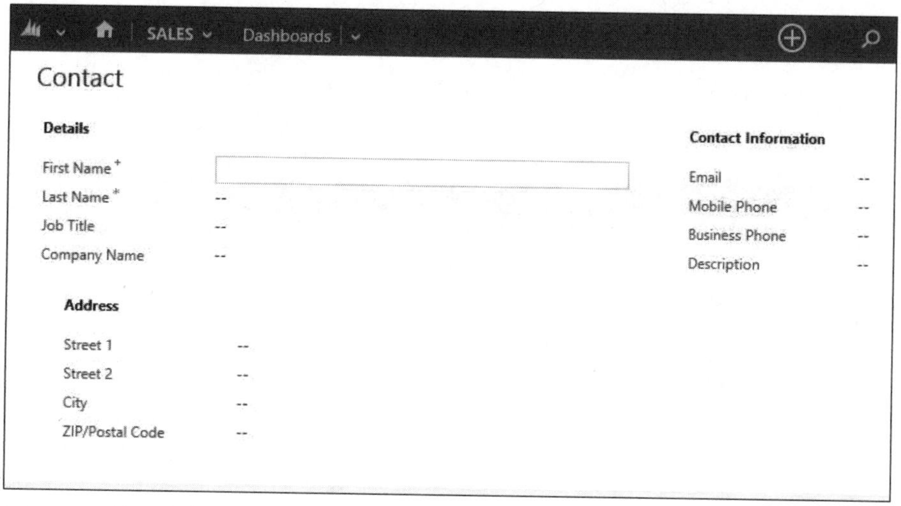

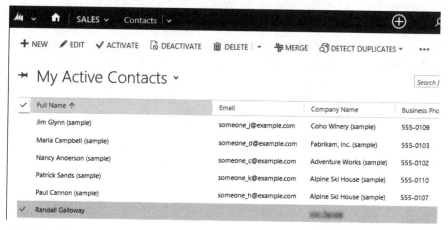

FIGURE 4-8 Enter information about the new contact.

3. When you're finished, click Save. The contact is created.

View and edit contacts

You can view your contacts from within your work area. Click Contacts on the navigation bar. Your contacts will appear in list form (see Figure 4-9). To view more information about a contact, click it in the list. A page for that contact opens (see Figure 4-10). On that page, you can edit the contact as necessary.

FIGURE 4-9 View your contacts.

FIGURE 4-10 Click a name to view more information about that contact.

> **TIP** If you have a lot of contacts, you might want to use the search function to locate the one you want. Enter the contact's name or other information about the contact in the Search field in the upper-right corner of the page to find it.

> **TIP** To call or email a contact, click the contact's phone number or email address in the contact list or contact page.

Work with accounts

As mentioned, you use accounts to keep track of companies with whom you do business. These might be clients or potential clients, vendors, business partners, or any organization that interacts with your organization.

Create accounts

To create an account, follow these steps:

1. On the Microsoft Dynamics CRM navigation bar, click Microsoft Dynamics CRM, and then click your work area.

2. Click the work area name on the navigation bar, and then click Accounts.

3. The My Active Accounts page opens (see Figure 4-11). Click New.

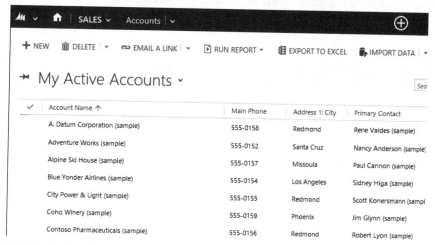

FIGURE 4-11 The My Active Accounts page lists your active accounts and their associated information.

4. The Account page opens (see Figure 4-12). Enter as much information about the account as you can. Then click Save. The account is created.

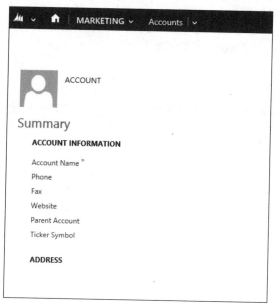

FIGURE 4-12 Enter as much information about the new account as you can.

View and edit accounts

As with contacts, you view your accounts from within your work area. Click the Accounts option in the navigation bar to display a list of your accounts (see Figure 4-11, shown earlier). To view more information about an account, click it in the list. A page for that account opens (see Figure 4-13). On that page, you can edit the account as necessary.

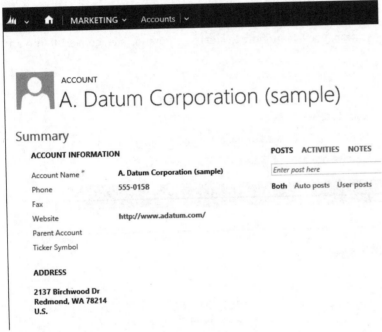

FIGURE 4-13 Click an account to view more information about it.

Associate contacts with an account

CRM is all about relationships with other organizations—your accounts—and the people within those organizations—your contacts. You will often want to associate one or more contacts with an account. Here's how to do it:

1. On the account's page, in the Contacts section, click the Add button. (It looks like a plus sign.)

2. To search for the contact you want to add, enter the contact's name in the Search field.

3. Click the contact's entry in the list of search results to add it to the account.

Work with leads and opportunities

A lead represents a potential sale. You might receive a lead through advertising, networking, or an email campaign. In contrast, an opportunity represents a target that is farther along in the sales process. In this section, you'll learn how to create a lead and, later, convert it into an opportunity.

Create a lead

To create a lead, follow these steps:

1. On the navigation bar of the Sales work area, click Sales. Then click Leads.

2. The My Open Leads page opens (see Figure 4-14). Click New.

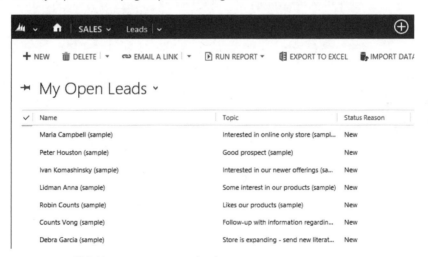

FIGURE 4-14 Click New to create a new lead.

3. The Lead page opens (see Figure 4-15). In the Summary area, enter your lead's company and contact information.

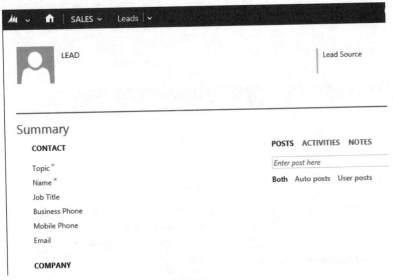

FIGURE 4-15 Enter information about the lead.

4. In the Details area of the Lead page, enter information about your lead's industry. Also enter the lead's preferred method of contact.

5. Enter any notes about the lead, such as phone calls made, emails sent, or other useful information. Then click Save. The lead is created.

View and edit a lead

You view your leads from within the Sales work area. Click Leads on the navigation bar to display a list of your leads (see Figure 4-14, shown earlier). To view more information about a lead, click it in the list. A page for that lead opens (see Figure 4-16). From there, you can edit your lead.

> **TIP** If you have a lot of leads, you might want to use the search function to locate the one you want. Enter the lead's name in the Search field in the upper-right corner of the page to find it.

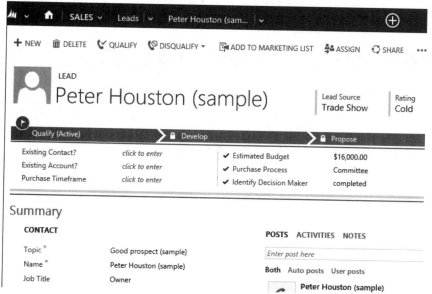

FIGURE 4-16 Click a lead to view more information about it.

Convert a lead to an opportunity

Ideally, you'll nurture your lead so effectively that you'll be able to qualify it—that is, convert it to an opportunity. Follow these steps:

1. On the navigation bar of the Sales work area, click Sales. Then click Leads.

2. Click the lead you want to qualify to open it.

3. In the Qualify section of the Lead page (see Figure 4-16, shown earlier), enter the requested information.

4. At the top of the Lead page, click Qualify.

5. Click Save. The lead is qualified and is converted to an opportunity.

View and edit your opportunities

As with your leads, you view your opportunities from within the Sales work area. Click Opportunities on the navigation bar to display a list of your opportunities (see Figure 4-17). To view more information about an opportunity, click it in the list. A page for that opportunity opens (see Figure 4-18). From there, you can edit your opportunity.

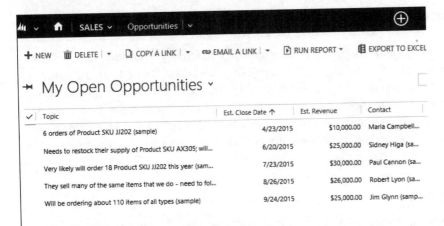

FIGURE 4-17 View your opportunities.

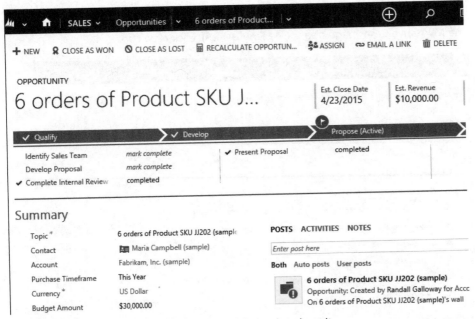

FIGURE 4-18 Click an opportunity to view more information about it.

> **TIP** If you have a lot of opportunities, you might want to use the search function to locate the one you want. Enter the opportunity's name in the Search field in the upper-right corner of the page to find it.

Create and manage cases

A key aspect of managing any customer relationship is effectively responding if there is a problem. To help with this, you can use Microsoft Dynamics CRM Online to create cases. (Some organizations call each case a ticket or an incident.) A case contains all the data about a customer issue, including the case priority, where it originated (for example, from a phone call, an email message, an inquiry on your website, an in-person conversation, or even a post on social media), whether there have been other cases associated with this customer, and how much time you have to resolve the case.

Create a case

After you receive a question or complaint from a customer—again, from a phone call, an email message, an inquiry on your website, an in-person conversation, or a post on social media—you can easily create a case. Here's how:

1. On the navigation bar of the Service work area, click Service. Then click Cases.

2. The My Active Cases page opens (see Figure 4-19). Click New Case.

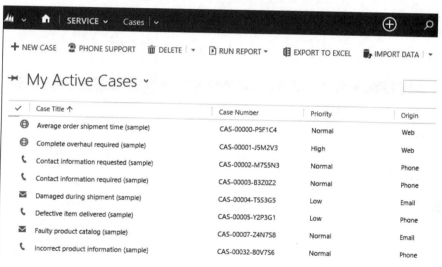

FIGURE 4-19 Click New Case to create a new case.

3. The New Case page opens (see Figure 4-20). Click Find Customer.

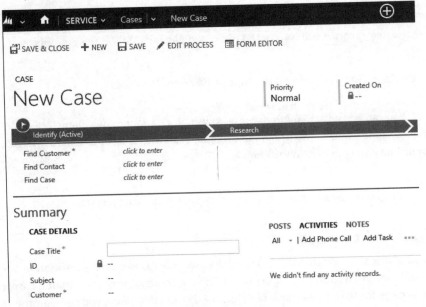

FIGURE 4-20 Click Find Customer on the New Case page.

4. In the list of account and contact records (see Figure 4-21), click the customer's record to select it.

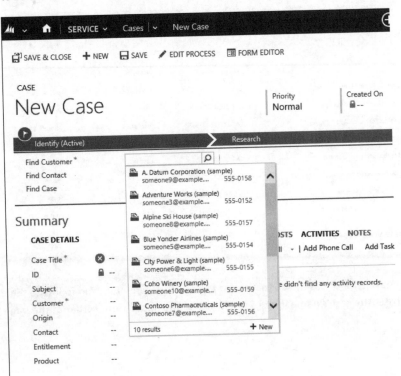

FIGURE 4-21 Click the customer's record in the list.

5. In the Case Title field, enter a descriptive name for the case.

6. Fill in any other details that apply, and click Save. The case is created.

View and edit a case

You view your cases from within the Service work area. Click Cases on the navigation bar to display your cases in list form (see Figure 4-22). To view more information about a case, click it in the list. A page for that case opens (see Figure 4-23). On that page, you can edit the case as necessary.

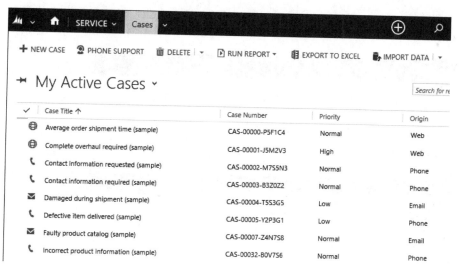

FIGURE 4-22 View your cases.

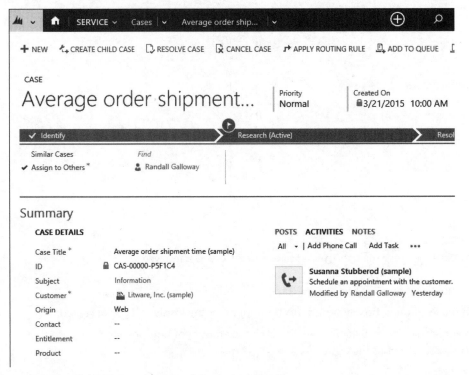

FIGURE 4-23 Click a case to view more information about it.

Mark a case as resolved

In business, there are few things that are as satisfying as resolving a customer issue. To mark that accomplishment, you should mark the associated case record as resolved. When you mark a case as resolved, it is removed from your list of open cases.

> **TIP** If you later discover that the issue has not been resolved after all, you can reactivate the case. Open the resolved case and click Reactivate Case. You can then edit the case.

To mark a case as resolved, follow these steps:

1. Open the case that you want to mark as resolved.
2. Click Resolve Case on the case page's command bar.
3. In the Resolve Case dialog box (see Figure 4-24), click the Resolution Type arrow and click the option in the list that best reflects how the case was resolved.

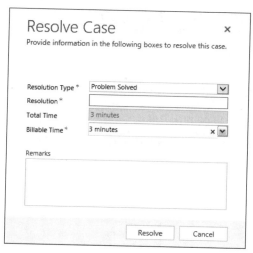

FIGURE 4-24 The Resolution Type indicates how the case was resolved.

4. In the Resolution Type list, click Problem Solved.

5. In the Resolution box, enter a short description of the resolution you achieved.

6. If applicable, in the Billable Time list, click the amount of time spent on the case that should be billed to the customer.

7. Click Resolve.

Track activities

In Microsoft Dynamics CRM Online, you use activities to keep track of all your interactions with a customer. For example, when you place a phone call to a customer, you can record it as an activity. The same is true for emails and other types of communications. You can also create activities to assign tasks to yourself.

> **TIP** To maximize the power of Microsoft Dynamics CRM Online, you should add an activity for every customer interaction. That way, you'll have a record of it.

Add a customer-related activity

You can add an activity to a contact, account, lead, opportunity, case, or other type of record to help you keep track of your interactions with that entity. When you do so, both you and your coworkers can review the history of your relationship with that customer.

The steps are slightly different depending on what type of activity you want to add to a customer record. To add an activity to log a call, follow these steps:

1. Open the record to which you want to add the call. As mentioned, this can be a contact, account, lead, opportunity, case, or other type of record.

2. On the record page, click Activities.

3. Click Add Phone Call (see Figure 4-25).

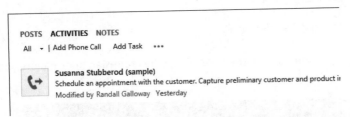

FIGURE 4-25 Click Add Phone Call in the Activities section of the page.

4. The Add Phone Call dialog box opens (see Figure 4-26). In the description area, enter a summary of the conversation with the customer.

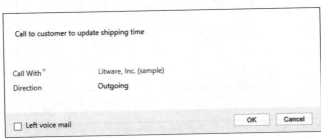

FIGURE 4-26 Enter a summary of the call in the Add Phone Call dialog box.

5. If the customer called you (rather than the other way around), click Direction to change the Outgoing setting to Incoming.

6. If you were unable to reach the customer but left a voice mail, select the Left Voice Mail check box.

7. Click OK to save the activity.

Adding an activity to log an email message is slightly different. Here's what you do:

1. Open the record to which you want to add the email message.

2. On the record page, click Activities.

3. Click More, indicated by an ellipsis (...). Then click Email (see Figure 4-27).

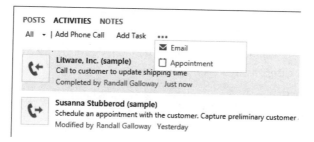

FIGURE 4-27 Click More and then click Email.

4. The New Email page opens (see Figure 4-28). Fill in the requested information, and click Save.

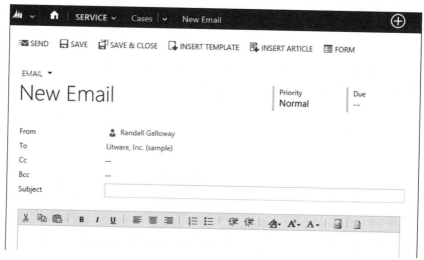

FIGURE 4-28 Fill in the information in the New Email page.

Explore the Microsoft Dynamics CRM Online ready-to-use business processes

As mentioned, one way that Microsoft Dynamics CRM Online helps to reduce the costs associated with acquiring new customers is by automating certain business processes. Microsoft Dynamics CRM Online includes several ready-to-use business processes for common scenarios in sales, service, and marketing. By using these processes, you ensure that your employees follow consistent steps every time they interact with customers.

So what business processes are available? Here's a list:

- **Phone sales campaign**   This business process is designed for employees who are charged with calling prospects, creating and qualifying leads, developing opportunities, and closing deals.

- **Email sales campaign**   This is similar to the phone sales campaign, but for email.

- **Multichannel sales campaign**   Use this business process if you plan to contact prospects by phone and email.

- **Marketing list builder**   This business process is ideal for creating targeted marketing lists for accounts, contacts, or leads; adding prospects; and gaining manager approval.

- **Service appointment scheduling**   If your business involves scheduling service appointments, setting up reminders, and making sure service activities are completed, you'll find this business process useful.

- **Service case upsell**   By using this business process, you can help employees introduce additional products or services to your customer while resolving a customer's service request. This process is known as an *upsell*.

- **Guided service case**   You can use this business process to make sure data is entered consistently for service cases and that required activities are completed to resolve a case.

- **Opportunity to invoice (business-to-business)**   Your organization can use this business process to follow a standard process for assessing needs, negotiating outcomes, fulfilling orders, and closing opportunities when selling to other businesses.

- **Contact to order**   Use this business process to target sales by using a consistent method to interact with customers.

- **Upsell after service interaction**   If you'd like your employees to turn a good service experience into an opportunity to upsell more products and services to the customer, activate this business process.

- **In-store excellence**   Use this business process to suggest orders for store owners and field personnel and gain acceptance from store managers for those orders.

You can also create custom business processes. For more information about using Microsoft Dynamics CRM Online business processes, including how to activate them and links to information on creating your own, visit *www.microsoft.com /en-us/dynamics/crm-customer-center/add-ready-to-use-business-processes.aspx*.

Add an activity for yourself

In addition to using activities to track your interactions with a customer, you can use them to keep track of tasks you need to perform for a particular customer. Follow these steps:

1. Open the record to which you want to add a task.

2. On the record page, click Activities.

3. Click Add Task (see Figure 4-25, shown earlier).

4. The Add Task dialog box opens (see Figure 4-29). Assign a subject title to your task. You can also enter a description and a due date, and you can assign a priority level to the task. Enter the name of the owner; each task must have an assigned owner.

FIGURE 4-29 Give your task a meaningful subject title in the Add Task dialog box.

> **TIP** By default, you are assigned as the Owner. To assign the task to someone else, click the lookup icon and choose the user you want.

5. Click OK to save the task. The task is created.

View and edit activities

To view and edit activities assigned to you, follow these steps:

1. Click the Activities tile in your work area to display a list of your activities (see Figure 4-30).

2. To view details about an activity, click it in the list. A page for the activity opens (see Figure 4-31). You can edit the details in this page as needed.

3. When you've finished the task, click Mark Complete on the page's command bar to mark it complete.

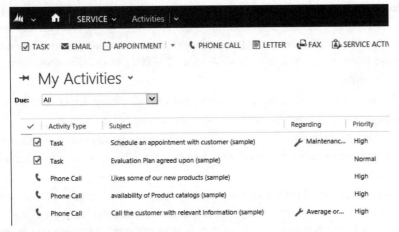

FIGURE 4-30 View a list of your activities.

FIGURE 4-31 Click an activity to view more information about it.

Microsoft Dynamics Marketing

Some Microsoft Dynamics CRM Online subscription plans offer access to Microsoft Dynamics Marketing. With this tool, your marketing team can plan, execute, and measure marketing campaigns. The software offers tools with which you can perform the following tasks:

- **Campaign management**   Microsoft Dynamics Marketing includes tools to help you plan, track, and analyze the return on investment of your marketing campaigns.

- **Campaign automation**   You can use the Microsoft Dynamics Marketing intuitive flowcharting tools to create automated rule-based campaigns.

- **Behavioral analysis**   How do your contacts engage with your campaigns, emails, landing pages, offers, events, and other touches? With Microsoft Dynamics Marketing, you can find out—and even use what you learn to score and qualify leads. In addition, you can use third-party behavioral analysis to track visitors from other sites, including social media sites.

Here are just a few of the specific features offered with Microsoft Dynamics Marketing:

- **A/B testing**   Are you torn between two marketing strategies? If so, you can use Microsoft Dynamics Marketing to perform A/B testing to identify the best approach. You can run your test as a simple bulk emailing or include it as part of a fully auto-mated campaign.

- **Marketing messages**   Email marketing messages are the cornerstone of many mar-keting campaigns. With Microsoft Dynamics Marketing, you can create graphically rich messages, which you can then save in template form and apply to future communica-tions.

- **Offers**   With Microsoft Dynamics Marketing, you can create special offers and extend them to selected clients via email. The system can then track the email open and click-through rates, in addition to sales resulting from the offer.

- **Webinars**   Conferences and trade shows are likely an important part of your com-pany's marketing strategy. But some customers just aren't able to attend these events. That's where webinars come in. By using tools in Microsoft Dynamics Marketing, you can organize webinars, sending invitations and tracking responses. Any user with a PC or mobile device running Microsoft Skype for Business—can join.

- **Reports**   Microsoft Dynamics Marketing includes dozens of system reports—that is, preconfigured reports that you can generate and print. Whether you need administra-tion reports, vendors and payables reports, or any report in between, you'll be able to generate the reports for your business needs.

> **TIP**   For more information about Microsoft Dynamics Marketing, visit *www.microsoft.com /en-us/dynamics/marketing-customer-center/*.

Microsoft Social Listening

According to *Forbes*, "78% of salespeople using social media outsell their peers" (*www.forbes.com /sites/markfidelman/2013/05/19/study-78-of-salespeople-using-social-media-outsell-their-peers/*). Because of social networks like Facebook and Twitter, millions of people are online and con-nected—and many of them might be airing their opinions about your organization, products, industry, or competitors. Knowing what people are saying—and taking the right action when they say it—can help you drive engagement, win business, and foster customer loyalty.

But how can you sift through the mountains of data available through social media? That's where Microsoft Social Listening comes in. Microsoft Social Listening scours social networks like Twitter and Facebook, in addition to blogs, YouTube videos, and news posts for mentions of terms you define and reports its results in easy-to-understand charts and graphs.

With these visuals, you can do the following:

- **Track the "buzz"**   If you want to know whether your search topic or category is "buzzing," check the Buzz Report. This report reveals the total and average numbers of posts in a specified time frame. To track how the number of posts is trending over time, check the Trend Report. Finally, the Volume History Report shows peaks and valleys in the volume of posts over time.

- **Track customer sentiment**   Several reports offer information about how customers are feeling about your product or company. For example, the Sentiment Volume Report displays a bar graph comparing the total number of positive and negative posts, whereas the Sentiment Share of Voice Report shows a comparison of positive, negative, and neutral posts. If you need to correlate sentiment with dates and events, you can view the Sentiment History Report, which tracks sentiment on a timeline. Finally, the Sentiment Summary by Sources Report shows you how, for example, sentiment on Twitter varies from sentiment on Facebook.

- **Find out where posts are coming from**   You can use the Sources Share of Voice and Sources Summary Reports to discover which channels are yielding the most posts—for example, Facebook or Twitter. To find out where posts are coming from geographically, you can view the Languages Report. (Microsoft Social Listening can track posts in English, French, German, Spanish, and Portuguese.) Finally, you can view the Key Influencers Report to find out precisely which people mention your search terms the most often.

NOTE   You can integrate data from Microsoft Social Listening into Microsoft Dynamics CRM Online and Microsoft Dynamics Marketing. This interoperability makes Microsoft Social Listening a powerful tool not just for those employees who run your company's social media program, but also for people in your sales, service, and broader marketing departments.

What can you do with all this information? That is, how can it help your business? Simply put, these visuals help you spot emerging trends. You can also use them to track marketing campaigns, respond to service issues before they escalate, and gain insights into your competitors.

TIP   For more information about Microsoft Social Listening, visit *www.microsoft.com /en-us/dynamics/crm-social.aspx*.

Go mobile with Microsoft Dynamics CRM Online

You aren't limited to using Microsoft Dynamics CRM Online on your desktop. You can also use it on your mobile devices—including Windows Phone, Android, and iOS smartphones, in addition to Microsoft Surface and iPad tablets.

Although you can use your mobile device's web browser to run Microsoft Dynamics CRM Online, you'll probably prefer to use the Microsoft Dynamics CRM Online app. This app is available from the following sites:

- **Windows Phone**   *aka.ms/windows-phone*
- **Microsoft Surface tablet (Windows 8)**   *aka.ms/windows-surface-apps8*
- **Microsoft Surface tablet (Windows 8.1)**   *aka.ms/windows-surface-app8.1*
- **Android (phone)**   *aka.ms/crm4android*
- **Android (tablet)**   *aka.ms/crm-android-tablets*
- **iOS (iPhone)**   *aka.ms/crm4iphone*
- **iOS (iPad)**   *aka.ms/crm4ipads*

> **NOTE** The app operates in much the same way as the desktop version you explored in this chapter.

Before you can use Microsoft Dynamics CRM Online on your mobile device, you might need to turn on this functionality. Follow these steps:

1. On the Microsoft Dynamics CRM Online navigation bar, click Microsoft Dynamics CRM.
2. Click Settings.
3. Click Customization.
4. The Customization window opens. Click Customize The System.
5. In the navigation pane, expand the Entities node. Then choose the entity you want. In this example, Address is selected.

> **NOTE** Creating an entity is like creating an entry in a table. Each account or contact that you create is an entity. Each bit of information you assign to those entities, such as a subject or address, is also an entity. Basically, an entity is a piece of information. These entities can all be linked, which makes it possible for you to have the information you need without pulling the pieces together yourself.

6. The Address page opens. If necessary, click the General tab (see Figure 4-32).

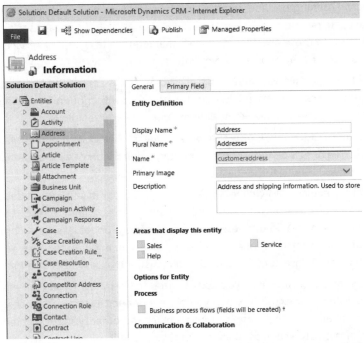

FIGURE 4-32 Customize an entity to enable CRM for your phone and tablet.

7. In the Outlook & Mobile section, select the CRM For Phones and CRM For Tablets check boxes.

8. On the Actions toolbar, click Save.

You now have access to your CRM data on your phone.

Summary

- With customer relationship management (CRM) software, companies can reduce the costs associated with acquiring new customers by organizing and automating certain business processes. Companies can also use CRM software to improve their customers' experience with sales, marketing, and customer service. Perhaps most importantly, CRM software offers one central, organized, easy-to-access place to store data about all your customers and prospects. Microsoft Dynamics CRM Online is such a program.

- Microsoft Dynamics Marketing includes a full suite of tools for data segmentation, behavior tracking, digital asset management, and brand management. It's geared for brand managers and campaign managers. Sales teams can also use this software for more insights into campaigns and targeting.

- Microsoft Social Listening provides volume and sentiment analysis of social networking data. It's ideal for those members of your staff who handle your business's social media efforts, in addition to those employees in sales, marketing, and customer service who want to get a sense of your products, competitors, and industry.

- Like many tools on the Microsoft public cloud, Microsoft Dynamics CRM Online is a SaaS suite and is subscription-based. Microsoft offers four subscription levels. You can mix and match these levels to accommodate the needs of your employees.

- Microsoft Dynamics CRM Online offers three work areas—Sales, Service, and Marketing. Each work area has its own dashboard, offering a quick view of various details. You'll also find tools tailored for that aspect of the business.

- With Microsoft Dynamics CRM Online, you can work with four main types of data. A contact is a record of a person you know and work with. An account is a record about a company with whom you do business. A lead represents a potential sale. An opportunity is a target that is farther along in the sales process. In addition to these, you can also work with cases. A case contains data about a customer question or complaint.

- In Microsoft Dynamics CRM Online, you use activities to keep track of all your interactions with a customer. For example, when you place a phone call to a customer, you can record it as an activity. The same is true for emails and other types of communications. You can also create activities to assign tasks to yourself.

- One way that Microsoft Dynamics CRM Online helps to reduce the costs associated with acquiring new customers is by automating certain business processes. Microsoft Dynamics CRM Online includes several ready-to-use business processes for common scenarios in sales, service, and marketing. By using these processes, you ensure that your employees follow consistent steps every time they interact with customers.

- You aren't limited to using Microsoft Dynamics CRM Online on your desktop. You can also use it on your mobile devices—including Windows Phone, Android, and iOS smartphones, in addition to Microsoft Surface and iPad tablets.

CHAPTER 5

Manage devices in the cloud by using Microsoft Intune

Introduction to Microsoft Intune

Gone are the days when employees were locked to their workstations, with only desktop computers to get things done. Now people expect to be able to work on a variety of devices—desktop computers, laptop computers, smartphones, tablets, and even devices that are both phones and tablets, also known as *phablets*. And they're no longer satisfied with the hardware they've been assigned by their employer. These days, people want to be able to work on their own devices—their own laptops, smartphones, tablets, or phablets. (This is referred to as *bring your own device*, or BYOD.)

All this means is that IT departments are faced with the task of empowering employee productivity across devices—but also with overseeing the security of corporate information on both personal and corporate-owned devices. That's where Microsoft Intune comes in.

Like Microsoft Office 365, Microsoft Intune is a software as a service (SaaS) offering. With Microsoft Intune, organizations can provide employees with access to corporate programs, data, and resources from virtually anywhere and on almost any device (including Windows, Windows Phone, Android, and iOS devices), while at the same time helping to protect corporate information—all from the Microsoft public cloud. With the stand-alone version of Microsoft Intune, which is the focus of this chapter, the administrator can use a web-based administration console to track what hardware is in use. The administrator can also apply policies on all devices and manage settings.

> **NOTE** You can watch videos about setting up your subscription and learn about device management at *aka.ms/go-intune*.

Set up your Microsoft Intune subscription

As you learned in Chapter 2, "Get started with Office 365," Office 365 offers many different subscription models depending on the size of your business and on which Office apps you want to use. In contrast, when used as a stand-alone solution, Microsoft Intune offers one basic subscription model, on a per-user/per-month basis. This subscription includes the following:

- 20 gigabytes (GB) of storage for distributing programs
- Software distribution
- Microsoft System Center 2012 Endpoint Protection (hybrid on-premises–based solution)
- Software licensing inventory reports
- Mobile device app publishing
- Alerts and monitoring
- Security policy management
- 99.9-percent scheduled uptime service level agreement
- Best-in-class support

> **TIP** Microsoft offers a 30-day trial for users who want to test-run the service. To start the trial, go to *aka.ms/go-intune*, click Try Now, and then follow the on-screen prompts. (If you've already signed up for another Microsoft service, such as Office 365, you should sign in using the same user name and password.) As with the Office 365 free trial, you have only 30 days from the time you activate your trial, so activate the trial when you are ready to go through this chapter.

You are not limited to using Microsoft Intune as a stand-alone app, however. You can also use it with Microsoft System Center 2012 R2 Configuration Manager. This extends Configuration Manager beyond "on-premises" PC management to devices in the cloud, including Android, iOS, and Windows Phone devices, all from a single console. This solution provides rich policy management and reporting. It also provides for greater scalability.

> **NOTE** This chapter focuses on using Microsoft Intune as a stand-alone app.

System Center Configuration Manager and Microsoft Intune

Many large organizations and businesses use System Center 2012 R2 to manage, monitor, virtualize, configure, and powerfully automate their information systems, datacenters, and programs, whether they are located on-premises, in the cloud, or in a hybrid environment.

Though a detailed discussion is beyond the scope of this book, it's worthwhile to include a brief introduction to how System Center 2012 R2—and particularly the component called Configuration Manager—can be used to manage devices. The good news is that with this approach, you combine the benefits of the cloud-based, heterogeneous device support provided by Microsoft Intune with the familiar experience that is Configuration Manager, so that you can perform all configuration, software deployment, and policy application for those devices by using one tool.

When you integrate System Center 2012 R2 Configuration Manager and Microsoft Intune, you can create a single management solution. This integration has the added benefit of allowing both domain-joined and non–domain-joined devices to be managed in the same, consistent way, through the Configuration Manager console. Although the complete details of making this integration happen are beyond the scope of this chapter, the outline of the process goes something like this:

1. Configure alternate universal principal name (UPN) suffixes.

2. Synchronize Active Directory Domain Services (AD DS) accounts to Microsoft Intune.

3. Activate accounts in Microsoft Intune.

4. Connect Configuration Manager to the Microsoft Intune subscription.

5. Add the Microsoft Intune Connector site system role.

6. Enable and configure various device platform management extensions.

Connecting to your Microsoft Intune subscription is pretty straightforward. Follow these steps:

1. In the Administration section of Configuration Manager, click Overview, Cloud Services, and then click Microsoft Intune Subscriptions.

2. On the Home tab of the toolbar, click Add Microsoft Intune Subscription.

3. The Create Microsoft Intune Subscription Wizard starts. Use this wizard to sign in to and connect with your subscription, set some general configuration options, choose device platforms you'll support, and more.

For complete documentation on how to use Configuration Manager and Microsoft Intune for device management, see the Microsoft TechNet documentation, "Manage Mobile Devices with Configuration Manager and Microsoft Intune" (*aka.ms /managemobile-configman-intune*). You can also try the process by using virtual machines running in a TechNet Virtual Lab. See "User and Device Management" (*aka.ms/UserAndDeviceManagement*).

Kevin Remde
Technical Evangelist – Microsoft Corporation

Explore the Account Portal

After you set up your Microsoft Intune subscription (or sign up for the free trial), you're ready to begin exploring the program. Your first stop is the Account Portal. As you might guess, the Account Portal is where you manage your Microsoft Intune account. You can access it by clicking the Account Portal link in the upper-right corner of the Microsoft Intune window.

When you first open the Account Portal, it displays the Dashboard (see Figure 5-1). From here, you can add users. To view other options or settings, click any of the links on the left side of the page. These links are divided into four categories—Setup, Management, Subscriptions, and Support—as described here:

- **Setup**
  - **Overview** This page offers support for those configuring services for Microsoft Intune.
- **Management**
  - **Users** From this page, you can add new users, view existing users, edit and delete user accounts, and more.
  - **Security Groups** From this page, you can create security groups and add users to those groups in Microsoft Azure Active Directory (discussed in Chapter 6, "Build and run servers without hardware"). This makes it easier to manage users and devices. You'll use security groups in the Microsoft Intune Administrator Console (discussed in this chapter).
  - **Domains** From this page, you can configure a custom domain that includes your company name for use with Microsoft Intune. (For more on this, see the next section.)

- **Subscriptions**
  - **Manage** From this page, you can view and manage your billing and subscription information. You can also convert your free trial version to a paid subscription from this page.
  - **Licenses** To find out how many Microsoft Intune licenses you have available, see this page.
  - **Purchase** Buy additional licenses from this page.
  - **Software** Go to this page to view any software that you have purchased to distribute to users' devices via Microsoft Intune.
- **Support**
  - **Overview** From this page, you can get help and support from the Microsoft Online Community and manage your delegated administrators—that is, those users to whom you have granted administrative privileges.
  - **Service Requests** Click this link to open the Microsoft Intune support page.
  - **Service Health** This page displays the current status of each service that is running.

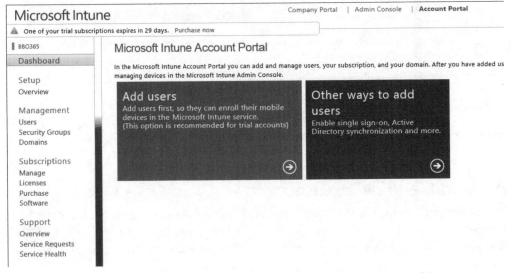

FIGURE 5-1 The Account Portal Dashboard displays links in categories on the left side of the page.

Configure a custom domain

As mentioned, you can configure a custom domain for use with Microsoft Intune, as you can with Office 365—but if you already configured your domain with Office 365, there's no need to do so again here. If, however, you have not configured your custom domain to work with Office 365 or any other Microsoft product, click the Domains link on the left side of the Account Portal (under the Management heading), click the Add A Domain link, and follow the on-screen prompts (see Figure 5-2). For more information about custom domains, see the "Configure a custom domain" section in Chapter 2.

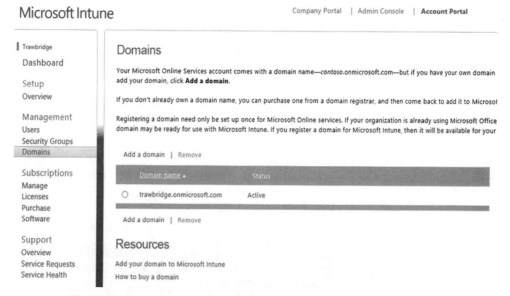

FIGURE 5-2 Click Add A Domain to get started with configuring your custom domain.

Add, edit, and delete users

If you want your company's employees to be able to take advantage of all that Microsoft Intune has to offer, create a user account for each one of them. In other words, add users. To add a user to Microsoft Intune, log on to Microsoft Intune and open the Account Portal. Then follow these steps:

1. On the Dashboard of the Account Portal, click the arrow on the Add Users tile, click New, and then click User. The New User Wizard starts.

2. On the Details page of the New User Wizard (see Figure 5-3), enter the new user's first name, last name, display name, and user name. Then click Next.

FIGURE 5-3 The Details page of the New User Wizard contains boxes for the First Name, Last Name, and User Name for the user who is being created by the administrator.

3. On the Settings page of the New User Wizard (see Figure 5-4), you can assign settings for the user. For example, you can indicate whether the user should have administrative privileges, assign roles to the user, and note where the user is located. When you are finished assigning settings, click Next.

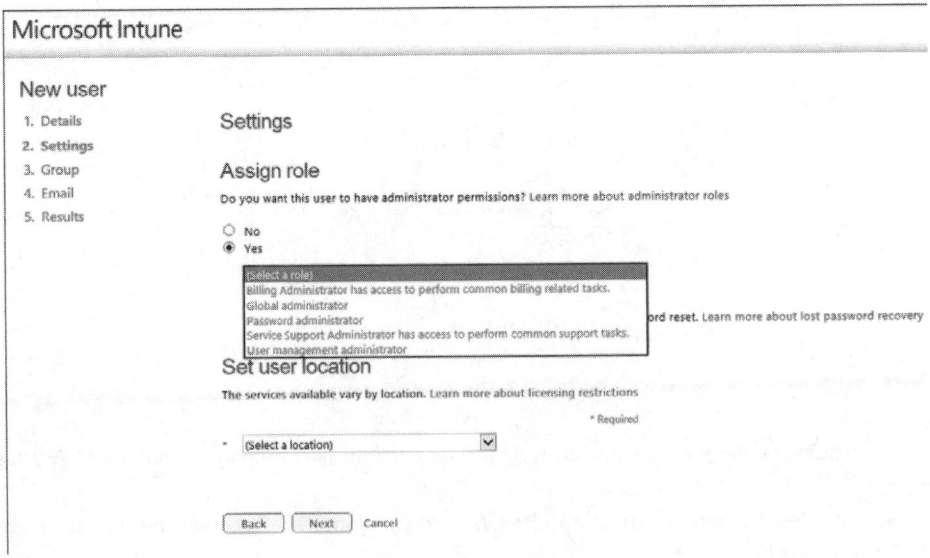

FIGURE 5-4 Assign settings on the Settings page of the New User Wizard.

4. On the Microsoft Intune User Group page of the New User Wizard (see Figure 5-5), you can assign the user to a group. (You'll learn more about groups later in this chapter.) When you're finished, click Next.

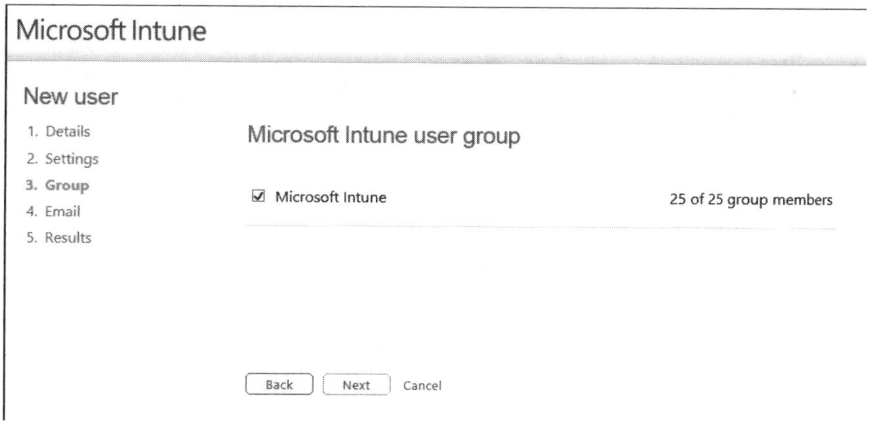

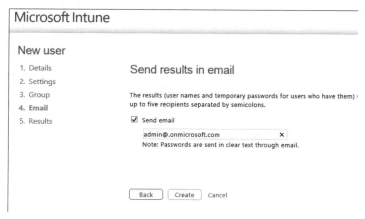

FIGURE 5-5 Assign users to groups on the Microsoft Intune User Group page of the New User Wizard.

5. On the Email page of the New User Wizard (see Figure 5-6), enter your own email address so that you, the administrator, will receive the password. That way, you have it for safekeeping. Optionally, you can enter the new user's email address so that the password can be sent to him or her. (If you don't choose to have the email sent to the user, be sure to devise some other method by which the user can obtain the user name and password.) Then click Create.

FIGURE 5-6 Enter an email address on the Send Results In Email page of the New User Wizard.

6. The Results page of the New User Wizard (see Figure 5-7) shows the new user's user name. Click Finish.

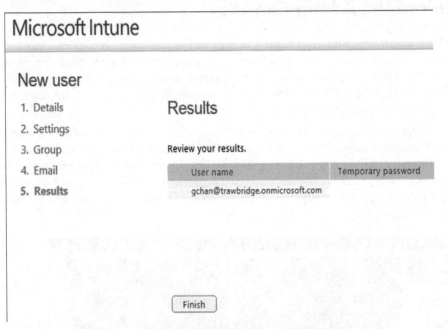

FIGURE 5-7 Click Finish on the Results page of the New User Wizard.

After you finish adding a new user, you will be directed to the Users page in the Account Portal (see Figure 5-8). (You can also access this page by clicking the Users link on the left side of the console, under the Management heading.) Here you can view a list of users. This is also the starting point if you want to edit or delete any user accounts. To edit or delete a user account, select the user whose account you want to edit or delete in the list, click the Edit or Delete link, and follow the on-screen prompts.

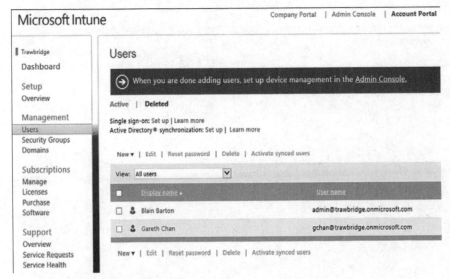

FIGURE 5-8 The user is added, as shown on the Users page. You can also access this page by clicking the Users link on the left side of the Account Portal, under the Management heading.

Explore the Admin Console

The Microsoft Intune Admin Console is where you manage your users' computers and devices—that is, where you deploy software, apply updates, configure policy, and monitor devices. The Admin Console is web browser–based, so you can access it from anywhere, with any device (assuming you have an Internet connection). From mobile devices, connect through *account.manage.microsoft.com*.

To access the Admin Console, click the Admin Console link in the center of the Microsoft Intune Dashboard page. The Admin Console Dashboard (shown in Figure 5-9) appears by default, showing options for getting started with managing mobile devices and getting started with managing computers). The right side of the Dashboard, shown in Figure 5-10, offers various links, including Getting Started, What's New, Forums, System Overview, and Mobile Device Management.

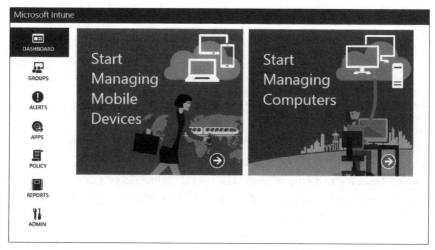

FIGURE 5-9 The Microsoft Intune Admin Console Dashboard helps you get started managing mobile devices and computers.

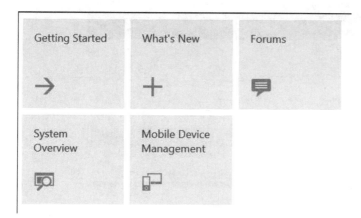

FIGURE 5-10 Access more information from these links, which are available from the Admin Console Dashboard.

In addition to the Dashboard, the Admin Console features a series of links on the left side of the page. These are as follows:

- **Groups**   Click this link to access settings with which you can create groups for users and devices. With these settings, you can more easily manage your devices and users. You'll learn how to create groups later in this chapter.

- **Alerts**   You can set up alerts to help you quickly assess the overall health of the devices you use Microsoft Intune to manage. You'll learn how to set up an alert later in this chapter.

- **Apps**   From here, you can view your app status, access a list of apps that Microsoft Intune has detected on computers you manage, and prepare apps for deployment to devices. You can also view various updates.

- **Policy**   Click this link to view high-level policy details such as policy conflicts, to add new policies, and to view the policies you already have.

- **Reports**   This link offers access to Microsoft Intune's reporting tools. By using these tools, you can generate a variety of useful reports, including computer and mobile device inventory reports, detected software reports, and license reports.

- **Admin**   Click the Admin link to view details about your subscription and cloud storage and to access links to manage updates, storage use, and more.

If you set up Microsoft Intune to manage computers in addition to devices, three other links will appear:

- **Updates**   Click this link to view information about your software update status and your cloud storage status. You can also manage the updates you plan to deploy to computers.

- **Protection**   From here, you can view high-level details for Endpoint Protection, including the current malware and computer status. You can also access links to tasks that help you protect your systems and investigate any malware found.

- **Licenses**   View and manage license agreements for software you have added to Microsoft Intune here.

What is Endpoint Protection?

Endpoint Protection is a built-in feature of Microsoft Intune. It provides real-time protection against malware, automatically scanning computers and keeping malware definitions up to date. Endpoint Protection also offers tools to help administrators in the event of a malware attack. (*Malware* refers to any software designed to damage or disable a computer or network.)

Create device and user groups

Creating device and user groups simplifies the management of user accounts and devices. For example, you could set up groups by geographic location, department, or hardware characteristics. After you have set up a group, you can perform a wide variety of administrative tasks on those groups rather than on individual users or devices. For example, you could set a policy for a group of users or deploy a program to a set of devices in one action.

To create a device group, follow these steps:

1. In the Microsoft Intune Admin Console, click Groups on the left side of the page.

2. If necessary, click Overview, as shown in Figure 5-11.

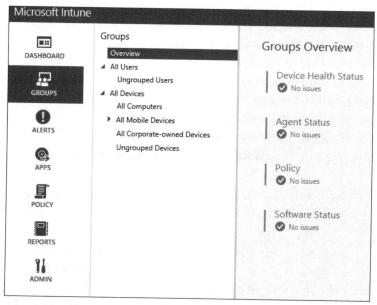

FIGURE 5-11 Click Overview to display a short visual of key information about groups.

3. On the Groups Overview page, click Create Group. The Create Group Wizard starts.

4. In the Group Name box, enter a name for the group (see Figure 5-12). Then click All Devices and click Next.

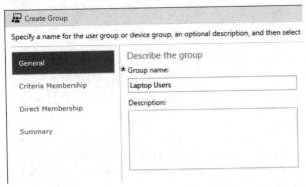

FIGURE 5-12 Create groups to form logical groupings of users.

5. On the Define Membership Criteria page, choose what types of devices you want to add. Then click Next.

6. On the Define Direct Membership page, specify which devices you want to add to the group. Then click Next.

7. Review your selections on the Summary page, and then click Finish.

The newly created group will appear in the Groups list, under All Devices, as shown in Figure 5-13.

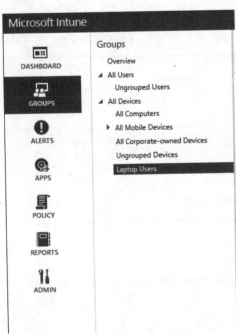

FIGURE 5-13 A newly created group, Laptop Users, appears under All Devices.

From here, you can edit or delete the group.

Creating a user group is similar to creating a device group. Follow these steps:

1. In the Microsoft Intune Admin Console, click Groups on the left side of the page.

2. If necessary, click Overview.

3. On the Overview page, click Create Group. The Create Group Wizard starts.

4. In the Group Name box, enter a name for the group. Then choose All Users from the list. Finally, click Next.

5. On the Define Membership Criteria page, click the Browse button next to the Exclude Members From These Security Groups box, and select Company Administrator. This way you can manage the group without affecting the Company Administrator account (also called the Tenant Administrator). Click Next.

6. On the Define Direct Membership page, specify the specific users you want to add to the group. Then click Next.

7. Review your selections on the Summary page, and then click Finish.

Set up alerts

An important part of managing any system is being notified when there are problems. To address this, you can use Microsoft Intune to set up alerts and notifications. For example, you might set up an alert for when malware is detected.

To set up an alert—in this example, for malware detection—follow these steps:

1. In the Microsoft Intune Admin Console, click Alerts on the left side of the page.

2. If necessary, click Overview.

3. On the Overview page, click Configure Alert Type Settings.

4. In the search box that appears, enter **malware**. Then click the Search icon.

> **TIP** If you want to create an alert for something else, enter a different keyword in the search box.

5. Right-click Investigate New Malware and choose Configure.

6. In the Configure Alert Type dialog box, shown in Figure 5-14, click the Severity list and choose Critical. Then click OK.

FIGURE 5-14 Select the Critical severity level so that you'll receive these alerts.

Next, you can set up Microsoft Intune to send you a notification via email if this alert is triggered. Follow these steps:

1. In the Microsoft Intune Admin Console, click Alerts.

2. If necessary, click Overview.

3. On the Overview page, click Configure Alert Type Settings.

4. Click the Notification Rules node, as shown in Figure 5-15, and then click the Create New Rule button.

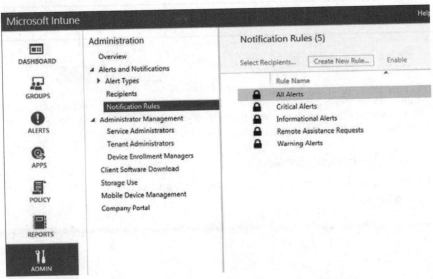

FIGURE 5-15 You create a rule to so that alerts trigger an email notification.

5. The Create Notification Rule Wizard starts. On the first page of the wizard, shown in Figure 5-16, enter a name for the notification, select the categories that apply (in this example, Endpoint Protection), and select the alert severity (Critical). Then click Next.

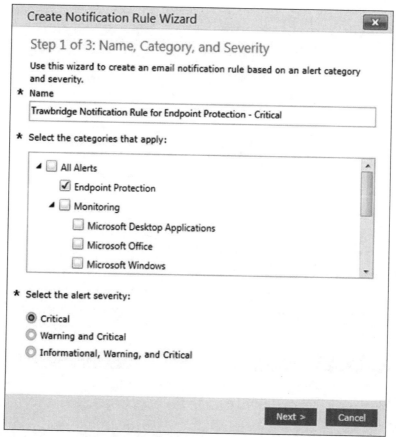

FIGURE 5-16 To create an email notification based on an alert category and severity, start by creating a name for the notification, and then identify the categories and alert severities you want to associate with this notification.

6. Select All Devices and click Next.

7. On the final page of the wizard, select the email address to which the notification should be sent.

Create policies

With Microsoft Intune, you can apply policies. A policy is a group of settings that controls features on a computer or mobile device. Microsoft Intune offers many types of preconfigured policies, which you can apply as needed. For example, there are preconfigured policies for managing Windows Firewall. Alternatively, you can create your own custom policies.

To create and deploy a policy—in this example, a mobile device security policy—follow these steps:

1. In the Microsoft Intune Admin Console, click Policy on the left side of the page.

2. If necessary, click Overview.

3. On the Policy Overview page, shown in Figure 5-17, click Add Policy.

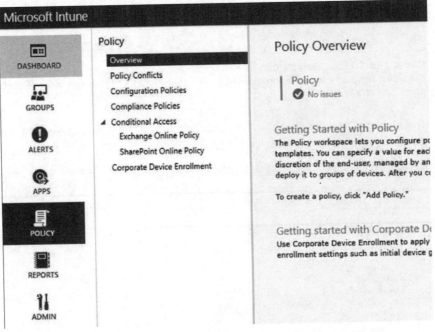

FIGURE 5-17 You can create your own policy from the Policy Overview page.

4. As shown in Figure 5-18, select a template for your new policy. Also specify how you want to use the template. The template provides the settings to configure your policy. In this example, select Mobile Device Security Policy, click Create And Deploy A Policy With The Recommended Settings, and then click Create Policy.

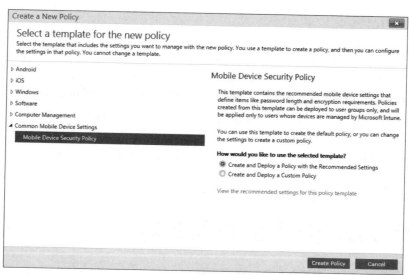

FIGURE 5-18 Select a template that contains settings you want to configure for your policy. You can select templates for common mobile devices, specific types of devices, software, and computer management.

5. The Manage Deployment dialog box, shown in Figure 5-19, opens. Select All Users so the policy applies to everyone, click Add, and click OK.

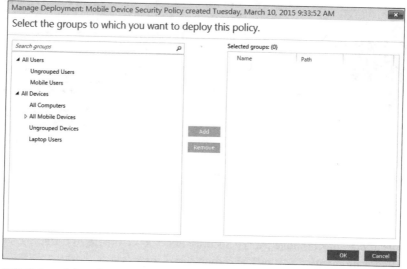

FIGURE 5-19 Select the groups to which you are deploying the policy.

As a result of this policy, all mobile devices you enroll in Microsoft Intune will lock after 15 minutes of inactivity, require a password to unlock, and permit only four consecutive sign-in failures before being wiped.

Install the Microsoft Intune client software on client computers

You must install the Microsoft Intune client software on your employees' computers so that they can work with Microsoft Intune. When you do, the computers will be able to do the following:

- Check for software updates.
- Scan for malicious software.
- Install programs from your Company Portal. (You'll learn more about the Company Portal later in this chapter.)

NOTE This chapter focuses on using Microsoft Intune as a stand-alone app. Go to *aka.ms /manageintuneapps* for more information about the application management capabilities of Microsoft Intune alone.

Before you can install the client software on a client computer, you must create a compressed file of the software and place it on a drive that is accessible from the client machine. To do so, follow these steps:

1. In the Microsoft Intune Admin Console, click Admin on the left side of the page.
2. Click Client Software Download on the Administration page. The Client Software Download page appears, as shown in Figure 5-20.

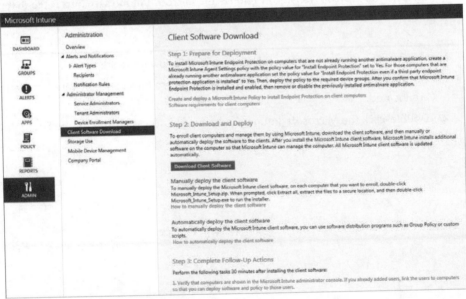

FIGURE 5-20 The Client Software Download page in the Admin Console explains how to prepare for, download, and deploy client software.

3. Click the Download Client Software button to download the compressed file, which is called Microsoft_Intune_Setup.zip, and save it in a secure location on your network.

4. Extract the contents of the compressed file to the same location on your network, as shown in Figure 5-21.

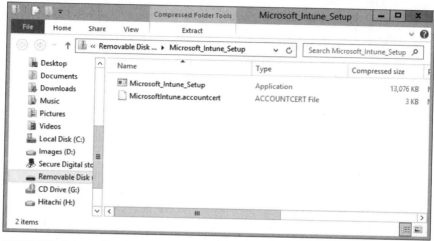

FIGURE 5-21 Extract the setup files to a location on your network.

IMPORTANT Do not rename or remove the MicrosoftIntune.accountcert file that is extracted. If you do remove or rename it, the client software installation will fail.

Next, install the software on the client computer. Follow these steps:

1. On the client computer, browse to the folder where the client software installation files are located.

2. Double-click the Microsoft_Intune_Setup.exe file. The Microsoft Intune Setup Wizard starts, as shown in Figure 5-22.

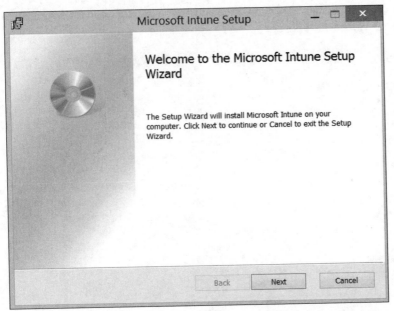

FIGURE 5-22 This is the Welcome page for the Microsoft Intune Setup Wizard.

3. Click Next to proceed, and then click Finish. The wizard installs Microsoft Intune on the client machine.

After the setup routine is complete, the client software continues to run in the background, configuring the computer for use with Microsoft Intune. Specifically, it does the following:

- It automatically enrolls the computer with Microsoft Intune.
- It submits an inventory of the computer's hardware and software.
- It configures Microsoft Intune policy, also installing Endpoint Protection (if configured to do so).
- It installs the Microsoft Intune Center app on the computer.

You'll know the client installation is complete and was successful when the Microsoft Intune Center, shown in Figure 5-23, appears on the client machine.

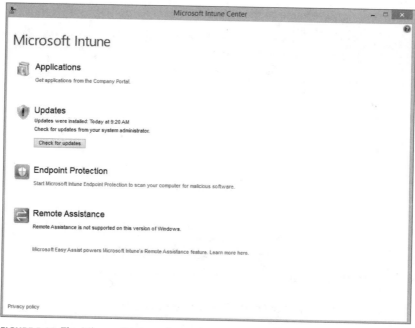

FIGURE 5-23 The Microsoft Intune Center is displayed when installation is complete.

The Microsoft Intune Center offers the user access to the following:

- **Applications** The user can click this option to download any programs that you have made available to him or her via the Microsoft Intune Company Portal.
- **Updates** These include updates that the administrator has made available or requires.
- **Endpoint Protection** Endpoint Protection offers real-time protection and scans for malware.
- **Remote Assistance** This is available for Windows 7 devices.

The client machine will also appear in the Admin Console. To view it, click Groups on the left side of the console, click All Devices, and click All Computers. As shown in Figure 5-24, the computer is listed in the pane on the right.

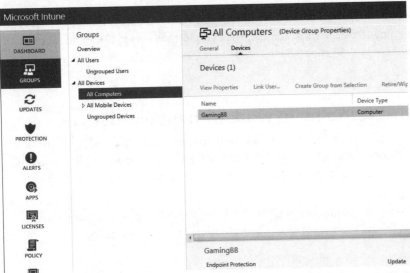

FIGURE 5-24 A computer on which the client software was installed appears in the All Computers pane in the Admin Console.

As shown in Figure 5-25, you can now right-click the computer in the All Computers list and perform many different tasks on it. For example, you can run a malware scan, restart the computer, or update malware definitions.

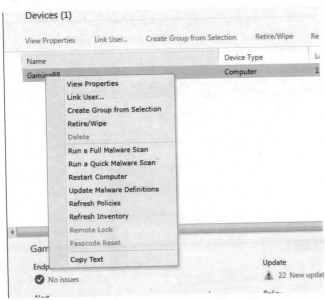

FIGURE 5-25 Right-click the computer in the Admin Console to view the tasks you can perform on it.

> **TIP** If you want to uninstall the Microsoft Intune client software from the computer—for example, if the computer belongs to someone who has left the company and no longer needs the software—you can choose Retire/Wipe to remove it.

Set up Microsoft Intune to work with mobile devices

You can set up Microsoft Intune to work with various types of mobile devices. These include Windows tablets, Windows Phones, Android devices, and iOS (Apple) devices. First, however, you must indicate that you want to use Microsoft Intune to manage your mobile devices.

> **TIP** After you set up Microsoft Intune to work with mobile devices, you must enroll the devices you want to use. You'll learn how to enroll devices later in this chapter.

Follow these steps:

1. In the Microsoft Intune Admin Console, click Admin on the left.
2. On the Administration Overview page, click Mobile Device Management.
3. In the Mobile Device Management pane, click Set Mobile Device Management Authority, as shown in Figure 5-26.

> **IMPORTANT** Plan carefully! If you choose this option, you cannot use System Center to manage mobile devices. After you choose an authority, you cannot change it again.

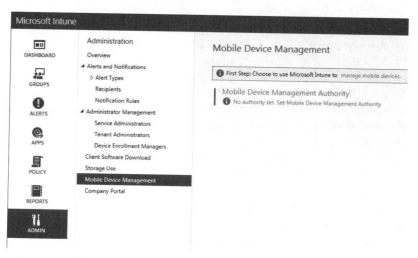

FIGURE 5-26 Click Set Mobile Device Management Authority to use Microsoft Intune to manage mobile devices.

4. The Manage Mobile Devices dialog box opens, as shown in Figure 5-27. Select the Use Microsoft Intune To Manage My Mobile Devices check box. Then click OK.

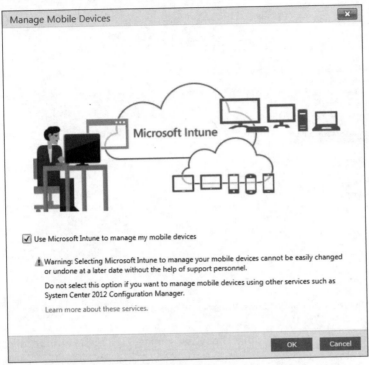

FIGURE 5-27 Indicate that you want to use Microsoft Intune to manage your mobile devices.

Microsoft Intune displays the available mobile platforms. As shown in Figure 5-28, you can now enroll Windows, Windows Phone, and Android devices. iOS devices, however, require a bit more configuration.

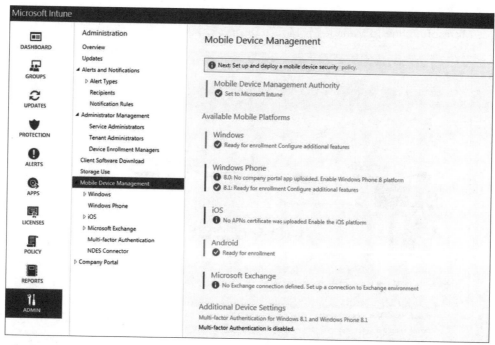

FIGURE 5-28 You are now set to enroll Windows, Windows Phone, and Android devices.

To set up Microsoft Intune to work with iOS devices, you need an Apple Push Notification service (APNs) certificate.

NOTE To complete the following steps, you must have an Apple ID. This should be a special Apple ID for your company rather than your personal Apple ID and should be passed along to your replacement if you leave the company. For more information, go to *applieid.apple.com*.

To obtain this certificate, follow these steps:

1. In the Microsoft Intune Admin Console, click Admin on the left.

2. On the Administration Overview page, click Mobile Device Management.

3. Under Mobile Device Management, click iOS and then click Upload An APNs Certificate to open the page shown in Figure 5-29.

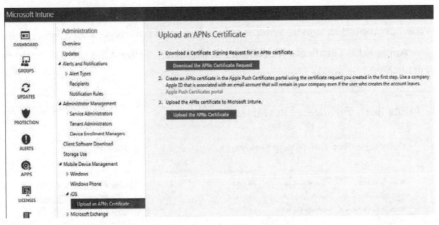

FIGURE 5-29 Start the process of uploading an APNs certificate.

4. In the Upload An APNs Certificate pane, click Download The APNs Certificate Request.

> **TIP** A quicker way to access the page shown in Figure 5-29 is to click the Enable The iOS Platform link shown earlier in Figure 5-28.

5. You will be prompted to save the certificate signing request (.csr) file in the certs ios folder on your computer. Enter a name for the file (in this example, **request.csr**), and click Save (see Figure 5-30). You need this file on your computer to complete the next step.

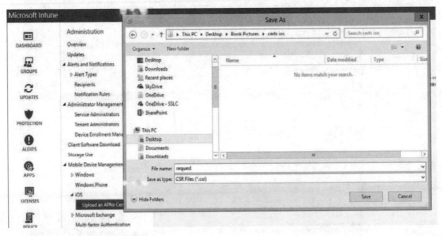

FIGURE 5-30 Save the .csr file.

6. In the Upload An APNs Certificate pane, click the Apple Push Certificates Portal link.

7. When prompted to sign in, enter your Apple ID and password. Then click Sign In.

8. The Apple Push Certificates Portal opens, as shown in Figure 5-31. Click Create A Certificate.

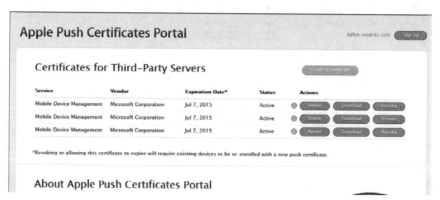

FIGURE 5-31 Click Create A Certificate in the Apple Push Certificates Portal.

9. When prompted, click Accept to agree to the terms of use.

10. The Create A New Push Certificate page appears. Click Browse.

11. The Choose File To Upload dialog box opens. Locate and select the .csr file you saved in step 5 (in this example, the request.csr file in the certs ios folder). Then click Open (see Figure 5-32).

FIGURE 5-32 Select the .csr file you saved in step 5.

12. Click Upload on the Create A New Push Certificate page (see Figure 5-33) to upload a new push certificate.

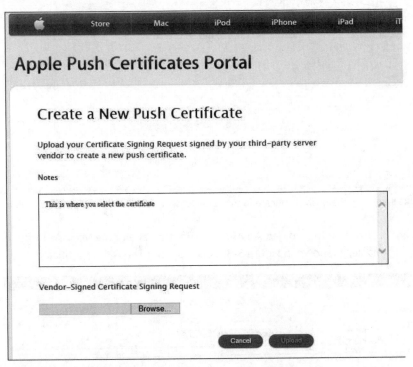

FIGURE 5-33 Upload the selected .csr file.

13. Windows asks you to confirm that you want to upload the push certificate. Click the arrow next to the Save button and click Save As, as shown in Figure 5-34.

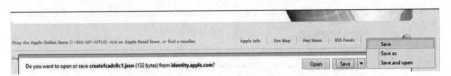

FIGURE 5-34 When prompted, click the arrow next to the Save button and click Save As.

14. The Save As dialog box opens. Select the folder in which you saved the .csr file (certs ios) and leave the push certificate file name as the default (createfcadc8c1 in this example), as shown in Figure 5-35. Then click Save.

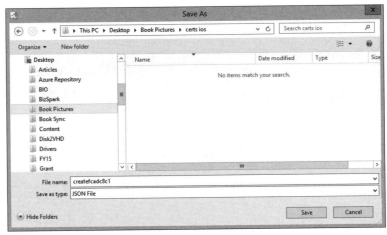

FIGURE 5-35 Save the push certificate in the same folder as the .csr file you created earlier.

15. You are returned to the Upload An APNs Certificate pane in the Microsoft Intune Admin Console, as shown in Figure 5-36. Click Upload The APNs Certificate.

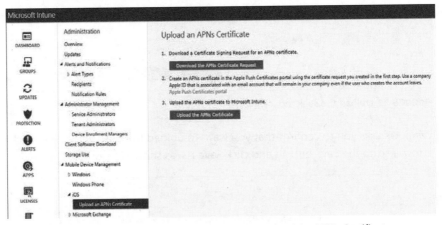

FIGURE 5-36 Click Upload the APNs Certificate in the Upload An APNs Certificate pane.

16. The Upload The APNs Certificate dialog box opens. Click Browse.

17. The Open dialog box appears. Locate and select the push file (now named MDM_Microsoft Corporation_Certificate) in the certs ios folder and click Open (see Figure 5-37).

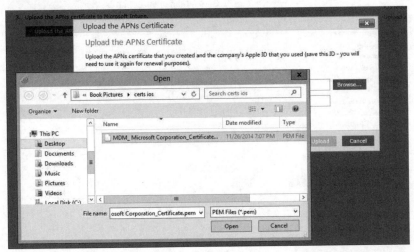

FIGURE 5-37 Locate and select the MDM_Microsoft Corporation_Certificate file and click Open.

18. In the Upload The APNs Certificate dialog box (see Figure 5-38), again enter your Apple ID. Then click Upload.

FIGURE 5-38 Enter your Apple ID and click Upload.

As shown in Figure 5-39, you can now enroll iOS mobile devices and set them up for use with Microsoft Intune. You'll learn how to enroll devices later in this chapter.

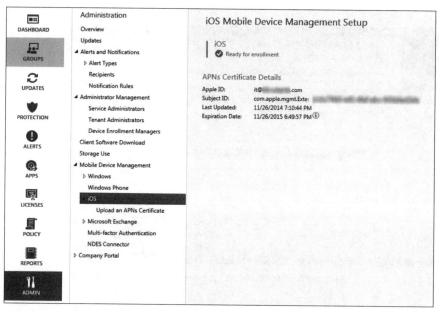

FIGURE 5-39 Microsoft Intune is now set to enroll iOS mobile devices.

Prepare software for distribution

One of the main benefits of using Microsoft Intune is that it offers an easy way to distribute software to your users, whether those users are using desktop computers or mobile devices. You can even control which groups of users have access to what software.

> **NOTE** When you prepare software for distribution as described in this section, the software is made available to users via your Company Portal. You'll learn more about the Company Portal—and how to download software from it—later in this chapter.

To prepare a program for distribution, follow these steps:

1. In the Microsoft Intune Admin Console, click Apps on the left side of the page to display the Apps page, as shown in Figure 5-40.

2. On the Apps page, under Tasks, click Add Apps.

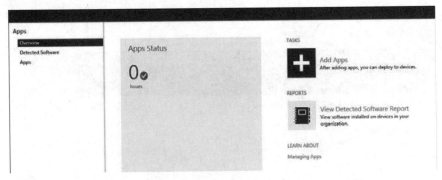

FIGURE 5-40 You can make apps available to users throughout your company.

3. On the Add Software – Sign In page, enter your Microsoft Intune user name and password.

4. The Microsoft Intune Software Publisher Wizard starts. On the Before You Begin page, click Next.

5. On the Software Setup page shown in Figure 5-41, for Select How This Software Is Made Available to Devices, click External Link. Next, enter the URL for the software in the Specify The URL field. Then click Next.

> **NOTE** To obtain a link to a policy-managed app (iOS and Android), from the App Store, find and note the URL of the policy-managed app you want to deploy. For example, the URL of the Microsoft Word for iPad app is *https://itunes.apple.com/us /app/microsoft-word-for-ipad/id586447913?mt=8*.

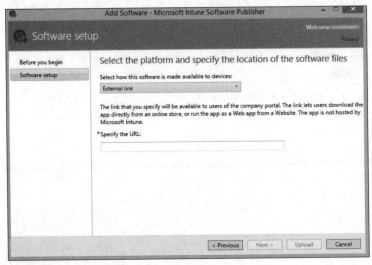

FIGURE 5-41 You create the link that will be available through the Company Portal so that users can download and run the app.

6. On the Software Description page shown in Figure 5-42, enter information about the software.

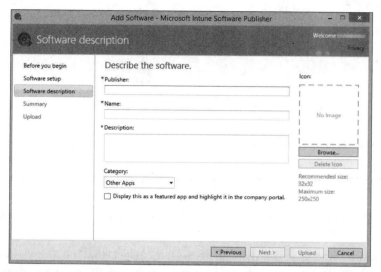

FIGURE 5-42 Enter information about the software. This information will appear in the Company Portal.

This information will appear in your Company Portal:

- **Publisher** This specifies the name of the publisher, which is usually the company name.

- **Name** This is the name of the software, which will appear in the Company Portal. Give each software package a unique name because the Company Portal will display only one app if there are multiple apps with the same name. Also, consider how users will search for this software when you create the name; it should be easy to find.

- **Description** Provide a brief description of the software that will appear in the Company Portal.

- **Category** This optional setting lets you classify the software in predefined categories, or as Other Apps if none of the predefined categories is applicable.

7. Optionally, make your software more visible with two additional settings:

   ■ Select the check box if you want the software to be displayed prominently on the Company Portal as a featured app.

   ■ Include an image for an icon to be associated with the app. The recommended size is 32 x 32 pixels, and the maximum size is 250 x 250 pixels.

8. After completing all the settings, click Next.

9. The Summary page appears. Verify the information you entered.

> **IMPORTANT**   Before you move on to the next step, test the URL from your Internet browser on a mobile device. You want to be sure the link is working before you publish the software.

10. Click Upload to publish the software. Then click Close to exit the wizard.

After you complete the Microsoft Intune Software Publisher Wizard, there's one more step you need to take: indicating which users will have access to the software.

1. In the Apps pane of the Admin Console (see Figure 5-43), click Manage Deployment.

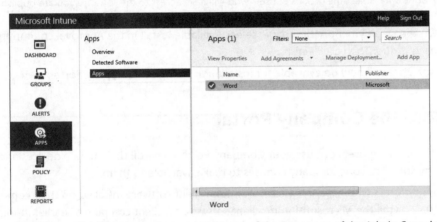

FIGURE 5-43 Click Manage Deployment at the top of the Apps pane of the Admin Console.

2. On the Select Groups page shown in Figure 5-44, select the group or groups to which you want to grant access to this software. Click Add, and then click Next.

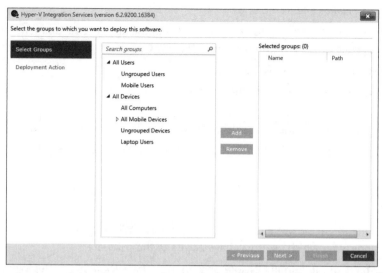

FIGURE 5-44 Select the groups of users who will have access to the software you are publishing.

3. On the Deployment Action page, select Available Install in the Approval column for each group. Then click Finish.

The software will now be available for installation from your Company Portal.

Explore the Company Portal

As mentioned, your users can use your Company Portal to enroll their mobile devices and to access any software your company chooses to make available to them.

Computer users who have the Microsoft Intune client software installed on their computers (see "Install the Microsoft Intune client software on client computers" earlier in this chapter for details) can access the Company Portal by clicking the Company Portal link in the upper-right area of the Microsoft Intune screen. From there, users can install apps and perform other tasks.

Mobile users must take a few additional steps to access the Company Portal. Specifically, they must install the Company Portal app on their devices. They must also enroll their devices from the Company Portal. (Computers are enrolled automatically when the Microsoft Intune client software is installed.) Read on to learn how to complete these tasks.

Create your Company Portal

Before you can use your Company Portal, you must create it. You do this from the Microsoft Intune Admin Console. Here's how:

1. In the Microsoft Intune Admin Console, click Admin on the left side of the page.
2. On the Administration Overview page, click Company Portal.
3. The Company Portal pane opens (see Figure 5-45). Enter the requested information and click Save.

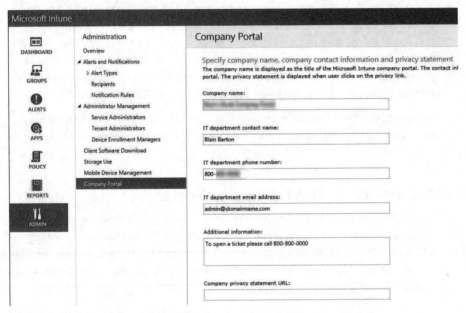

FIGURE 5-45 Enter the requested information to set up your Company Portal.

Install the Company Portal app on your mobile device

To install the Company Portal app, which is free, on a mobile device, you (or the user) must obtain the app from the appropriate outlet. That is, Windows Phone users can obtain the app from the Windows Phone Store, Android users can obtain the app from Google Play, and iPhone and iPad users can obtain the app from the App Store.

- For Windows devices, go to *aka.ms/windowscompanyportal*.
- For Windows Phone, go to *aka.ms/winphonecompanyportal*.
- For Android devices, go to *aka.ms/androidcompanyportal*.
- For iOS devices, go to *aka.ms/ioscompanyportal*.

After they install the app, users should start it. When they do, they'll be asked to provide credentials. These should be the user name and password the user received after his or her user account was created (unless the user has changed the password, in which case the new password should be used). The first time the user starts the app, he or she will also be required to accept the app's terms and conditions.

Terms and conditions

You're familiar with these. Everyone has terms and conditions attached to the use of their products. You can include terms and conditions that your users will find the first time they use the Company Portal from any device. Each user will need to accept the terms and conditions to gain access to the Company Portal. Also, if you update the terms and conditions, you can create a new version that requires users to accept them again the next time they open the Company Portal.

Terms and conditions apply to users (not devices). Users accept each version only once, and then they can access the Company Portal from any of their devices.

Enroll a device in the Company Portal

In addition to downloading the Company Portal app, mobile users must enroll their devices with Microsoft Intune. The specific steps for enrolling vary by device. If you are using the Microsoft Intune client on a Windows-based device, you can go to the Company Portal link or click the Software icon located in the notification area on your device. You will then select the software you want to install.

> **NOTE** For more information about enrolling mobile devices by using Microsoft Intune, go to *https://technet.microsoft.com/en-us/library/dn646957.aspx.*

Install software on a computer or device from the Company Portal

Earlier, you learned how to prepare software for distribution on Microsoft Intune. In this example, the software is Adobe Reader. After you have installed the Microsoft Intune client software on your computer or downloaded the Company Portal app to your mobile device and enrolled the device with Microsoft Intune, you can install the software from the Company Portal.

To install software on a computer, follow these steps:

1. Go to the notification area, click the Microsoft Intune icon as shown in Figure 5-46, and click Company Portal.

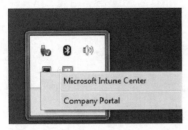

FIGURE 5-46 You open the Company Portal from the notification area.

2. Sign in to your account, as shown in Figure 5-47. Use the account that was set up as a user in the Microsoft Intune Admin Portal. Make sure you use the client software that comes from within the portal.

FIGURE 5-47 Sign In to Microsoft Intune.

3. When the Microsoft Intune Center opens (see Figure 5-48), click Applications.

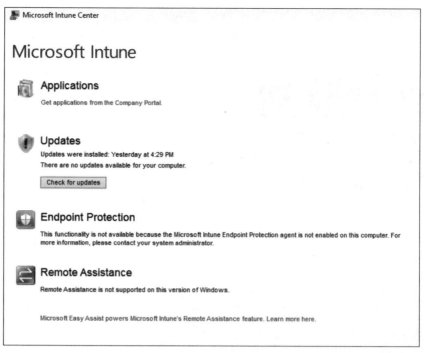

FIGURE 5-48 Select Applications from the Microsoft Intune Center.

4. In the dialog box shown in Figure 5-49, link your device to the Microsoft Intune portal by clicking Yes, indicating that you are the primary user of the device.

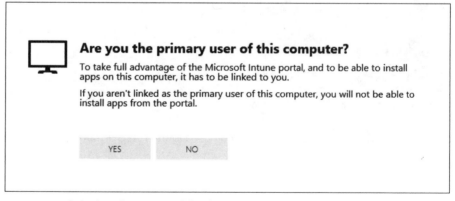

FIGURE 5-49 Only the primary user of the device can install apps from the Microsoft Intune portal.

5. When the Company Portal opens, it will have an informational message at the top, indicating that your device either is not enrolled or can't be identified (see Figure 5-50). Click Click Here To Select Your Device.

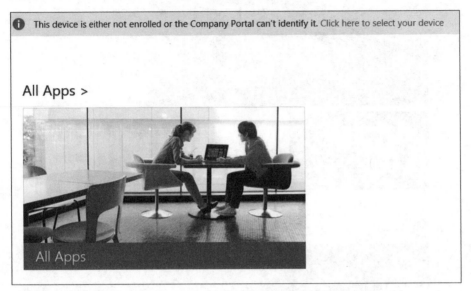

FIGURE 5-50 You must identify your device to access the Company Portal.

6. You are prompted to select your local device (see Figure 5-51). This is the device on which this app will be installed. Select your device and click OK.

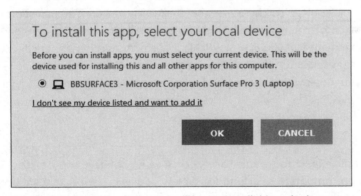

FIGURE 5-51 Select the device you will use to install this and other apps.

7. When this process is complete, the Company Portal displays both the apps that are available and your device, as shown in Figure 5-52.

FIGURE 5-52 Your device and your app are visible in the Company Portal.

Depending on which portal you choose—either the Microsoft Store Company Portal for devices or the Microsoft Intune Company Portal—users will have access to apps and to the device management that you make available to them. Apps communicate directly with an on-premises server (Configuration Manager) or with the Microsoft Intune service, depending on your deployment strategy and management requirements.

Summary

- These days, people expect to be able to work on a variety of devices—desktop computers, laptop computers, smartphones, tablets, and even devices that are both phones and tablets, also known as *phablets*. Moreover, they want to be able to work on their *own* devices. This is referred to as *bring your own device*, or *BYOD*.

- With Microsoft Intune, organizations can provide employees with access to corporate software, data, and resources from virtually anywhere and on almost any device (including Windows, Windows Phone, Android, and iOS devices), while at the same time protecting corporate information—all from the Microsoft public cloud.

- When used as a stand-alone solution, Microsoft Intune offers one basic subscription model, on a per-user/per-month basis.

- The Account Portal is where you manage your Microsoft Intune account. You can access it by clicking the Account Portal link in the upper-right corner of the Microsoft Intune window.

- You can configure a custom domain for use with Microsoft Intune, as you can with Office 365—but if you already configured your domain with Office 365, there's no need to do so again.

- For your company's employees to be able to take advantage of all that Microsoft Intune has to offer, you must create a user account for each one of them. In other words, you must add users. You add, edit, and delete user accounts via the Account Portal.

- The Microsoft Intune Admin Console is where you manage your users' computers and devices—that is, where you deploy software, apply updates, configure policy, and monitor devices. The Admin Console is web-based, so you can access it from anywhere (assuming you have an Internet connection).

- Creating device and user groups simplifies the management of user accounts and devices. After you have set up a group, you can perform a wide variety of administrative tasks on that group rather than on individual users or devices.

- With Microsoft Intune, you can apply policies. A *policy* is a group of settings that controls features on a computer or mobile device. Microsoft Intune offers a variety of preconfigured policies, which you can apply as needed. Alternatively, you can create your own custom policies.

- For your employees' computers to work with Microsoft Intune, you must install the Microsoft Intune client on them. When you do, the computers will be able to check for software updates, scan for malicious software, and install software from the Company Portal.

- You can set up Microsoft Intune to work with various types of mobile devices, including Windows tablets, Windows Phones, Android devices, and iOS (Apple) devices. First, however, you must set up Microsoft Intune to manage your mobile devices.

- Microsoft Intune offers an easy way to distribute software to your users, whether they're using desktop computers or mobile devices. You can even control which groups of users have access to what software.

- The Company Portal is a repository for all the apps that your company chooses to make available to users. It's also where users enroll devices for use with Microsoft Intune.

CHAPTER 6

Build and run servers without using hardware

What is IaaS?

Traditional businesses operate with a server room, or at least one server in a closet somewhere on-premises. But having servers on site means providing maintenance and support. Unfortunately, when it comes to small businesses, that maintenance and support is often provided by non-technical employees. They do the best they can, but it's quite a challenge for the business. Moreover, expenses add up because servers require electricity, cooling systems, backup power systems, and more.

Another major challenge is poor network connectivity. Many small businesses cope with slow Internet connections. Perhaps worse, security is too often a secondary consideration in business decisions. And, of course, data is lost when a hard drive crashes and backup routines have been neglected.

Luckily, in today's world, businesses both small and large have a new option: public cloud services and, more specifically, infrastructure as a service (IaaS). As mentioned in Chapter 1, "What the cloud can do for your business," with IaaS users can rent compute, storage, and networking resources by using datacenter hardware to deploy virtual machines (VMs). The service provider maintains this infrastructure. Users pay for these resources as they would a utility, like power or water, with the cost reflecting the actual amount of resources consumed.

If you go the IaaS route, does that mean your business buys a physical server in a data-center somewhere? No. It means that you buy compute cycles, storage space, and networking resources on the IaaS cloud platform, without the need to manage the hardware. But even though the compute, storage, and networking resources are owned by the service provider, you still control the operating system and programs, which are hosted on the provider's datacenters. So, regardless of what type of software your business uses, you can deploy it in an IaaS platform.

Microsoft offers a formidable IaaS platform: Microsoft Azure. With Azure, you get compute, storage, and networking services, as shown in Figure 6-1. You, however, are responsible for the elements at the top of the stack shown in the figure. Azure also offers websites and web hosting, SQL platform as a service (PaaS), predictive analytics, mobile back ends, and more. Some of these features will be discussed elsewhere in this book.

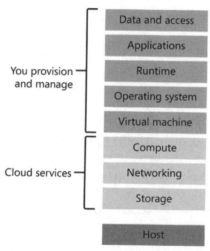

FIGURE 6-1 Azure handles the items in the bottom of the stack. The items on the top are managed by you.

MICROSOFT VIRTUAL ACADEMY Watch a video about Azure IaaS for IT pros at *aka.ms/go-mva/azureitpros.*

Azure in Action

Though this chapter primarily discusses VMs, you can benefit from understanding the overall breadth and depth of Azure. My website, *virtuallycloud9.com*, runs on Azure. This website is hosted on WordPress and is backed by a Windows VM. The data resides in a MySQL database at Microsoft's partner, ClearDB. In this case, the website is deployed as a cloud service with the normal WordPress setup execution completed in the background for the administrator. The VM is set up in the process and runs without the administrator's involvement. This would be using Azure in the platform-as-a-service (PaaS) model. As you learned in Chapter 1, with PaaS users can develop, run, and manage web apps in a ready-made, cloud-based environment.

Conversely, during the Azure IT Pro Camps in 2015, the technical team helped administrators learn how to deploy VMs for custom programs or operating system deployments. The VMs can connect to and use websites deployed in the same Azure subscription, and they can also interact with SQL databases deployed in the same account.

Tommy Patterson
Senior Technical Evangelist – Microsoft Corporation

Set up your Azure subscription

Azure is an IaaS. In other words, it's a subscription service. Microsoft offers two types of subscriptions for Azure:

- **Pay as you go**   With this type of subscription, you pay for what you use each month, with no commitment. There is no minimum purchase, and you can cancel anytime.
- **Enterprise agreement**   This subscription model is designed for large organizations. With this model, organizations commit to a certain level of usage per month. In exchange, they get reduced prices for the service.

TIP   For those who want to try the service before committing to using it, Microsoft offers a 30-day trial subscription. For more information, visit *aka.ms/try-azure.* After the trial expires, you can convert it to a pay-as-you-go subscription.

Virtual machines are priced by using a tier system. For Windows-based VMs, you must first select whether you want to choose from the Basic tier options or the Standard tier options. VMs in the Basic tier cannot be automatically scaled (that is, their numbers automatically increased or decreased), nor can they engage in load balancing. VMs in the Standard tier, however, are unrestricted in both regards. If you are deploying a VM as a one-time test, choosing one in the Basic tier is probably just fine. VMs in the Standard tier are best for production apps that need to scale based on demand.

Within each tier are several additional options, each with its own set of parameters. For example, the Basic tier for Windows-based VMs offers the choices outlined in Table 6-1. (For more details about the two tiers and VM sizes, go to *aka.ms/vmsizes*.)

TABLE 6-1 Basic tier choices

Option	Number of cores	RAM	Disk size
A0	1	768 MB	20 GB
A1	1	1.75 GB	40 GB
A2	2	3.5 GB	60 GB
A3	4	7 GB	120 GB
A4	8	14 GB	240 GB

Table 6-2 outlines the Standard tier choices for Windows-based VMs.

TABLE 6-2 Standard tier choices

Option	Number of cores	RAM	Disk size
A0	1	768 MB	20 GB
A1	1	1.75 GB	70 GB
A2	2	3.5 GB	135 GB
A3	4	7 GB	285 GB
A4	8	14 GB	605 GB
A5	2	14 GB	135 GB
A6	4	28 GB	285 GB
A7	8	56 GB	605 GB

NOTE Pricing information is not included here because it frequently changes. Indeed, prices in the cloud are nearly as fluid as water. And fortunately, like water, these prices seem to be streaming downward. For the latest in pricing, and to find out what additional plans are available, visit *azure.microsoft.com/en-us/pricing/calculator/?scenario-virtual-machines*.

Azure does not bill on a per-month or even a per-hour basis. Rather, VMs in Azure are billed by the minute. If you run a VM for only a few minutes each month, your bill will be smaller than if you run it for a few hours, reflecting the low usage.

> **TIP** To help you estimate your VM bill, you can use the Azure Cost Estimator tool. You can download this tool from *microsoft.com/en-us/download/details.aspx?id=43376*.

Get started with Azure

At the time of this writing, there were two portals or user interfaces for Azure. One is the classic portal, which has the most comprehensive set of options for deployment. The other is the preview portal. You can switch portals from either portal. The classic portal can be found at *manage.windowsazure.com*.

When you sign up for an Azure account, you have dozens of features and options at your disposal. Virtual machines, websites, databases, and other types of cloud services are readily available for deployment. Before you use these, however, you must complete a couple of key tasks:

- **Create a storage account** For maximum control over your deployment, create a storage account with a "friendly" name of your choosing. (Otherwise, Azure will create one for you, with an abominable name like Pyxverrsses1023456.)

> **TIP** A useful naming convention would be to use your initials, the type (such as "vm" for virtual machine and "sa" for storage account), and the number—for example, bbvmsa01. This not only helps you identify what is inside the storage account, it also makes it easier to use scripting tools such as Windows PowerShell.

- **Set up a virtual network** Virtual machines reside on virtual networks. Before you start working with VMs in Azure, you must set up a network on which they can reside.

After you complete these key steps, you can start building your VMs.

Create a storage account

Your next step is to create a "friendly" storage account—that is, a storage account with a meaningful name and with other settings you apply. Otherwise, the system will create one for you automatically—which is not ideal. Your Azure storage account gives you access to services in Azure Storage. By default, your data will be available only to you, the account owner.

How many storage accounts can you have?

By default, each Azure subscription can have up to 20 storage accounts. (This can be extended to 50 storage accounts.) Each storage account can grow to as much as 500 terabytes (TB)! That equates to nearly 10 petabytes (PB) of disk space available for each subscription, extendable to more than 24 PB. To put that in perspective, you can fit more than 256 million average-sized documents or pictures in a single Azure subscription on disk.

Although it's possible to create a storage account when you set up your first virtual machine, it's better to do so beforehand by using the Storage Account Creation Wizard. As you walk through the following steps, the reason will be clear.

To create a storage account through the Storage Account Creation Wizard:

1. Click the New button in the lower-left corner of the Azure portal (see Figure 6-2).

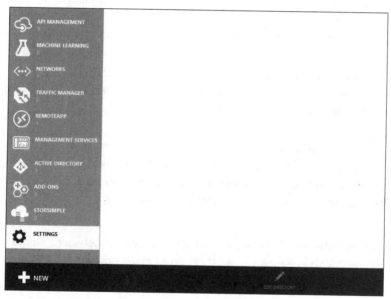

FIGURE 6-2 Select New to create a storage account.

2. On the New page, select Data Services, Storage, Quick Create, as shown in Figure 6-3.

FIGURE 6-3 On the New page, click Data Services, Storage, Quick Create.

3. Enter a meaningful name for your storage account in the URL box. Choose a short descriptive name followed by a couple of numbers, such as **contoso01**, as shown in Figure 6-4.

> **NOTE** You must enter a name that is not already in use. If you enter a name that has already been taken, you'll get an error message, as shown in Figure 6-4.

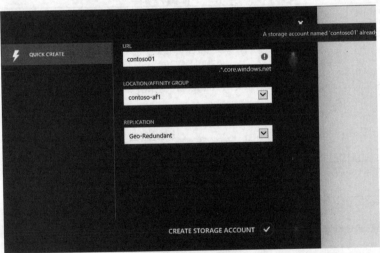

FIGURE 6-4 Enter a name for your storage account in the URL field. Be sure to choose a name that is not already in use.

4. You must associate your storage account with the same location where the primary workloads or VMs will be accessing the storage. Select the group you just created in the Location/Affinity Group list. In this example, it is contoso-af1.

5. In the Replication list, select Geo-Redundant.

6. Click Create Storage Account.

What is geo-redundancy?

To help protect your data, every block of data is written to three separate physical disks in the regional datacenter (see Figure 6-5). To allay fears of data loss if the entire region experiences a communications failure, the Azure subscription administrator (in this case, you) can set the storage account to replicate all data in the account from one area of the country/region to the opposite side of the country/region. This is known as *geo-redundancy*. In other words, the data is written three additional times to three additional physical disks in a different geographical location (see Figure 6-6). This greatly increases the protection of your data against physical disk failure. As an added benefit, replicating your data six times—three in a separate geolocation, but within the same country/region—meets compliancy regulation restrictions.

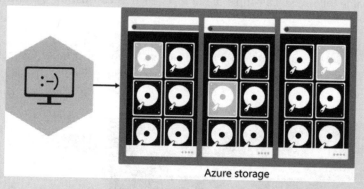

FIGURE 6-5 With Azure, data is written to three separate physical disks in the datacenter.

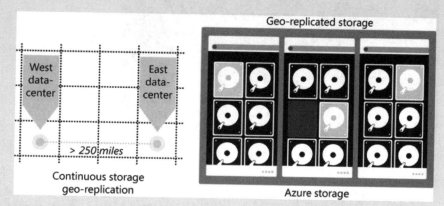

FIGURE 6-6 Geo-redundancy helps protect data with replication in multiple geographic locations.

Set up a virtual network

Virtual machines and other cloud services need a virtual network on which to reside. A virtual network is an isolated networking environment in the Azure subscription. That is, it is separate from all other Azure subscriptions, making it more secure. You must create a virtual network before you can build your VMs.

Before you can set up your virtual network, you must register a DNS server. A *DNS server* is used to map a computer's domain name to its IP address. DNS servers are an essential part of the Internet. It is because of a DNS server that you can enter **www.microsoft.com** in your Internet browser to access the computer that hosts the main Microsoft website, rather than the more cumbersome (and harder to remember) IP address. (The assumption here is that your business will use a router that is connected to an ISP, providing a connection to the Internet.)

What's an IP address?

An Internet Protocol address—usually shortened to *IP address*—is a number that is assigned to each device on a network (including a DNS server). The IP address identifies the device. IP addresses that use the Internet Protocol version 4 (IPv4) numbering scheme have four blocks of numbers, with as many as three digits in each block. For example, the IP address for the computer that hosts the main Microsoft website is 104.68.131.39. (Another type of IP numbering scheme, called IPv6, uses a different type of notation.)

To register a DNS server, follow these steps:

1. In the navigation pane of the Azure portal, click Networks.
2. Click the New button in the lower-left corner of the page.
3. On the New page, select Network Services, Virtual Network, Register DNS Server.
4. In the Name field, enter a name for this registration. (This is only for your reference. It will not be resolved.)
5. Enter the IP address you want in the DNS Server IP Address field (see Figure 6-7).

FIGURE 6-7 Register your DNS server.

6. Click Register DNS Server.

Next you need to create the virtual network and point it to the DNS server you just registered. To create the virtual network, follow these steps:

1. In the navigation pane of the Azure portal, click Networks.

2. Click the New button in the lower-left corner of the Azure portal.

3. Select Virtual Network, Quick Create.

4. On the New page, in the Name field, enter a meaningful name for your network—in this example, **contosovnet001**.

5. Select your IP address space from the Address Space list.

6. Select the maximum number of VMs on the network from the Maximum VM Count list.

7. In the Location list, select the same location—in this case, East US.

8. In the DNS Server list, select the newly created DNS entry (see Figure 6-8).

FIGURE 6-8 Create a virtual network.

9. Click Create A Virtual Network.

Understand virtual machine templates

VM deployments in Azure are typically done by using predefined operating system templates. As shown in Figure 6-9, there are different templates for different operating systems. These templates come with the correct drivers and are available either from the Azure repository or from custom operating system images.

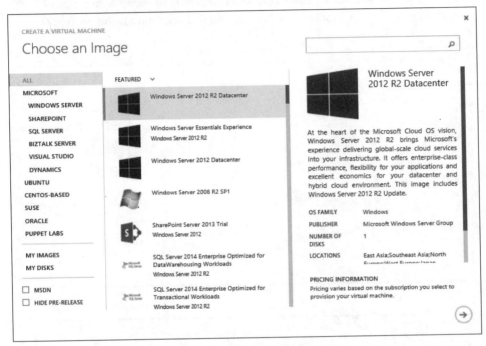

FIGURE 6-9 There are different templates for different operating systems.

The gallery lists the available supported templates by operating system. The My Images and My Disks categories are also listed. The My Images category displays *sysprepped* images. These are images that you, as the administrator, have imported into the library for your subscription. The My Disks category lists VM disks that are not sysprepped but that are operating system disks that are not currently deployed or in use. In other words, administrators can "spin up" a VM and then decide later to remove the VM from the deployment but not necessarily delete the disk. These disks are then available for redeployment at a later time from the Create A Virtual Machine Wizard.

Open-source and third-party software

In the past few years, Microsoft has announced numerous partnerships in correlation with the Azure cloud platform. For example, as of this writing, Oracle has chosen Microsoft as the only third-party cloud provider that it is willing to support for Oracle-based VMs. Administrators can also deploy VMs based on various Linux operating systems, including Ubuntu, CentOS, Oracle Linux, Chef and Puppet (see Figure 6-10).

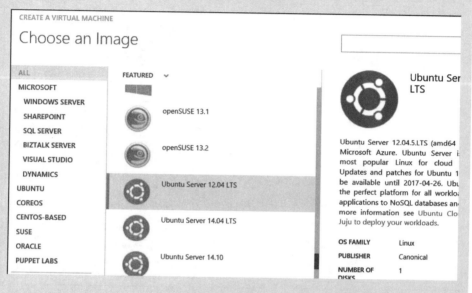

FIGURE 6-10 You can choose to create open-source and third-party VMs.

Build your first virtual machine

You are now ready to build your first VM (server) in the cloud. Your first server will be a domain controller. A *domain controller* holds all user, computer, group, and other account information for managing security.

> **NOTE** To plan for growth, start with a dedicated domain controller. While your business is still small, you can opt to also use this server for additional roles. You can add more domain controllers for redundancy and workload balance later if you want.

To create a virtual machine, follow these steps:

1. In the navigation pane of the Azure portal, click Virtual Machines.
2. Click the New button in the lower-left corner of the Azure portal.
3. Select Compute, Virtual Machine, From Gallery.
4. The Create A Virtual Machine Wizard starts. On the Choose An Image page (see Figure 6-9, shown earlier), click Windows Server 2012 R2 Datacenter. Then click the Next button (the right-pointing arrow) at the bottom of the page.
5. On the Virtual Machine Configuration page, in the Version Release Date field, select the most recent version release date so that your new VM includes the most recent operating system updates.
6. In the Virtual Machine Name field, enter a name for your virtual machine. This example uses **ContosoDC01**.

> **TIP** Define a naming scheme by location, function, or other helpful criteria.

7. For the tier, select Standard.
8. In the Size list, select A1 (1 Core, 1.75 GB Memory).

> **NOTE** A VM's size affects the cost associated with using it.

9. In the New User Name field, enter a secure local administrator user account to provision inside the virtual machine operating system. In this example, the **ContosoAdmin** account is used. Remember this name, because you will need it to log on to the virtual machine.

10. Enter a password for the VM and enter it again to confirm it (see Figure 6-11). Then click the Next button to continue.

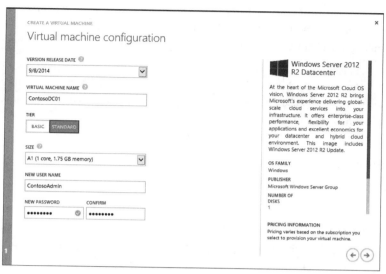

FIGURE 6-11 Set up the configuration of the new VM.

> **TIP** It's imperative that you use secure passwords for administrator, user, and service accounts—and that you remember and protect them. Consider using sentences (with or without spaces) for passwords, including letters of different cases and symbols. These passwords can be easier to remember than some cryptic code. You can read about creating secure passwords at *aka.ms/secure-passwords*.

11. On the second Virtual Machine Configuration page, in the Cloud Service list, select Create A New Cloud Service.

> **NOTE** Cloud services must be uniquely named, because each service must be accessible via the Internet for administrative access and monitoring, and possibly for user access. It's a good practice to give the cloud service a name that reflects the service being provided. As you build additional VMs, a list will appear from which you can select the cloud service created during the original VM's creation.

12. In the Cloud Service DNS Name field, enter a name for the cloud service (in this example, **ContosoAuth**). This name becomes part of the URL used to contact the VM.

NOTE In this example, by including *Auth* (which stands for authentication) in the name, you denote that this particular cloud service will hold only domain controller machines. Creating a cloud service name that encompasses many virtual machines of the same type of service helps to organize and provide connectivity to a set of virtual machines serving the same purpose.

13. In the Region/Affinity Group/Virtual Network list, select the location you defined earlier; in this case, it is East US.

14. In the Storage Account list, select contoso01. This is the storage account you created earlier in this chapter.

15. In the Availability Set list, select Create An Availability Set.

NOTE An *availability set* is a set of VMs that are grouped together to help guarantee that they will be highly available. Creating an availability set allows for redundancy if there is a server or rack outage, because each VM in the availability set resides on separate hardware. Note that all VMs in an availability set should run identical workload types. For example, they should all be domain controllers or file servers.

16. In the Availability Set Name field, enter the same name you entered in the Cloud Service DNS Name field—in this case, **ContosoAuth**.

17. Leave the settings in the Endpoints section as they are (see Figure 6-12). Then click the Next button.

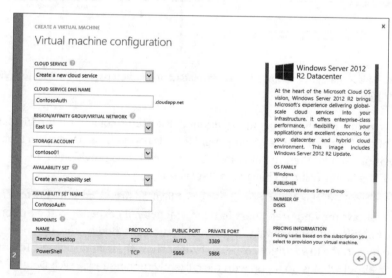

FIGURE 6-12 Use the settings shown here on the second Virtual Machine Configuration page of the Create A Virtual Machine Wizard.

18. At the top of the third and final Virtual Machine Configuration page, the Install The VM Agent check box should be selected by default, as shown in Figure 6-13. The VM Agent serves many purposes, such as allowing for the injection of a new administrator password into the VM if the administrator needs to change it. Click the check mark in the lower-right corner of the page to complete the process and close the wizard.

> **NOTE** Notice the configuration extension options on the final Virtual Machine Configuration page. These allow for deeper operating system management, such as additional security, runtime, debugging, and other features that can help increase the productivity and reliability of VMs. If you own the proper licensing, you can enable these. For more information about extensions, visit *msdn.microsoft.com/en-us/library/azure/dn606311.aspx.*

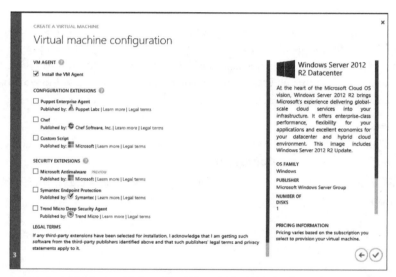

FIGURE 6-13 This is the third and final Virtual Machine Configuration page of the Create A Virtual Machine Wizard.

While the new virtual machine is being provisioned, the Status column on the Virtual Machines page of the Microsoft Azure Management Portal changes from displaying Stopped to Stopped (Provisioning) and then to Running (Provisioning). When provisioning for this new VM is completed, the Status column changes to display Running.

As shown in Figure 6-14, the Azure portal has a notification area along the bottom of the screen, which shows moving green bars to denote activity. By expanding the ribbon at the bottom, you can display more details for each operation initiated by the administrator. You can click the bars in the lower-right corner to hide or show these notifications. To display more information about what is going on with the currently running tasks, click Details. When a task is finished, click OK for that task or click Dismiss Completed to dismiss the status ribbon shown in the figure.

FIGURE 6-14 The notification area is expanded.

After the new virtual machine has finished being provisioned and the status is Running, do the following:

1. Click the name of the new VM that is displayed on the Virtual Machines page of the Azure portal (in this case, ContosoDC01).

2. Click Dashboard.

3. On the Dashboard page, make a note of the internal IP address.

In this example, it should be listed as 192.168.0.4. If a different internal IP address is displayed, the virtual network and/or virtual machine was not created correctly. In that case, click Delete on the toolbar of the VM details page for the machine, and repeat the steps in this section and, if necessary, in the "Set up a virtual network" section.

Define a data disk within the virtual machine

Before you use a new VM you should define a data disk on the server so you have a place to store data and settings. The operating system drive that comes with all VMs has caching enabled. In addition, most programs write to a persistent disk where caching does not occur in case of a power failure.

To create a data disk, follow these steps:

1. On the VM Dashboard for ContosoDC01, as shown in Figure 6-15, click Attach on the command bar and select Attach Empty Disk.

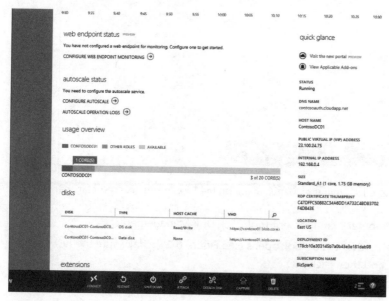

FIGURE 6-15 Click the Attach button to add a new disk or to attach an existing disk to the VM.

2. The Attach An Empty Disk To The Virtual Machine Wizard starts. On the first page, enter a name for the new disk in the File Name field—in this example, **ContosoDC-data01**.

3. In the Size field, enter **120 GB**.

4. In the Host Cache Preference field, select None. This is important for data persistency.

5. Click the check mark to create and attach the new virtual hard disk to the VM.

6. On the VM Dashboard, click Connect on the command bar and select Open. This starts a Remote Desktop connection to the console of this virtual machine.

7. Accept the authorization messages and then log on at the console of your VM by using the local administrator credentials.

8. From the Remote Desktop console of the VM, you must create a new partition on the data disk that you just attached and then format this partition as a new volume with the NTFS file system. This new volume will be where the Active Directory Domain Services (AD DS) database, logs, and other pertinent files are held, plus any other data you want to store on this server in the future. To begin, open Server Manager, click the Tools menu, and click Computer Management (see Figure 6-16). The Computer Management tool starts.

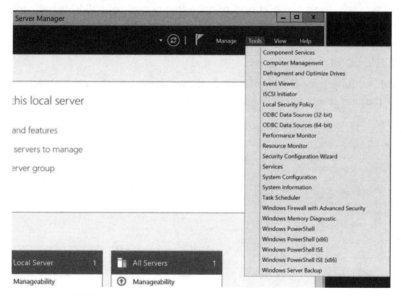

FIGURE 6-16 Click Computer Management on the Tools menu in Server Manager.

9. In the Computer Management tool, click Disk Management.

10. The Initialize Disk dialog box opens (see Figure 6-17). Make sure the new disk is selected, and then click OK.

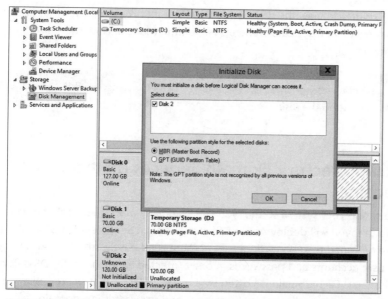

FIGURE 6-17 Make sure the new disk is selected in the Initialize Disk dialog box.

11. Right-click the Unallocated Space entry on Disk 2 and click New Simple Volume.

12. The New Simple Volume Wizard starts. On the Welcome page, click Next.

13. On the Specify Volume Size page, click Next again.

14. The drive letter should be preconfigured to F. Click Next twice. Review your selected settings, as shown in Figure 6-18, and then click Finish.

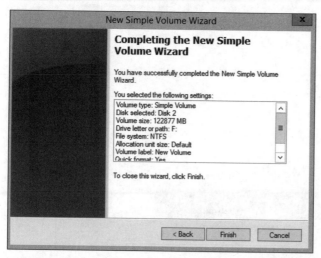

FIGURE 6-18 Review your settings after completing the wizard.

15. Start File Explorer to view the drive. Note that it might take a while for it to appear. When the new drive F appears in the upper volume window, close the Computer Management tool.

> **NOTE** If you get a message that asks whether you want to format the drive, click Cancel. You already formatted the disk.

Install Active Directory Domain Services on the virtual machine

You will want to set up your system so that you can granularly manage security between users. To achieve this, you will deploy Active Directory Domain Services (AD DS). AD DS is a type of database designed to keep track of user accounts and passwords. With AD DS, you can store these user accounts and passwords in one protected location. An AD DS database is made up of domains. Each domain is hosted by a server called a domain controller. As you learned earlier, a *domain controller* holds all accounts and passwords in a domain.

To install AD DS on your VM, follow these steps:

1. From the Remote Desktop console of the VM, open Server Manager, click Manage, and click Add Roles And Features (see Figure 6-19). The Add Roles And Features Wizard starts.

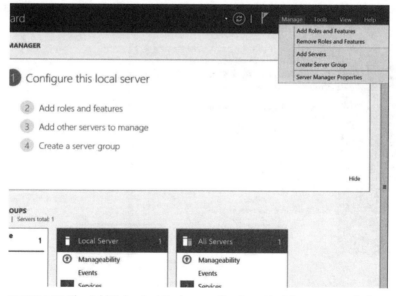

FIGURE 6-19 The Add Roles And Features option is on the Manage menu in Server Manager.

2. On the Before You Begin page of the Add Roles And Features Wizard, click Next.

3. On the Select Installation Type page, click Role-Based or Feature-Based Installation. Then click Next.

4. Ensure that the current server is selected. Then click Next.

5. On the Select Server Roles page, click Active Directory Domain Services.

6. The Add Roles And Features Wizard dialog box opens. Click Add Features (see Figure 6-20).

> **NOTE** Management tools, such as ADSIEdit and Active Directory Users and Computers, will also be installed if the Include Management Tools check box is selected.

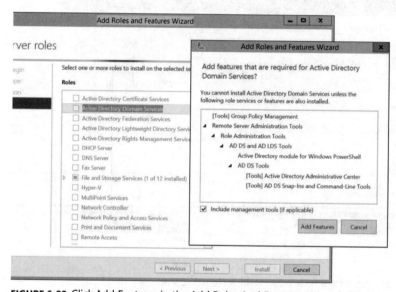

FIGURE 6-20 Click Add Features in the Add Roles And Features Wizard dialog box.

7. On the Select Server Roles page of the wizard, click Next. Then click Next on the Select Features page and on the Active Directory Domain Services page.

8. On the Confirm Installation Selections page, select the Restart The Destination Server Automatically If Required check box.

9. In the Restart dialog box, select Yes. Then click Install. The installation will take a few minutes. When it's finished, click Close.

Promote the server

An AD DS framework is divided into three levels: domain, tree, and forest. A *domain* is a group of computers, users, and devices—that is, a group of network objects—that share the same AD DS database. A *tree* is a collection of one or more domains. A *forest* is a collection of one or more trees.

Your next step, then, is to promote the VM (server) you just created to a domain controller in a new forest. To promote the server, follow these steps:

1. From the Remote Desktop console of the VM, open Server Manager, click the caution icon in the upper-right corner of the screen, and click Promote This Server To A Domain Controller in the menu that appears (see Figure 6-21).

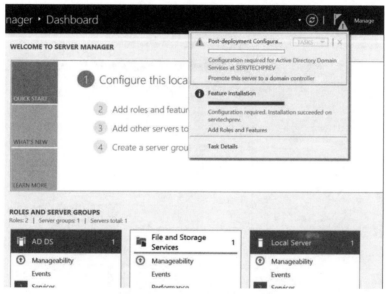

FIGURE 6-21 Click Promote This Server To A Domain Controller.

2. The Active Directory Domain Services Configuration Wizard starts, with the Deployment Configuration page displayed. Under Select The Deployment Operation, select Add A New Forest.

3. In the Root Domain Name field, enter **contoso.com** (see Figure 6-22). Then click Next.

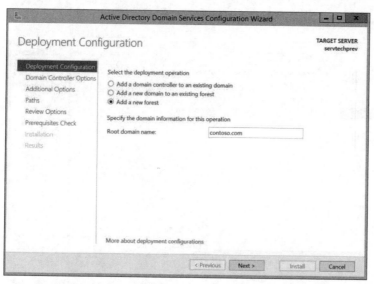

FIGURE 6-22 Choose Add A New Forest on the first page of the Active Directory Domain Services Configuration Wizard.

TIP If your business is a small one and you don't have anyone with significant technical expertise, consider entering *yourcompanyname*.loc in the Root Domain Name field (where *yourcompanyname* is the name of your company). It's less work than configuring a public name space (such as contoso.com, as shown in this example). However, if you expect to grow rapidly, go ahead and use a public name space, as long as you actually own that domain. For more information on naming conventions, visit *support.microsoft.com/kb/909264*.

4. The Domain Controller Options page opens. Enter a secure password and enter it again to confirm it. (Be sure to remember this password.) Then click Next.

5. The DNS Options page opens. Ignore the warnings and click Next. Then click Next again on the Additional Options page.

6. On the Paths page, shown in Figure 6-23, change the Database Folder, Log Files Folder, and SYSVOL Folder paths so they start with **F:** rather than C:\. (Drive F is the drive you defined earlier in this chapter.) Then click Next.

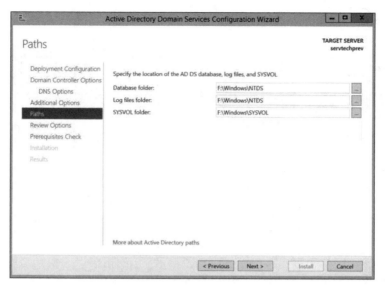

FIGURE 6-23 Change the paths so they start with F:\ instead of C:\.

> **NOTE** In production environments, it's important to use a drive and folder that is not on the standard C drive to house the AD DS data. Having this data separated also makes for easier backups.

7. On the Review Options page, click Next.

8. On the Prerequisites Check page, review any issues and then click Install. You can ignore any warnings that appear. The last line should say that all prerequisite checks passed successfully. This will take some time (20 minutes or more) to complete.

9. When the check is complete, restart your VM.

Your VM (server) is now ready for use. At this point, you can install a new VM, connect it to the domain, and add applications. Or, if your business is small, feel free to add the business applications to this server. For example, you can download and install QuickBooks and Microsoft Office on the server.

> **NOTE** You might need to adjust the server's CPU and memory for additional performance by adjusting the VM size in the Azure management portal. Do so while the VM is shut down.

Set up users and authentication

Your server is up and running. Before it will be useful, however, you need to set up additional users, file shares, user rights, shared applications, and whatever else you want to add. To achieve this, you will use the Active Directory Users and Computers tool. This tool is for managing users and computers in a domain.

NOTE When you add a user to the domain, you give him or her the ability to log on to the domain. However, the user must also be given the right to log on to the new server.

To set up a user and authentication, follow these steps:

1. From the Remote Desktop console of the VM, open Server Manager, click Tools, and click Active Directory Users And Computers (see Figure 6-24). The Active Directory Users and Computers tool starts.

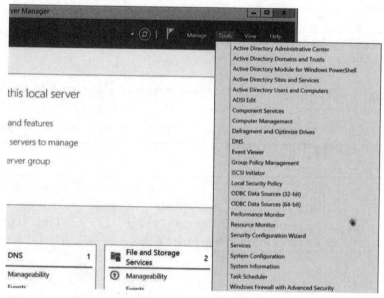

FIGURE 6-24 Choose Active Directory Users And Computers from the Tools menu in Server Manager.

2. In the Active Directory Users and Computers tool, expand the domain (in this case, contoso.com), right-click the Users folder, click New, and click User (see Figure 6-25).

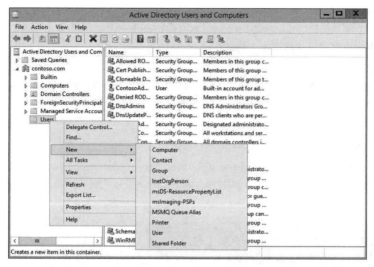

FIGURE 6-25 Create a new user.

3. In this example, add a user named Dan to the domain. Enter a user name, first name, and last name (if you want), and click Next.

4. Enter a password for the new user and enter it a second time to confirm it. This password should be strong. Then click Next.

5. Click Finish to add the user.

6. For Dan to be able to log on to the server, you need to add him to the proper group. In this example, you will add him to the Administrators group. (Note that it is not recommended that you add everyone to this group.) To begin, right-click Dan's entry in the Users list and click Add To A Group (see Figure 6-26).

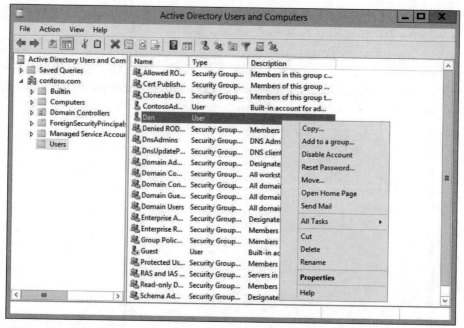

FIGURE 6-26 Right-click the user in the list and click Add To A Group.

7. Enter **Administrators** and click Check Names to verify that this group exists. When the group name appears underlined, the group has been verified. Click OK.

8. Log off from the server and click the Connect button from the Azure portal. This time, however, use the user account you just created (with your domain) to log on—in this example, contoso\dan. A new desktop should appear, and any applications that were previously installed should be accessible to the user.

Azure monitoring and alerts

As robust as Azure is, issues will inevitably arise. To detect these issues, you can set up cloud service monitoring and metric-based alerts.

With cloud service monitoring, the administrator can set up probes. These probes ensure that a specified cloud service is working properly. This monitoring does not reveal whether a VM or the programs it runs are working properly, but whether the cloud service itself is available on the Internet. If the probe detects an issue, it notifies the administrator via email.

To activate cloud service monitoring:

1. On the VM Dashboard, click the Configure tab.

2. Scroll down to the Monitoring section. Here you can add probes to monitor the cloud service from many geographic locations (see Figure 6-27). Azure service endpoints determine whether your application is deployed to and managed by the global Azure platform. Enter the required information and click Save.

FIGURE 6-27 Activate cloud service monitoring in the Monitoring section of the VM Dashboard.

> **NOTE** Monitoring the cloud service provides peace of mind to the administrator. Unless informed otherwise, all is well in the Azure cloud platform.

Administrators use alerts to watch the utilization (or inactivity) of the VMs. They can set up multiple alerts per VM to watch for spikes in processor usage, memory consumption, disk throughput, and networking. These alerts can be set up based on conditions (rules) set forth by the administrator. If an alert is triggered, the administrator is notified via email. Figure 6-28 shows the Create Alert Rule Wizard, which you use to create an alert. (To access this wizard, click the Monitor tab on the VM Dashboard and click Add Rule on the command bar at the bottom of the window.)

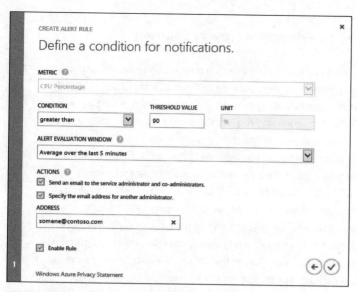

FIGURE 6-28 Use the Create Alert Rule Wizard to create alerts.

Back up your files with Azure Recovery Services

Backing up your files is crucial to your business. If you lose valuable data within your company, it could be the beginning of the end of your business. Backing up is not just an option, it is a necessity.

One option is to back up locally—that is, on a tape, disk, or other computer on site. Although this is certainly better than nothing, it will prove useless if there is a natural or human-caused disaster at your place of business. In that case, both your source data and your backup data might become unavailable.

A better option is to back up your data to the cloud by using Azure Recovery Services. The example in this section demonstrates this by showing how to back up file shares stored on a Windows Server 2012 server. The instructions would be identical if you were backing up a workstation.

Azure Site Recovery as a disaster recovery solution

Azure Site Recovery is an end-to-end disaster recovery (DR) system running in the Microsoft cloud. *Disaster recovery* can be defined as a set of policies and procedures that facilitates the recovery and continuation of vital technology infrastructure and systems following a disaster that disables the primary infrastructure and systems. Compared to a high availability (HA) system, such as clustering, the DR is usually offsite and has an orchestrated recovery workflow to bring up an infrastructure and systems brought down by a natural or human-caused disaster. Also, unlike an HA system, a DR system such as Azure Site Recovery replicates backups of the VM and the physical environment. However, DR systems need to be started and brought online when recovery is instituted. In the past, DR systems have been difficult and costly to institute. As a result, many enterprises do not have a complete DR system in place. Azure Site Recovery solves the DR implementation problem by using a straightforward web interface to instrument the many moving parts of a working DR solution.

Azure Site Recovery starts with a replication of VMs or physical machine disks between site locations, but it goes far beyond replication. In a typical app scenario, multiple servers are required to run in concert to deliver that application. For example, an external-facing website might not only have a web server but might also rely on a database server, along with a separate app server, all pulled together with security through an AD DS domain controller. Of course, all these servers are communicating over a network. So a successful failover requires that all the servers be replicated in unison and that all the servers start back up in a specific order within a compatible network, all tied to security. Azure Site Recovery delivers all the tools to manage this type of disaster recovery orchestration through a web interface.

Joe Homnick
Homnick Systems

Create a backup vault

Before you can back up your files, you must create a backup vault. Follow these steps:

1. From the server you want to back up, open the Azure portal, and select Recovery Services, New, Backup Vault, Quick Create.

2. In the Name field, enter a name for the backup vault. This can be any name you like. A good practice is to name it so there is a clear understanding of what it will ultimately store. In this example, the server name is used, because this particular vault will only back up one server. If you have multiple sites, multiple servers, multiple departments, or other variables, you might consider using a short code in your naming conventions.

3. In the Region list, select the appropriate region (in this example, East US).

4. Click Create Vault (see Figure 6-29). Azure creates the backup vault.

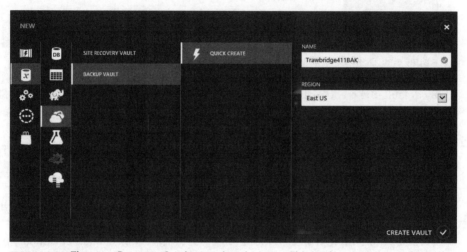

FIGURE 6-29 These are Recovery Services settings in Azure. This is where you create the backup vault to store your Windows Server backups.

Download the vault credentials, install the Azure Backup Agent, and register your server

Next, you need to download the vault credentials, install the Azure Backup Agent, and register your server for backup. Here's how:

1. After the backup vault is created, the name of the vault (in this example, Trawbridge-411BAK) appears in the list. Click the name to open the dashboard.

2. The page shown in Figure 6-30 appears. Click Download Vault Credentials.

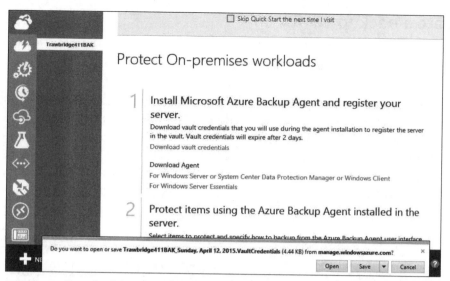

FIGURE 6-30 Download the vault credentials.

3. By default, the credentials will be saved in the Downloads folder if you select the Save or Save As option. In this example, the name of the file that contains the credentials is Trawbridge411BAK_Sunday, April 12, 2015.VaultCredentials. Click Save.

4. The vault credentials are downloaded. To continue, under Download Agent, click For Windows Server Or System Center Data Protection Manager Or Windows Client.

NOTE If you are performing procedures from a server or a workstation that is locked down, you will need to turn off Enhanced IE Protection (from Server Manager, Local Server) and turn off IE Protected Mode (on the Security tab under Internet Options) because you are downloading an .exe file. Don't forget to change those setting back when you are finished.

5. When prompted, click Run to run the Backup Agent installer, which is called MARSAgentInstaller.exe.

6. The Microsoft Azure Recovery Services Agent Setup Wizard starts, with the Installation Settings page displayed (see Figure 6-31). Leave the Installation Folder and Cache Location settings as is, and click Next.

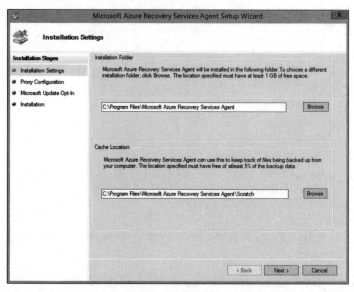

FIGURE 6-31 This is the Installation Settings page of the Microsoft Azure Recovery Services Agent Setup Wizard. Here you choose the installation folder and cache location.

7. On the Proxy Configuration page of the wizard, if you need proxy information to connect to the Internet, go ahead and enter that information. Click Next to continue.

8. On the Microsoft Update Opt-In page of the wizard, choose whichever option you want. The recommended setting is Use Microsoft Update When I Check For Updates.

9. On the Installation page of the wizard, click Install. The Azure Recovery Services Agent and any other necessary software is installed.

10. When the installation is complete, the page shown in Figure 6-32 is displayed. Click Proceed To Registration to register your server.

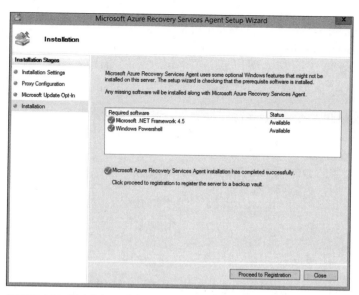

FIGURE 6-32 Click Proceed To Registration to proceed.

11. The Register Server Wizard starts, with the Vault Identification page displayed (see Figure 6-33). Click Browse.

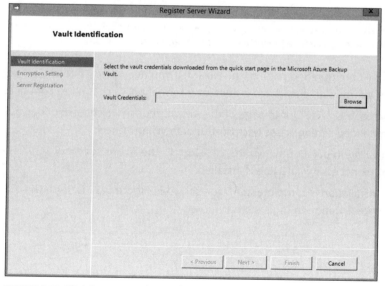

FIGURE 6-33 Click Browse on the Vault Identification page of the Register Server Wizard.

12. Locate and select the file that contains the vault credentials you downloaded in steps 1 and 2. Then click Open.

13. Click Next on the Vault Identification page to continue.

14. On the Encryption Setting page of the Register Server Wizard (see Figure 6-34), you set a passphrase for the backups you create. Enter the passphrase in the Enter Passphrase box and again in the Confirm Passphrase box. If you want to use a system-generated passphrase, just click the Generate Passphrase button. Browse or enter a location to store a text file containing the passphrase. Then click Finish.

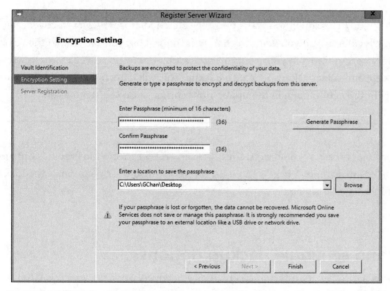

FIGURE 6-34 On the Encryption Setting page of the Register Server Wizard, you configure encryption for the backups you create.

15. The Server Registration page of the Register Server Wizard (see Figure 6-35) indicates where the passphrase you created was saved and notifies you that you must configure and schedule backup options so that your server can be backed up. To do so, make sure the Launch Microsoft Azure Recovery Services Agent check box is selected. Then click Close.

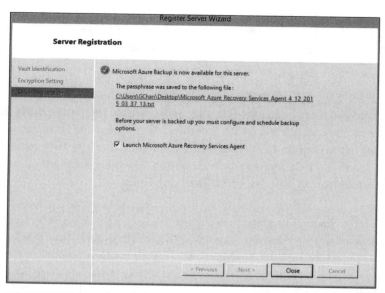

FIGURE 6-35 You can launch the Azure Recovery Services Agent from this page.

TIP If you already closed without selecting the Launch Microsoft Azure Recovery Services Agent check box, or if you want to change settings later, you can launch the Azure Recovery Services Agent from your computer's Start menu. To do so, click **Start**, enter **Azure Backup**, and select Microsoft Azure Backup. This will launch the Microsoft Azure Backup app. In the action pane in the upper-right corner, click Register Server.

NOTE If you get an error when registering the server, try clicking the Previous button, and then click Finish again. A lock is required for performing the operation. If the lock fails, you might have to try again.

Configure and schedule backup options

You will now notice a difference in terminology. *Azure Recovery Services*, which is what you have just finished setting up, is the set of online Azure backup components. The elements of the backup that reside on the client, server, or backed-up computer are referred to as *Microsoft Azure Backup*. Installing the Azure Recovery Agent embeds additional code through very tight integration with Windows Backup. The resulting product is called Microsoft Azure

Backup (or just Azure Backup). Microsoft Azure Backup connects to Azure Recovery Services in Azure for its target destination. You can set up Azure Backup to back up your files and folders automatically, on a schedule that you set.

To configure and schedule your backup options, follow these steps:

1. If you chose to launch the Azure Recovery Services Agent in step 13 in the previous set of steps, the Getting Started page of the Schedule Backup Wizard is displayed. If not, you can launch this wizard from within the server you are backing up by clicking Start, entering **Azure Backup**, and selecting Microsoft Azure Backup. (You might also want to right-click Microsoft Azure Backup and select Pin To Start so it is easy to find later.) This launches the Microsoft Azure Backup app. In the action pane on the right, click Schedule Backup to launch the Getting Started Wizard. Click Next to proceed with setting up the schedule.

2. On the Select Items To Backup page, to add files or folders to the list of items to be backed up, click Add Items.

3. In the dialog box that appears, expand the drive and folders, and then select the items you want to back up. Then click OK.

4. A list of the items you selected (in this example, the F:\Shares folder) is displayed, as shown in Figure 6-36. Click Next to proceed.

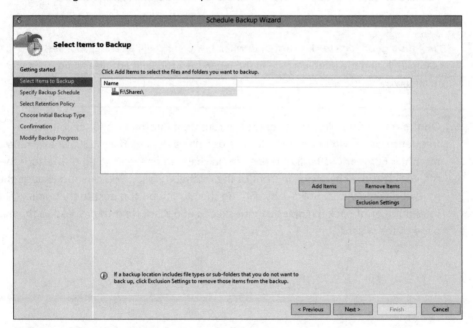

FIGURE 6-36 Choose the items you want to back up.

5. On the Specify Backup Schedule page (see Figure 6-37) select Day or Week. In the At Following Times section, click the time when you want the backup operation to occur in the Available Times list. You can enter up to three times per day. Generally, once per day is sufficient. If you choose weekly instead of daily, you'll also need to enter the day or days on which the backup should occur and how many weeks should pass between backup operations.

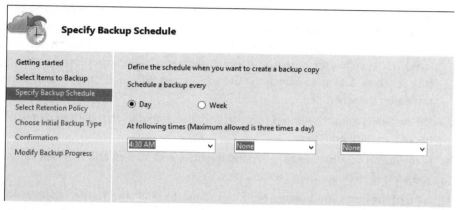

FIGURE 6-37 Set the frequency and time of day for the creation of backup copies.

TIP It's a good idea to choose a time when few people will be using your system—for example, during the middle of the night, when the probability of files being open is much lower.

6. On the retention policy page, enter the retention information for each backup frequency, as shown in Figure 6-38. The default values are: daily=180, weekly=104, monthly=60, yearly=10. All of these can be changed or even turned off. To turn them off, just clear the check box in front of the retention policy. You can also change the schedule of individual policies by clicking the Modify button next to that policy. The total number of backup copies cannot exceed 366. Click Next to proceed to the next page of the wizard.

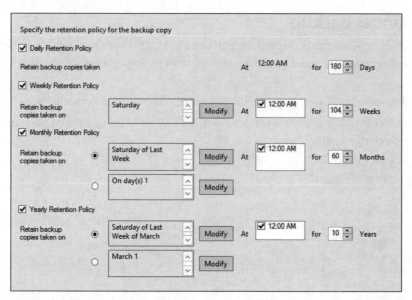

FIGURE 6-38 Choose the retention policy (how long Microsoft Azure Backup should retain the backup copies of your files and folders) for each type of backup.

7. On the Choose Initial Backup Type page, choose the initial backup type (the choices are Automatically Over The Network or Offline). If you choose Offline for your initial backup, you can save the backup to a USB drive that can then be shipped to Microsoft to import into your storage account. You will need to provide all of the information needed by Microsoft to gain access to your account and storage and to place the files where you want them. Unless you want to do an initial offline backup, just keep the default and click Next.

8. On the Confirmation page, review your selections and click Finish to complete the configuration.

9. The Modify Backup Progress page appears, notifying you that you have successfully created a backup schedule. Click Close.

Run a manual backup

In addition to setting up a backup schedule, you can also run backups manually. You might do so if, for example, you're about to make a system change. To run a manual backup, follow these steps:

1. Start Azure Backup by clicking Microsoft Azure Backup on your computer's Start menu.

2. In the Microsoft Azure Backup window, click Back Up Now in the Actions pane on the right side of the window (see Figure 6-39).

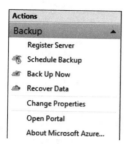

FIGURE 6-39 Click Back Up Now in the Actions pane to start a manual backup.

3. The Back Up Now Wizard starts, with the Confirmation page displayed. Click Back Up.

4. The Backup Progress page appears, indicating the progress of the manual backup. When it's complete, the page will notify you accordingly. Click Close. If you click Close before the backup is complete, it will continue to work in the background.

Recover data

Sometimes disaster strikes, and you lose your data. Maybe your hard drive crashes. Maybe your office is flooded or someone accidentally deletes a file. Whatever the reason, you can rest assured that as long as you've backed up your data (and you have the passphrase needed to retrieve it—see Figure 6-35, shown earlier), you can recover it. Here's how:

1. Start Azure Backup by clicking Microsoft Azure Backup on the Start menu.

2. In the Microsoft Azure Backup window, click Recover Data in the Actions pane on the right side of the window (see Figure 6-40).

3. The Recover Data Wizard starts, with the Getting Started page displayed. If the data you want to recover is on the server from which you originally created the backup, choose This Server, as shown in Figure 6-41. Then click Next.

> **NOTE** If you are recovering to a different server, click Another Server, and then browse to the downloaded vault credentials. Remember, you can download vault credentials by signing in to Azure and going to the dashboard of the recovery vault that stores the data you want to restore. Then click Recover. Azure will validate the credentials, and then you can proceed.

FIGURE 6-40 Click Recover Data to recover your data.

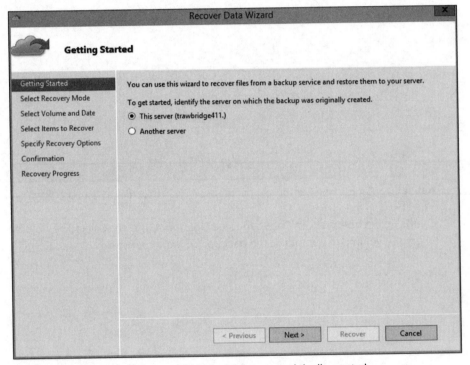

FIGURE 6-41 Choose the server on which the backup was originally created.

4. The Select Recovery Mode page is displayed (see Figure 6-42). If you know where the files you want to restore are located, choose Browse For Files, as shown here. Otherwise, choose Search For Files. Then click Next.

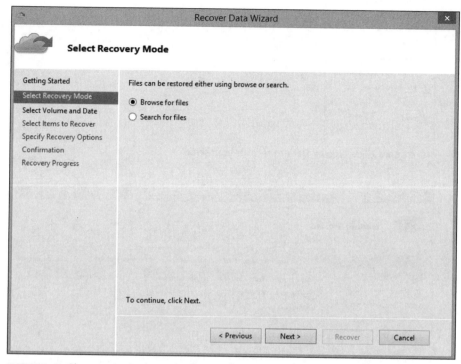

FIGURE 6-42 Choose whether you want to browse or search for files to restore.

5. On the Select Volume And Date page (see Figure 6-43), in the Select The Volume list, select the volume that contains the backup you want to restore.

6. In the Available Backups section, select the date and time of the backup you want to use for recovery. Then click Next.

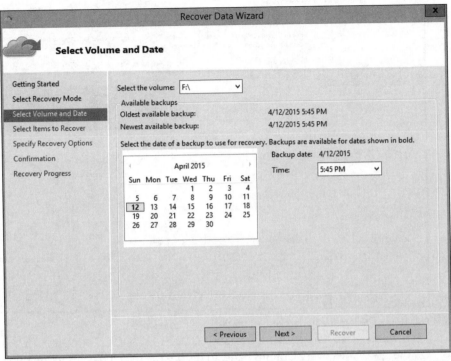

FIGURE 6-43 Select the volume containing the backup you want to restore and the date and time of the backup.

7. On the Select Items To Recover page (see Figure 6-44), in the Available Items pane, select the folder that contains the items you want to restore. All items in that folder will be restored by default. If you'd prefer to restore only certain items in the folder, select them in the Items To Recover pane. Then click Next.

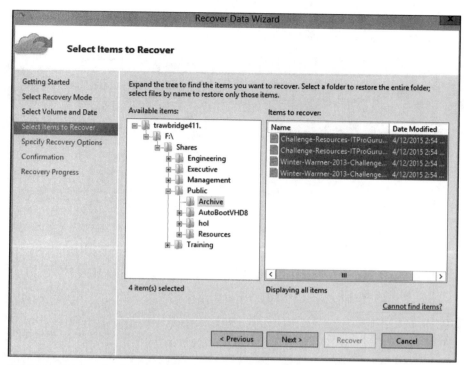

FIGURE 6-44 Select the folders or files that you want to restore.

8. On the Specify Recovery Options page, to restore the selected items to the original location, click Original Location. You could also restore to another location, by clicking Browse to go to the new location. You might want to do this if you want to look at the files that are recovered before you overwrite the files that are in the original location.

9. The Browse For Folder dialog box opens (see Figure 6-45). Select the folder where you want to save the recovered items or click Make New Folder to create a new folder, and then click OK.

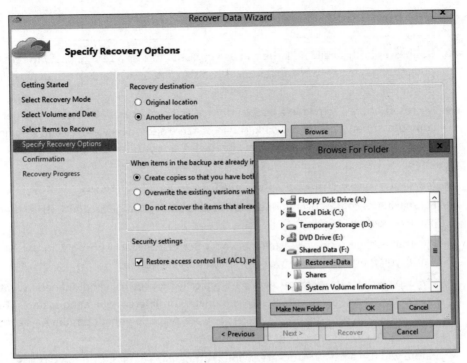

FIGURE 6-45 Select where you want to store the recovered backup.

10. In the When Items In The Backup Are Already In The Recovery Destination section, choose Create Copies So That You Have Both Versions, Overwrite The Existing Versions With The Recovered Versions, or Do Not Recover The Items That Already Exist On The Recovery Destination. In this example, the backup is being restored to a different location, so Create Copies is selected.

11. In the Security Settings section, select the Restore Access Control List (ACL) Permissions check box. This setting restores the permissions that the files had when they were backed up. If you do not turn this on, the restored files will inherit the permissions of the destination folder. Then click Next.

12. On the Confirmation page, review the selections you've made, and then click Recover.

13. The Recovery Progress page appears, indicating the progress of the recovery. When it's complete, the page will notify you accordingly. The actual time to restore depends on how many files and how much data you are restoring, and on your network bandwidth. It will be roughly the same amount of time it took to back up the files. Click Close.

Summary

- Businesses both small and large can use infrastructure as a service (IaaS) to rent compute, storage, and networking resources by using datacenter hardware to deploy virtual machines (VMs).

- Microsoft offers a formidable IaaS platform: Microsoft Azure. With Azure, you get compute, storage, and networking services. Azure also offers websites and web hosting, SQL database as a service (DaaS), predictive analytics, mobile back ends, and more.

- Microsoft Azure is an IaaS. In other words, it's a subscription service.

- For maximum control over your deployment, create a storage account with a "friendly" name of your choosing.

- Virtual machines reside on virtual networks. Before you start working with VMs in Azure, you must set up a network on which they can reside.

- VM deployments in Microsoft Azure are typically done by using predefined operating system templates. There are different templates for different operating systems. These templates come with the proper drivers and are available either from the Azure repository or from custom operating system images.

- Before you use a new VM, or server, you must define a data disk on the server so you have a place to store data and settings.

- Active Directory Domain Services (AD DS) is a type of database designed to keep track of user accounts and passwords. With AD DS, you can store these user accounts and passwords in one protected location. An AD DS database is made up of domains. Each domain is hosted by a server called a domain controller. A domain controller holds all accounts and passwords in a domain.

- After you get your server up and running, you must set up users, file shares, user rights, shared programs, and more. To achieve this, you use the Active Directory Users and Computers tool. This tool is for managing users and computers in a domain.

- As robust as Azure is, issues will inevitably arise. To detect these issues, you can set up cloud service monitoring and metric-based alerts.

- Backing up your files is crucial to your business. If you lose valuable data within your company, it could be the beginning of the end of your business. Backing up is not just an option, it is a necessity. One option is to back up locally—that is, on a tape, disk, or other computer on site. Though this is certainly better than nothing, it will prove useless in the event of a natural or human-caused disaster at your place of business. In that case, both your source data and your backup data might become unavailable. A better option is to back up your data to the cloud by using Microsoft Azure Recovery Services.

CHAPTER 7

Understand Server Manager

What is Server Manager?

In Chapter 6, "Build and run servers without hardware," you used Server Manager to configure a virtual machine (VM) for use as a file server. That's not surprising. Server Manager is the primary administrative tool for Windows Server 2012 R2, which in turn is the core server operating system in the cloud. With Server Manager, you deploy, configure, and maintain local and remote instances of other servers, all from one centralized console. Provisioning and managing servers is essential. Using Server Manager, then, is critical to normal business operations.

This chapter introduces Server Manager for Windows Server 2012 R2. More importantly, it also covers the Windows Server Essentials Experience role. Whether you are building servers in the cloud or on-premises, you should have a working understanding of Windows Server. By the end of this chapter, you'll know how to set your server environment up so you can better manage your administrative responsibilities if you choose to learn IT server management.

> **IMPORTANT** Server Manager is an administrative tool. You must have administrator privileges to run Server Manager. You will be prompted to provide the administrator's credentials.

Get started with Server Manager

In Windows Server 2012 R2, you can monitor the health of all servers through the Server Manager console. This console is installed by default. When you log on to Windows Server 2012 R2, Server Manager starts and opens the Server Manager Dashboard page,

shown in Figure 7-1. This page displays the status of your servers, including the roles and features that are currently active, in addition to other services. The navigation pane on the left details the roles that are managed and whether the console is local to the server or remote. The file and storage services are enabled by default.

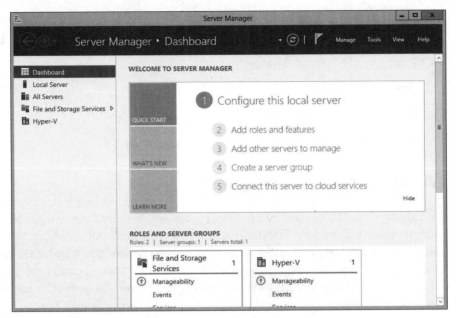

FIGURE 7-1 The Server Manager Dashboard page opens when Server Manager starts.

Add roles and features

With Server Manager, you can deploy and configure roles and features. A *role* is a service that a computer uses to perform a specific function for multiple users or other computers on a network, whereas a *feature* is software that supports or augments a role. Examples of roles include (but are not limited to) the following:

- **Active Directory Domain Services** When this role is applied, the server stores information about users, computers, and other devices on the network. With Active Directory Domain Services, administrators can manage this information. In addition, it helps to facilitate resource sharing and collaboration among users.

- **Application Server** With the Application Server role, a server can host and manage the design, development, and deployment of high-performance distributed business applications.

- **Dynamic Host Configuration Protocol Server** With this role, a server can serve as a Dynamic Host Configuration Protocol (DHCP) server. This type of server is used to assign or lease IP addresses to computers and other devices.

- **DNS Server**   With this role, a server can act as a Domain Name System (DNS) server. DNS servers are an essential part of the Internet. As you learned in Chapter 6, DNS is used to map an easy-to-remember domain name, such as *www.microsoft.com*, to an IP address.

- **Fax Server**   You can apply this role to configure your server to send and receive faxes.

- **File Services**   With this role, a server can be used for storage management, file replication, and more.

- **Print and Document Services**   Servers with this role can centralize printer access and tasks.

- **Remote Desktop Services**   With this role, users can access programs installed on a remote desktop server or access the Windows desktop itself from almost any computing device.

- **Web Server (IIS)**   With this role, you can share information with users on the Internet, an intranet, or an extranet by using Internet Information Services (IIS).

To add or remove roles and features, follow these steps:

1. On the Server Manager Dashboard page, under Configure This Local Server, click Add Roles And Features. Alternatively, click the Manage menu in the upper-right corner of the page and click Add Roles And Features (see Figure 7-2).

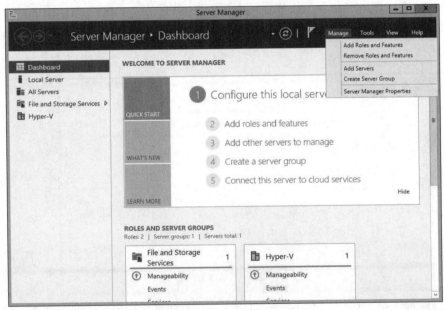

FIGURE 7-2 Click Add Roles And Features on the Dashboard page or in the Manage menu.

2. The Add Roles And Features Wizard starts, with the Before You Begin page displayed (see Figure 7-3). Click Next to begin.

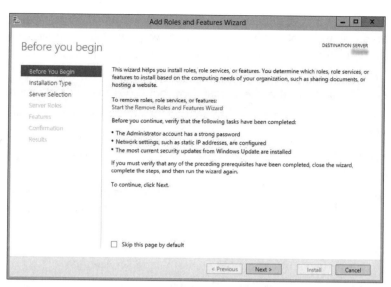

FIGURE 7-3 Click Next on the Before You Begin page of the Add Roles And Features Wizard.

3. On the Select Installation Type page, as shown in Figure 7-4, select Role-Based Or Feature-Based Installation. When you choose this option you can configure roles, features, and services for a single server. Then click Next.

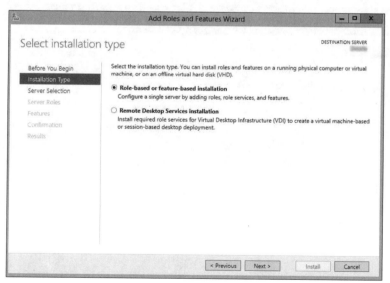

FIGURE 7-4 Choose Role-Based Or Feature-Based Installation on the Select Installation Type page of the Add Roles And Features Wizard.

4. On the Select Destination Server page (see Figure 7-5), you specify the server on which the roles and features should be installed. The Select A Server From The Server Pool option is selected by default, as is the server on which you want to install the roles and

features. This is because there is currently only one server in the server pool. Accept these defaults and click Next.

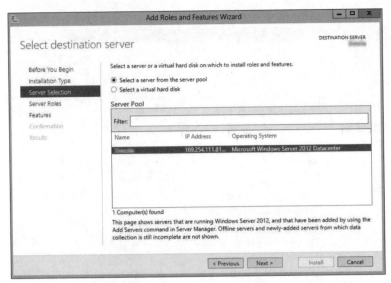

FIGURE 7-5 Leave the defaults selected and click Next.

5. On the Select Server Roles page (see Figure 7-6), you can deploy any of the roles included with Windows Server 2012 R2. Select a role—in this example, File And iSCSI Services\File Server—and click Next.

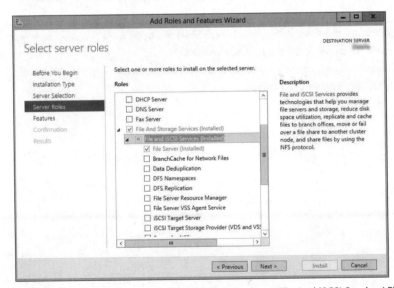

FIGURE 7-6 Choose the role you want to deploy—here, File And iSCSI Services\File Server—and click Next.

6. On the Select Features page (see Figure 7-7), you can select features associated with the chosen role to install on the server. Select any of the features you want, and then click Next.

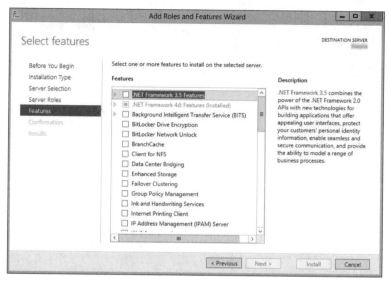

FIGURE 7-7 Select any features you want, and then click Next.

7. On the Confirm Installation Selections page, click Install.
8. The Results page opens. Click Close. The role and selected features are installed.

> **TIP** If you decide you no longer need a role or feature that you have installed on a server, you can remove it. To begin, click the Manage menu in the upper-right corner of the Server Manager Dashboard page and click Remove Roles And Features (see Figure 7-2, shown earlier in this chapter). Follow the prompts.

The Windows Server Essentials Experience role

The Windows Server Essentials Experience role is a special role available in Windows Server 2012 R2. When you install this role on a Microsoft Azure VM, you gain access to a set of features designed for managing a server in the cloud. Specifically, with the Windows Server Essentials Experience role you can do the following:

- Protect your server and client data by backing up the server and all client computers on your network.
- Manage your users and groups through a simplified server dashboard.
- Allow easy data access for Microsoft Online Services users (for example, Microsoft Office 365 users) through their domain credentials.
- Store your company's data in a centralized location.
- Integrate your server with Microsoft Online Services such as Office 365, Microsoft Intune, and Microsoft SharePoint.
- Synchronize and manage Office 365 user accounts and access through the dashboard.
- Create and manage SharePoint libraries through the dashboard.
- Access your server, network computers, and data from remote locations in a highly secure manner.
- Access data from any location and on any device by using the customized web portal for your organization.
- Manage mobile devices that access your company's emails.
- Monitor network health and obtain customized health reports, which can be created on demand, customized, and sent by email to specified recipients.

MICROSOFT VIRTUAL ACADEMY   Learn more about Windows Server 2012 R2 Essentials at *aka.ms/server2012ess*.

Set up the Windows Server Essentials Experience role

To install the Windows Server Essentials Experience role on a VM, follow these steps:

1. Follow the steps in the "Build your first virtual machine" section in Chapter 6. When prompted to choose a template or image for the new VM, however, click Windows Server Essentials Experience, as shown in Figure 7-8.

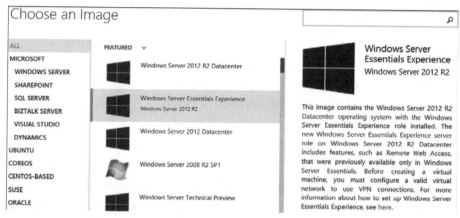

FIGURE 7-8 Click Windows Server Essentials Experience.

2. Instead of installing the File Server role on this new virtual machine, as you did in Chapter 6, you'll install the Windows Server Essentials Experience role. To begin, from the Remote Desktop console of the VM, open Server Manager, click the Manage menu, and click Add Roles And Features.

3. The Add Roles And Features Wizard starts. Step through the first three pages of the wizard as you did earlier in this chapter.

4. On the fourth page of the wizard, Select Server Roles, Windows Server Essentials Experience is selected by default. Click Next (see Figure 7-9).

> **TIP** If you accidentally close the wizard without clicking the deployment link highlighted in blue within the summary page, click the caution icon in the upper-right corner of the Server Manager Dashboard screen and click Configure Windows Server Essentials on the menu that appears.

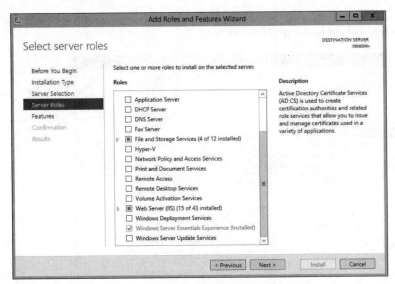

FIGURE 7-9 Add the Windows Server Essentials Experience role.

5. The Configure Windows Server Essentials page opens (see Figure 7-10). Click Next.

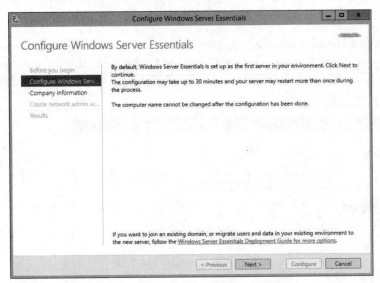

FIGURE 7-10 Click Next to configure the Windows Server Essentials experience role.

6. On the Company Information page shown in Figure 7-11, enter your company name and internal domain name, and then click Next.

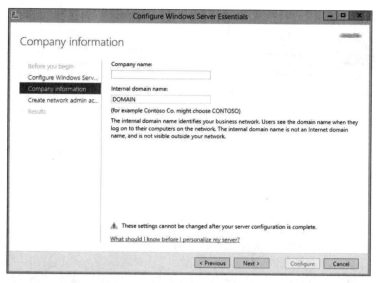

FIGURE 7-11   Enter the domain name that you or your organization owns, in addition to the company name.

7. On the Create A Network Administrator Account page, shown in Figure 7-12, enter an administrator account name and create a password for this account. You'll use these credentials to perform server management tasks that require administrator privileges. Click Configure to continue.

FIGURE 7-12   Provide your administrator account name and create a password that you will use to perform server management.

On the Results page shown in Figure 7-13, the progress bar shows the progress while the server configures the role. The process can take up to 30 minutes and will restart upon completion. When it is done, the Windows Server Essentials setup is complete. You can then sign in to the server to add resources to the role.

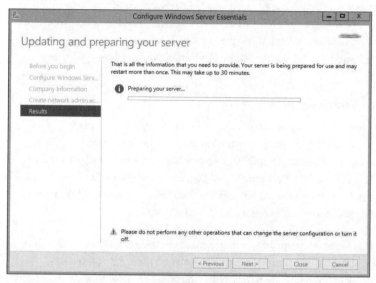

FIGURE 7-13 The Windows Server Essentials Experience Role is being configured.

TIP You could also set up the Windows Server Essentials Experience role by using Windows PowerShell. Specifically, you'd use the following command (cmdlet).

```
Add-WindowsFeature ServerEssentialsRole
```

For more information about Windows PowerShell, see the "Why learn Windows PowerShell?" sidebar later in this chapter.

Why Learn Windows PowerShell?

Every once in a while I am asked, "Why should I learn Windows PowerShell?" And to be honest, that is always a bit of a troublesome question. Why? Well, I am not certain I ever asked myself this question before. I just assumed I would learn it as soon as I first heard about it. But I guess not everyone is like that, so I decided to look at the issue from two perspectives—why and why not learn Windows PowerShell.

Don't learn Windows PowerShell

Don't bother learning Windows PowerShell if you already have scripts for everything and can perform all of your automation needs with those existing scripts. There is absolutely no reason to translate a perfectly working Microsoft Visual Basic Scripting Edition (VBScript), Perl script, or T-SQL script into Windows PowerShell if you don't need to. The purpose of writing a script is to avoid work. If the process of writing a script just generates more work, don't bother.

> **NOTE** There are probably a few environments in this state. They have highly developed automation systems in place, are not on the cutting edge of technology, and are perfectly happy with what they do, how they do it, and the capabilities it provides. If you find yourself in this situation, don't bother learning Windows PowerShell. It will not do you any good.

If you are planning to leave the IT profession in the next six months, you probably don't need to learn Windows PowerShell. I would also recommend that you not bother learning Windows PowerShell if your particular piece of technology does not have Windows PowerShell coverage. Of course, with complete access to the Microsoft .NET Framework, Windows Management Instrumentation (WMI), Active Directory Service Interface (ADSI), and the Win32 application programming interface, it is pretty hard to imagine anyone having a technology that Windows PowerShell cannot talk to, but if you do, it probably is not worth the effort to learn Windows PowerShell.

Learn Windows PowerShell

If you have more than one system to manage, and if those systems run a version of an operating system that was created since, perhaps, 2003, you should learn Windows PowerShell. But maybe you're accustomed to using VBScript or Perl to manage those systems. OK, fine—see the previous section of this sidebar. But if you find yourself needing to create new scripts or do new things to your system, you should begin using Windows PowerShell. Why? Because VBScript has not been improved since the release of Windows XP, and Perl is not even standard in the Windows build environment.

How hard is it to learn Windows PowerShell? Learning Windows PowerShell can be as easy as opening the Windows PowerShell console or Integrated Scripting Environment (ISE) and typing **Get-Process**. This one command provides information about all the processes running on your local system. To retrieve them from a remote system, use **Get-Process -ComputerName mycomputer**. It is that simple. Yes, it gets harder as you attempt more complex operations. But after you learn the basics, they transfer to other Windows PowerShell commands, or *cmdlets*, and to other technologies.

There are many resources to help you learn about Windows PowerShell. One of the best ones—which is also free—is the Hey Scripting Guy blog (*blogs.technet.com/b /heyscriptingguy/*). Published twice a day, seven days a week, it is the largest collection of Windows PowerShell information on the Internet. Of course, there are also local user groups, online user groups, Twitter feeds, Facebook groups, LinkedIn resources, and more. In addition, there are hundreds of YouTube videos related to Windows PowerShell. The problem is not finding helpful information, it is sifting through the plethora of resources. But that is better than not finding anything— a lot better!

Ed Wilson, Microsoft Scripting Guy
Author of Windows PowerShell Best Practices (Microsoft Press, 2014)

MICROSOFT VIRTUAL ACADEMY To get started with Windows Server 2012 R2: Server Management and Automation, take the course at *aka.ms/go-mva/serverman*.

TIP For more information on managing multiple remote servers, read "Manage Multiple, Remote Servers with Server Manager" at *aka.ms/remoteservers* and "Remote, Multiserver Management: Scenario Overview" at *aka.ms/remoteservers-scenario*.

Summary

- Server Manager is the primary administrative tool for Windows Server 2012 R2, which in turn is the core server operating system in the cloud. With Server Manager, you deploy, configure, and maintain local and remote instances of other servers, all from one centralized console.

- In Windows Server 2012 R2, you can monitor the health of all servers through the Server Manager console. This console is installed by default.

- When you log on to Windows Server 2012 R2, Server Manager starts and opens the Server Manager Dashboard page. This page displays the status of your servers, including the roles and features that are currently active, in addition to other services. The navigation pane on the left details the roles that are managed and whether the console is local to the server or remote.

- With Server Manager, you can deploy and configure roles and features. A *role* is a set of programs with which a computer can perform a specific function for multiple users or other computers on a network, whereas a *feature* is software that supports or augments a role. Examples of roles include Application Server, DNS Server, Fax Server, File Services, Print and Document Services, Remote Desktop Services, and Web Server (IIS).

- The Windows Server Essentials Experience role is a special role available in Windows Server 2012 R2. When you install this role on a Microsoft Azure VM, you gain access to a set of features designed for managing a server in the cloud.

- In earlier versions of the Windows Server operating system, you had to be physically present to gain access to a server. Alternatively, you could gain access to a server through the use of a Remote Desktop connection. Now, with Windows Server 2012 R2 and Server Manager, you can manage multiple remote servers—even configure deployment and perform maintenance—from one console. Before you can use the Server Manager console to manage a server remotely, you must add it to Server Manager.

CHAPTER 8

Run Windows apps remotely

Introduction to Azure RemoteApp

Apps are central to the success of any organization. Indeed, one of IT's key roles is to make sure apps are both running and accessible so that the organization can keep the business operational and thriving. Today, however, IT administrators have an additional challenge: to ensure that apps are accessible on multiple platforms, devices, and operating systems.

Microsoft Azure RemoteApp makes all that possible. RemoteApp runs on Windows Server in the Microsoft public cloud unlike Microsoft Intune, which runs locally on your computer or mobile device. When you use RemoteApp to run your apps, workers can access them from any Internet-connected Mac or PC desktop or laptop computer, in addition to any Windows Phone, Android, or iOS mobile device. Also, by using RemoteApp, your organization can take advantage of storage, scalability, a global reach, security, redundancy, and reduced hardware cost and configuration.

There are two types of Microsoft Azure RemoteApp deployments:

- **Cloud deployment** With this type of deployment, your apps and all data associated with them are stored in the Microsoft public cloud. You'll learn how to set up a cloud deployment in this chapter.

- **Hybrid deployment** With this type of deployment, your apps and data are stored in the cloud, but users can also access them locally, from the on-premises network. By using this approach, you can assemble a custom set of apps for your users.

Set up your RemoteApp subscription

You pay for Microsoft Azure RemoteApp as you use the services. There are no up-front costs and no termination fees. Azure payment is based on the services you consume. It is just like running a website, virtual machine, or database, where each service in Azure carries a different charge.

With RemoteApp, there are two tiers of service available:

- **Basic**   This tier is for lightweight apps—for example, apps for data entry or expense reporting. It's ideal for task workers.
- **Standard**   This tier is for those programs commonly known as "productivity apps," such as the Microsoft Office 365 suite. This works best for information workers.

Both tiers offer 50 gigabytes (GB) of storage per user.

You can try RemoteApp free for 30 days, after which you can transition to a paid subscription or discontinue using the service.

To start using the trial, complete the following steps:

1. Navigate to *manage.windowsazure.com* and create a new instance of RemoteApp as shown in Figure 8-1. Click Create A RemoteApp Collection.
2. When prompted, sign in with your Microsoft account credentials.
3. On the screen that appears, click the Sign Up For A Subscription button.

    The RemoteApp trial is added to your Azure portal. Note that this may take some time. When it is added, the RemoteApp feature will be active. You will now be able to manage the RemoteApp feature in Azure.

FIGURE 8-1 Create a collection to install the trial software on your machine.

Create a RemoteApp service

When you have RemoteApp running on your computer, you're ready to create a RemoteApp service. In other words, you're ready to set up your RemoteApp collection in the cloud. Follow these steps:

1. On the Azure portal page, click the New button. Then click App Services, RemoteApp, Quick Create to set up the RemoteApp service (see Figure 8-2).

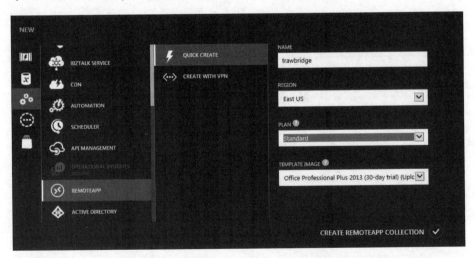

FIGURE 8-2 Set up RemoteApp as a service.

2. In the Name box, give your RemoteApp service a name. This can be anything you want, such as the name of your company.

3. In the Region list, click the region closest to you to minimize the connection time and improve performance.

4. In the Plan list, click Basic or Standard, depending on the number of remote users your service will serve.

5. In the Template Image list, click the Microsoft Office Professional Plus 2013 template image, which is available by default.

6. Click Create RemoteApp Collection.

> **NOTE** It might take a few minutes for your RemoteApp service to become active.

> **MICROSOFT VIRTUAL ACADEMY** For more information, see "Corporate Apps Anywhere, Anytime with Microsoft Azure RemoteApp" at *at aka.ms/go-mva/remoteapps.*

Add users to your RemoteApp service

After you've set up your RemoteApp service, it's time to specify who will be permitted to gain access to whichever Windows apps you choose to share through RemoteApp. Follow these steps:

1. In the left pane of the Azure portal, click Active Directory, as shown in Figure 8-3. The Active Directory page opens, displaying your directories (see Figure 8-4).

FIGURE 8-3 Click Active Directory in the navigation pane.

FIGURE 8-4 On the Active Directory page, you can choose which users will have access to the apps you share via RemoteApp.

TIP In Chapter 2, "Get started with Office 365," you set up users for Office 365. Those users can be imported into Microsoft Azure. Read on to learn how.

2. On the Active Directory page, click the directory you want to use. The Quick Start page opens (see Figure 8-5).

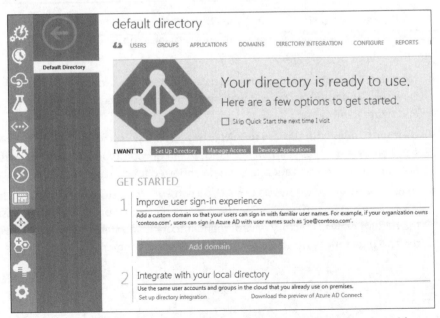

FIGURE 8-5 The Quick Start page offers options to help you configure the selected feature.

3. Click Users in the upper-left corner of the page to display the currently configured users within your Azure Active Directory.

4. To add or import a user, click Add User at the bottom of the page (see Figure 8-6).

FIGURE 8-6 Click Add User to add or import a user.

5. The Add User Wizard starts. In the Type Of User list, click the type of user you want to add (see Figure 8-7). Select New User In Your Organization.

   The three types of users are:

   - **New user in your organization** You can create a new user for your Azure Active Directory. This user's access will span across multiple services, including Office 365 and Azure RemoteApp.

   - **User with an existing Microsoft Account** This is a user with a regular Microsoft email address, such as *yourname*@outlook.com or *yourname*@live.com. This user is not part of your organization but can be imported for management purposes.

   - **User in another Windows Azure AD Directory** You can give users from other Azure Active Directory environments access to your directory if you have access to their Azure Active Directory environment. If there is an established access between the two directories, users can be used for either environment.

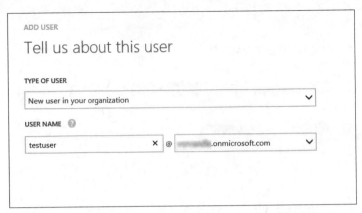

FIGURE 8-7 Add a user by identifying the type of user and providing a user name.

6. Enter the user's email address in the field provided. Then click the Next arrow in the lower-right corner of the page.

7. On the User Profile page, enter information in the First Name, Last Name, and Display Name boxes, and assign the new user a role from the Role list (see Figure 8-8). Then click the Next arrow in the lower-right corner of the page.

FIGURE 8-8 Provide a display name and assign a role to the user.

8. On the Get Temporary Password page, click Create to assign a temporary password to the new user account (see Figure 8-9).

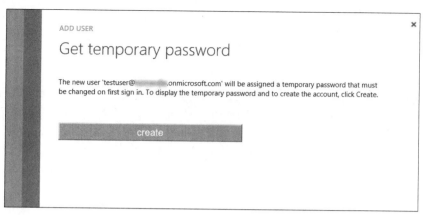

FIGURE 8-9 Create a temporary password for the user's first sign in.

9. The new password is displayed for the newly created user account. This password can be sent by email if you enter an address into the Send Password In Email box. Finally, click the check mark to send the password in email to the provided email address (see Figure 8-10).

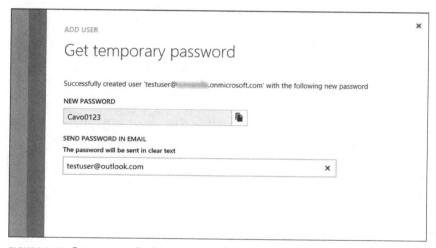

FIGURE 8-10 Enter an email address to send the temporary password to the user.

Publish an app

To make a Windows app available to your users, you must publish it. In this section, you'll learn how to publish various Office apps.

To publish an app, follow these steps:

1. In the Azure navigation pane, click RemoteApp.

2. Click the RemoteApp service you created earlier in this chapter. A dashboard screen appears, as shown in Figure 8-11.

3. Click the Publish RemoteApp Programs button.

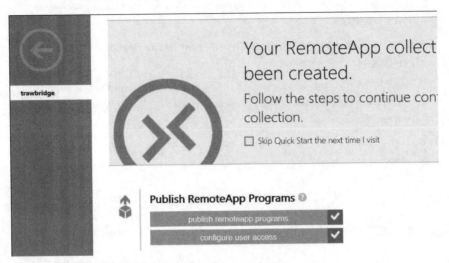

FIGURE 8-11 Click the Publish RemoteApp Programs button.

4. The Select RemoteApp Programs page opens (see Figure 8-12). Select the check box next to each app you want to share. Then click the check mark in the lower-right corner of the page.

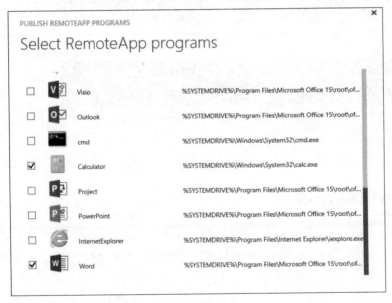

FIGURE 8-12 Select the apps you want to share.

Remove an app

If you no longer want to make an app available to users, you can unpublish it. Follow these steps:

1. Click Publishing at the top of the RemoteApp service dashboard screen (see Figure 8-11, shown earlier).

2. The Publishing page appears. Click the app you want to unpublish. Then click Unpublish at the bottom of the page (see Figure 8-13). The app's status changes to Unpublished.

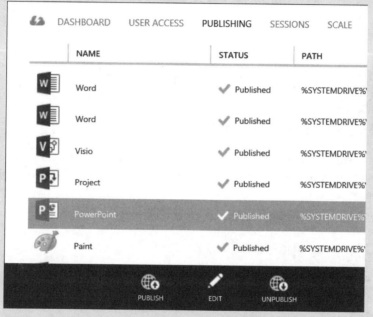

FIGURE 8-13 Select the app you want to remove and click Unpublish.

Configure user access

You've added users and groups to your RemoteApp service. You've published the Windows apps you want to share. Now it's time to specify which users are allowed access to which apps. Here's how:

1. On the RemoteApp dashboard screen (see Figure 8-11, shown earlier), click the Configure User Access button.

2. The User Access page opens (see Figure 8-14). Here you can add individual users. To add an individual user, enter that person's email address in the Users box and press Enter. When you're finished, click Save at the bottom of the page.

FIGURE 8-14 Give users or groups access to the apps you share via RemoteApp.

Set up RemoteApp on a client computer or mobile device

Now that you've set up your RemoteApp service, published apps, and configured user and group access, it's time to set up RemoteApp on your users' client computers and devices. These might be desktop computers, laptops, or mobile devices, such as smartphones, tablets, or phablets.

> **NOTE** RemoteApp works with mobile devices that run the Windows Phone, Android, and iOS operating systems.

To install RemoteApp on a client computer or mobile device, follow these steps:

1. On the client computer, open an Internet browser and go to *aka.ms/remoteapp-clients*. On the page that appears, click Download 'RemoteApp' Client for *Device* (see Figure 8-15). The client will be installed. (This might take a few minutes.)

FIGURE 8-15 Click Download 'RemoteApp' Client for *Device*.

> **NOTE** These steps demonstrate how to install the client software on a PC running the Windows operating system. If you are installing the software on some other type of device, the steps will vary slightly. Just follow the prompts.

2. After the installation is complete, the dialog box shown in Figure 8-16 appears. Click Get Started.

3. A sign-in page opens. Enter your Windows account's user ID (usually this is your email address) and click Continue (see Figure 8-17).

FIGURE 8-16 Click Get Started to set up the RemoteApp client.

FIGURE 8-17 Enter your email address and click Continue.

4. In the Azure RemoteApp dialog box, select the Work Resources check box, and click Done to continue (see Figure 8-18).

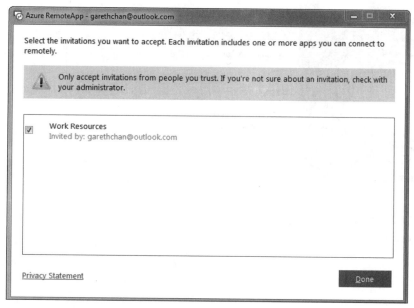

FIGURE 8-18 Select the invitation to share the app.

5. RemoteApp verifies your identity. After the verification is complete, you will get a list of apps that your organization has published to which you have access. To start an app, double-click it (see Figure 8-19). The app opens and you can open your file, as shown in Figure 8-20.

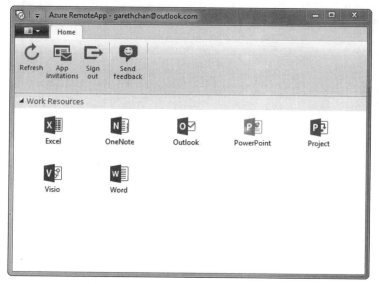

FIGURE 8-19 Double-click an app to start it.

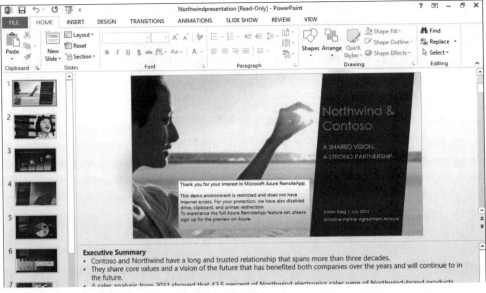

FIGURE 8-20 The app opens and you can open your files.

Summary

- One of IT's key roles is to make sure apps are both running and accessible so that the organization can keep the business operational and thriving. Today, however, IT administrators have an additional challenge: to ensure that apps are accessible on multiple platforms, devices, and operating systems.

- Microsoft Azure RemoteApp runs on Windows Server in the Microsoft public cloud. When you use RemoteApp to run your apps, workers can access them from any Internet-connected Mac or PC desktop or laptop computer, in addition to any Windows Phone, Android, or iOS mobile device.

- By using RemoteApp, your organization can take advantage of storage, scalability, a global reach, security, redundancy, and reduced hardware cost and configuration.

- There are two types of RemoteApp deployments: cloud deployments and hybrid deployments. With cloud deployments, your apps and all data associated with them are stored in the Microsoft public cloud. In a hybrid deployment, your apps and data are stored in the cloud, but users can also access them locally, from the on-premises network.

- You pay for Microsoft Azure RemoteApp on a per-user, per-month basis. There are no up-front costs and no termination fees.

- With RemoteApp, there are two tiers of service available: Basic and Standard. The Basic tier is for lightweight apps—for example, apps for data entry or expense reporting. It's ideal for task workers. The Standard tier is for "productivity apps," such as the Office 365 suite. This works best for information workers. Both tiers offer 50 GB of storage per user.

- The first step in setting up your business to use RemoteApp is to create a RemoteApp service in the cloud.

- You can add users and groups to your RemoteApp service.

- To make an app available to users, you must *publish* it.

- Before users can access the apps you publish, you must give them permission to do so. You must also install a RemoteApp client on the user's client computer or mobile device.

CHAPTER 9

Give users access to third-party apps

Share third-party apps in the cloud

Many people who are new to the Microsoft public cloud believe that it can be used only to share Microsoft products like Microsoft Office, Windows, SQL Server, and Visual Studio. This is not true. You can provision many third-party products from the Microsoft public cloud, including Oracle and Apache products and Linux, SAP, MYSQL, and PHP. In this chapter, you will learn how to use Microsoft Azure to do just that. Specifically, you'll find out how to use Azure to share Intuit's QuickBooks Online app. Users can then access the app directly from their web browsers.

> **NOTE** Of course, you must have the appropriate license for an app before you can use Azure to share it with your users. If you want to follow along with the steps in this chapter, you must get set up with the app's vendor beforehand. Remember to use the user name and password in Azure that you used for setting up the vendor app. To sign up for a free 30-day QuickBooks Online trial, go to *quickbooks.intuit.com* and click Start My Free Trial.

Set up your directory

To set up Azure to share a third-party app, you use a directory. This can be a new directory that you create or one that already exists. (See the "Start out in the cloud with just a directory" sidebar later in this chapter for more information.)

When you create your Azure subscription, you automatically create a new directory. You use this directory to manage all your users. As you'll discover in this section, you can set up this directory to share third-party apps. Follow these steps:

1. Sign in to the Azure portal at *manage.windowsazure.com*.

2. In the navigation pane, click Active Directory (see Figure 9-1).

FIGURE 9-1 Start here to set up your directory.

3. Click the New button at the bottom of the screen. Then click Directory, Custom Create.

4. The Add Directory dialog box opens, as shown in Figure 9-2. In the Directory list, click Use Existing Directory.

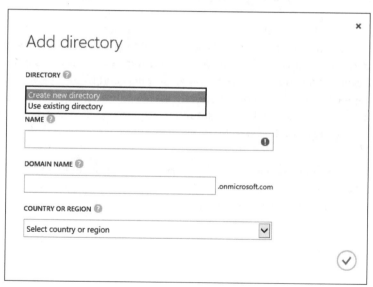

FIGURE 9-2 Click Use Existing Directory in the Add Directory dialog box.

5. Before you can set up the existing directory to share third-party apps, you must sign out and sign back in using an organizational account. Select the I Am Ready To Be Signed Out Now check box and then click the check mark in the lower-right corner of the dialog box (see Figure 9-3).

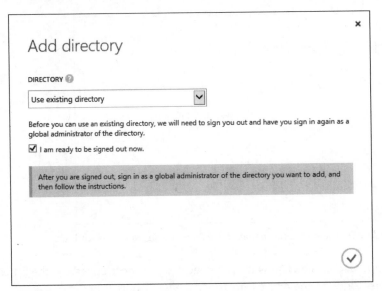

FIGURE 9-3 You'll need to sign out and sign back in as the global administrator.

6. When prompted to sign in, click Use Another Account (see Figure 9-4).

FIGURE 9-4 On the Sign In page, click Use Another Account.

7. Enter the account credentials (user name and password) for your organizational account, and click Sign In.

8. Azure asks you to confirm that you want to use the existing directory with Microsoft Azure. Click Continue (see Figure 9-5).

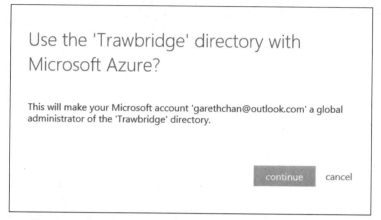

FIGURE 9-5 Click Continue to confirm that you want to use the directory with Azure.

9. When prompted, click Sign Out Now. The directory you chose appears in the list of available directories on the Active Directory page (see Figure 9-6).

FIGURE 9-6 The directory you added appears on the Active Directory page.

Start out in the cloud with just a directory

You've got a business. You're thinking about taking advantage of some of the public cloud offerings, but you haven't decided which ones yet. Microsoft Azure? Office 365? Just because you haven't decided, however, doesn't mean you can't put your stake in the ground by setting up your organizational account directory.

There are two basic ways to manage your identity within the Microsoft public cloud: with your Microsoft account (formerly Windows Live ID, such as *your-name*@hotmail.com) or with an organizational account. This determines who or what entity manages your account. Most people, when they start experimenting with cloud services, access them with a Microsoft account. This is often the email address they use to sign in to other consumer Microsoft services—such as OneDrive and Outlook.com. Or they might create a new Microsoft account with a work email address. When you sign up for a cloud service (like Azure) with your existing Microsoft account, you end up with a default directory, also known as a *tenant*, in the *onmicrosoft.com* domain with a name that is derived from your Microsoft account, like yourname*hotmail.onmicrosoft.com*. This is a free domain that comes with your service.

After you set up a directory, you can connect your official domain name, but if you want to use your *onmicrosoft.com* domain name for public-facing services, you might want it to align with your business name. To make that happen, you can create your tenancy (your default directory) *before* you connect any services to it. Just test to find out what names are available, choose the name you want, and then create the users within it. That way, instead of ending up with a directory of yourname*hotmail.onmicrosoft.com*, you can end up with something much nicer, like yourbusiness.*onmicrosoft.com*. To do this, follow these steps:

1. In your Internet browser, go to *https://account.windowsazure.com/organization*.

2. You'll be prompted to create your first account. When you do, you can enter the name you want to use for your directory and test for its availability. You don't need a credit card for this process, only a phone number to verify that you are human.

3. After you have completed this process, you will be led to a page where you can sign up for a cloud service, like Azure, on a trial basis. If you aren't ready to start an Azure trial or haven't yet made a decision about Office 365 or Microsoft Intune (each of which has its own 30-day trial), you can stop right there. You have claimed your directory.

After your directory is created, you can access it from the portals related to whatever cloud service you sign up for—Azure, Office 365, or Microsoft Intune. In this example, you *haven't* signed up for a service, so only the Office 365 and Microsoft Intune portals show your directory, without any services attached. You can find the portals here:

- **Azure**   *https://manage.windowsazure.com*
- **Office 365**   *https://portal.office.com*
- **Microsoft Intune**   *https://account.manage.microsoft.com*

   IMPORTANT   If you are going to use Office 365 or are using it, set up your tenant for Office 365 first, then Microsoft Intune, followed by Microsoft Azure Active Directory integration.

After you have signed in to the Office 365 or Microsoft Intune portal with your newly created account, you'll be able to create new users, give them additional permissions to manage your directory, and add your custom domain if you have one. For everything else, you'll be alerted that you aren't subscribed to anything.

At this point, you can be assured that you've claimed your directory, and you can take your time reviewing the other services, activate trials, and purchase the services you need, when you need them.

Jennelle Crothers
Technical Evangelist – Microsoft Corporation

Share the Intuit QuickBooks Online app

Now that your directory is set up, you're ready to configure it to share the Intuit QuickBooks Online app. (Remember, you need to have established a QuickBooks Online account first. This is done at the vendor's website.) Follow these steps:

1. On the Active Directory page (see Figure 9-6, shown earlier), click the directory you just added.

   TIP   If the Active Directory page is not currently displayed, click Active Directory in the Azure portal's navigation pane to open it.

2. The Quick Start page opens (see Figure 9-7). Click Applications at the top of the page.

FIGURE 9-7 Click Applications at the top of the Quick Start page.

3. On the Applications page, click Add An Application, as shown in Figure 9-8.

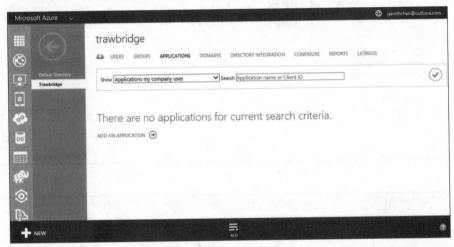

FIGURE 9-8 Click Add An Application to proceed.

4. You'll be asked what you want to do. Click Add An Application From The Gallery (see Figure 9-9).

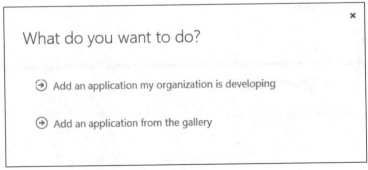

FIGURE 9-9 When asked what you want to do, click Add An Application From The Gallery.

5. The Application Gallery opens. In the search box in the upper-right corner of the page, enter **quickbooks** and then click the search icon. Then click QuickBooks Online in the list that appears. Finally, click the check mark in the lower-right corner of the page (see Figure 9-10). As shown in Figure 9-11, the app is added.

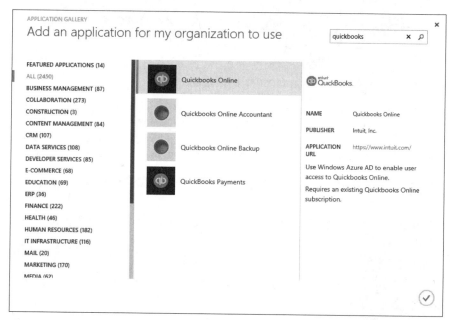

FIGURE 9-10 Click the app you want in the Application Gallery.

FIGURE 9-11 The app is added.

Set up the Access Panel Extension

Users will log on to the QuickBooks Online or other third-party app by using a web browser add-on called the *Access Panel*. When the user enters his or her credentials in the Access Panel, that user will automatically be passed to the third-party app. That way, the user needs to sign in only once. This is called *single sign-on*.

To make single sign-on possible, you as the administrator must install the Access Panel Extension. (To view your apps on your device, go to *manage.windowsazure.com* to get the Access Panel Extension.) Here's how:

1. In the QuickBooks Online page shown earlier in Figure 9-11, click the Configure Single Sign-On button.

2. You'll be asked whether you want to run or save the Access Panel Extension.msi file (see Figure 9-12). Click Run.

FIGURE 9-12 Click Run to install the Access Panel Extension.

3. The Access Panel Extension Setup Wizard starts, with the Welcome page displayed (see Figure 9-13). Click Next to continue.

FIGURE 9-13 Click Next on the Welcome page of the Access Panel Extension Setup Wizard.

4. The Install Access Panel Extension page opens (see Figure 9-14). Click Install.

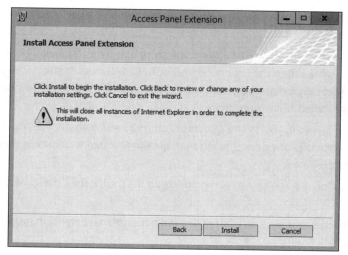

FIGURE 9-14 Click Install to install the Access Panel Extension.

5. The Access Panel Extension is installed (see Figure 9-15). Click Finish.

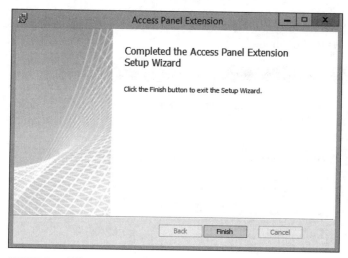

FIGURE 9-15 When prompted, click Finish.

6. As a final step, you must enable the Access Panel Extension and restart your web browser. Click the Enable button (see Figure 9-16), and then restart your browser as instructed.

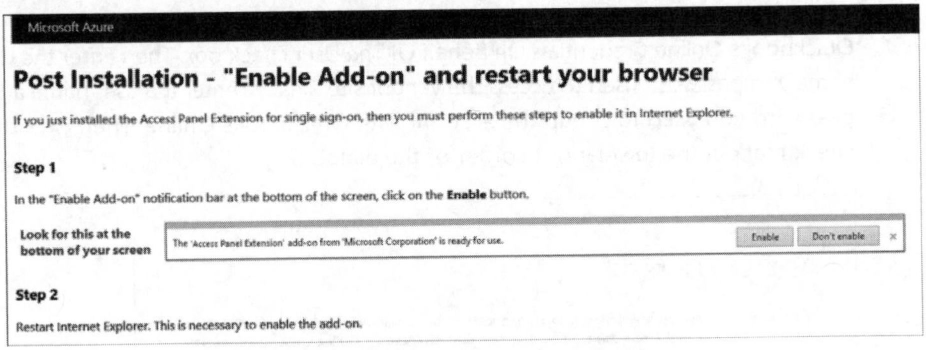

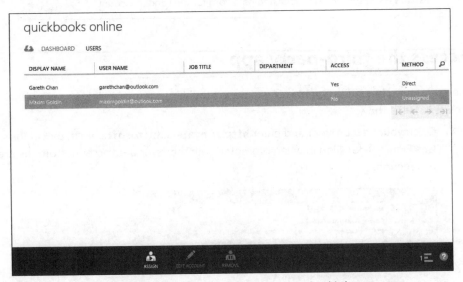

FIGURE 9-16 Enable the Access Panel Extension and restart your browser.

Allow users access to the third-party app

As the administrator, you can specify which users have access to this third-party app. You do so from the Azure portal. Follow these steps:

1. On the QuickBooks Online page (see Figure 9-11, shown earlier), click the Assign Users button.

2. On the QuickBooks Online Users page, select a user to whom you want to give access to the third-party app (see Figure 9-17). Click Assign.

FIGURE 9-17 Select a user to whom you want to give access to the third-party app.

3. The Assign Users dialog box opens (see Figure 9-18). Select the I Want To Enter Quickbooks Online Credentials On Behalf Of The User check box. Then enter the user name and password used to access the vendor site. That is, enter the user name and password you used to set up the account with QuickBooks Online. Then click the check mark in the lower-right corner of the dialog box.

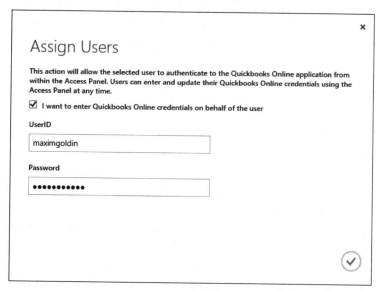

FIGURE 9-18 Enter the user name and password for the vendor account.

Access the third-party app

Users who have been given permission to access the third-party app do so by using their web browsers. Here's how:

1. Open your web browser and enter **http://myapps.microsoft.com** in the address box (see Figure 9-19). Sign in when prompted with the associated account from the previous section.

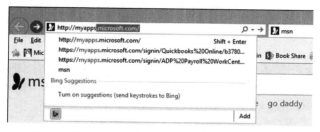

FIGURE 9-19 Direct your web browser to *http://myapps.microsoft.com*.

2. A page like the one shown in Figure 9-20 appears. Click the directory that is associated with the app in the menu.

FIGURE 9-20 Click the directory that is associated with the app in the menu, as shown here.

3. A list of the apps on the directory to which you have been given access appears (see Figure 9-21). Double-click QuickBooks Online to start the app.

FIGURE 9-21 Double-click QuickBooks Online to start the app.

4. A QuickBooks Online dialog box appears, with an Install Now button. Or, if you are using a Windows-based computer, you can click Here in the Tip to be redirected to a page from which you can install the Access Panel (see Figure 9-22).

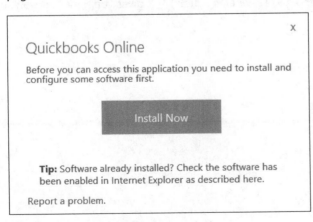

FIGURE 9-22 Install the app before continuing.

5. If this is the first time you've started this QuickBooks Online trial, you'll get the message shown in Figure 9-23. Then you'll be prompted to enter some information about yourself and your company, as shown in Figure 9-24. Enter the requested information, and then click Sign Up.

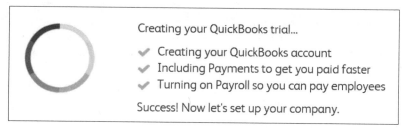

FIGURE 9-23 If this is the first time you have started the QuickBooks Online trial, you'll get this message.

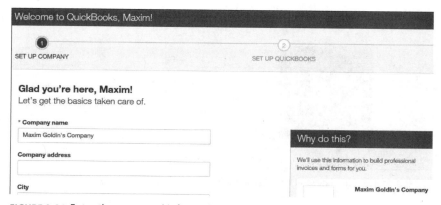

FIGURE 9-24 Enter the requested information.

6. On the next page, your User ID and Password credentials are entered for you, as shown in Figure 9-25. (This is the Access Panel in action.) This gives you single sign-on access to QuickBooks Online.

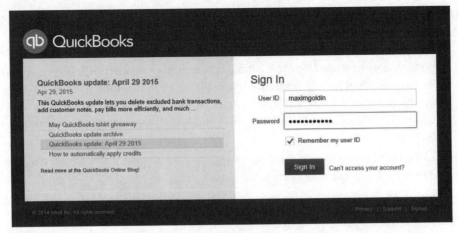

FIGURE 9-25 Enter your Windows user ID and password.

After you sign in, the QuickBooks Online app is ready for use (see Figure 9-26).

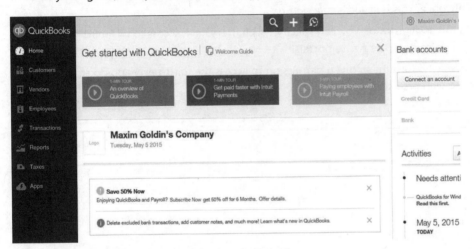

FIGURE 9-26 QuickBooks Online is open and ready for business.

Summary

- Although many people who are new to the Microsoft public cloud believe that it can be used only to share Microsoft products like Office, Windows, SQL Server, and Visual Studio, this is not true. You can use Microsoft Azure to provision many third-party products from the Microsoft public cloud, including Oracle and Apache products and Linux, SAP, MYSQL, and PHP. Users can then access these apps directly from their web browsers.

- To set up Azure to share a third-party app, you use a directory. This can be a new directory that you create or one that already exists.

- You must add the third-party app you want to share to the directory you have selected. You do so from the Application Gallery.

- Users will log on to the third-party app by using a web browser add-on called the *Access Panel*. When the user enters his or her credentials in the Access Panel, that user will automatically be passed to the third-party app. That way, the user needs to sign in only once. This is called *single sign-on*.

- As the administrator, you can specify which users have access to this third-party app. You do so from the Azure portal.

- Users who have been given permission to access the third-party app do so by using their web browsers.

CHAPTER 10

Build a website for your business

Azure websites

It is difficult to imagine a business that could not benefit from having a website. Fortunately, with Microsoft Azure, you can easily build your own custom site in the Microsoft public cloud.

By using Azure, you can deploy scalable web apps and mobile apps that use your programming language of choice. It does not restrict you to a particular programming platform but offers a wide selection of today's modern web technologies and source control providers. With Azure's easy-to-use management portal, you can select the type of site you want to deploy, such as .NET, Java, PHP, Node.js, or Python. You can also choose from many content management systems (CMSs) like WordPress, Drupal, Joomla!, DukeNetNuke (DNN), and many more—all from the cloud. The rest of this chapter refers to websites in WordPress, although there are many web apps and mobile apps that can be developed by using Microsoft Azure, which will be covered in Chapter 11, "Build a Windows app by using Windows App Studio."

> **NOTE** In this chapter, you'll use WordPress to build your site.

Plan your website

Before you use WordPress in Azure to create your website, you'll want to do some planning. Here are a few points to consider:

- **Purpose** What is the purpose of your website? What do you want it to do? You must clearly define what you expect of your website.

- **Contents** What will your website contain? At a minimum, it should provide information about the services you offer, your organization's background, your expertise, and any affiliations you have; links to any social media accounts you manage; and information about how to contact you.

- **Layout** How do you want to present the site content? What will the "look" of the site be?

> **TIP** Creating an outline or mockup of your site can help you determine how best to organize it.

You must also determine what level of resources you need from Azure. For example, how much storage will you need? Do you want to create more than one web app for your organization? Table 10-1 outlines your options (which are subject to change).

TABLE 10-1 Azure web app options

	Free develop and test apps	Shared dev/ test with higher limits	Basic Go live with basic apps	Standard Go live with web, mobile, logic apps	Premium maximum scale and enterprise integration
Web, mobile, or API apps	10	100	Unlimited	Unlimited	Unlimited
Logic apps	10	10	10	20 per core	20 per core
Integration	Dev/Test	Dev/Test	Dev/Test	Standard Connectors	Premium Connectors + Microsoft BizTalk Services
Disk space	1 GB	1 GB	10 GB	50 GB	500 GB
Maximum instances	--	--	Up to 3	Up to 10	Up to 50
App Service Environments	--	--	--	--	Supported
SLA	--	--	99.90%	99.95%	99.95%

For full details about app service plans, visit azure.microsoft.com/en-us/pricing/details/app-service/.

Create your website

In this section, you'll use Azure and WordPress to create your own website. A popular Content Management System (CMS), WordPress is an open-source project that offers a lot of enhancements, such as plug-ins, themes, and services. Most of these enhancements are free, and others are available for purchase. Although many WordPress sites are blogs, the highly customizable nature of WordPress makes it a popular choice as the core web platform for many large companies and educational institutions.

What is open-source software?

Open-source software is software that, according to the Open Source Initiative, "can be freely used, changed, and shared (in modified or unmodified form) by anyone." The initiative goes on to say, "Open source software is made by many people, and distributed under licenses that comply with the Open Source Definition." Many types of open-source software, including WordPress, are built and supported by groups of volunteers. For more information, visit *opensource.org*.

To create your website, follow these steps:

1. Sign in to the Azure portal at *https://manage.windowsazure.com*. The default view when you sign in to Azure is the All Items list.

2. Click the newly named Web Apps category (formerly named Websites), as shown in Figure 10-1.

FIGURE 10-1 Click the Web Apps category.

3. Click Create A Web App.

4. There are three options for creating a new web app (see Figure 10-2):

   - **Quick Create**   Quickly create your web app by specifying a URL. You can perform tasks such as deployment and configuration later.

   - **Custom Create**   Create a web app with additional options, such as a new or existing database, or with continuous deployment from source control.

   - **From Gallery**   Choose a web app from the gallery.

FIGURE 10-2 There are three options for creating a new web app.

Click From Gallery to continue.

5. On the Find Apps For Microsoft Azure page (see Figure 10-3), scroll down to WordPress and click it.

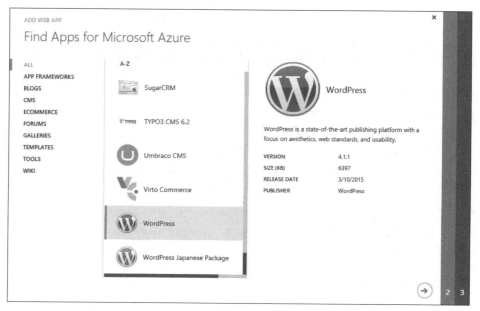

FIGURE 10-3 Click WordPress in the gallery.

6. Click the right arrow to continue.

7. On the Configure Your App page (see Figure 10-4), you will need to provide a unique URL for your site in the URL field. In the figure, notice that *trawbridge* has not been used; this is verified with a green check mark. If you enter a name that has already been used, you will receive a red exclamation mark.

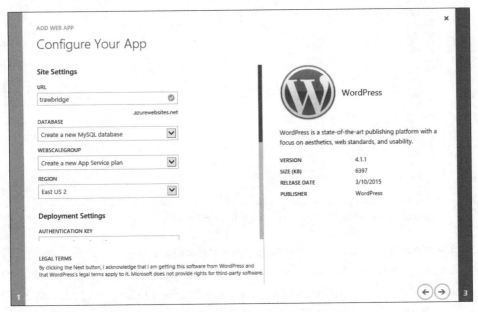

FIGURE 10-4 The Trawbridge URL is listed.

8. The Database field is preset to Create A New MySQL Database. If you have previously created a MySQL database, you can select it here from the menu.

9. The Webscalegroup setting is also preset to Create A New App Service Plan. If you have created an App Service plan, you can select it here from the menu.

10. On the Region menu, select the region that is closest to you.

11. The deployment settings are optional at this time. These settings add an extra layer of security to your cookies and passwords by using WordPress Security Keys, which consist of four authentication keys and four hashing salts (random bits of data) that work together (visit *digwp.com/2010/09/wordpress-security-keys/* for more information). Click the right arrow to continue.

12. On the New MySQL Database page (see Figure 10-5), either use the default database name that has been generated or rename it.

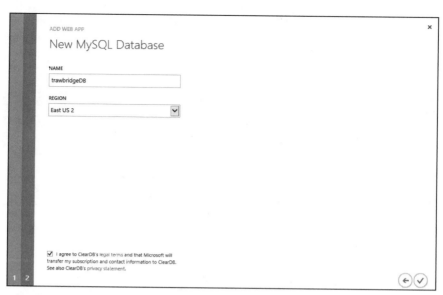

FIGURE 10-5 The new database is named TrawbridgeDB.

13. Select the region closest to you for the database location.

14. Select the check box to accept the legal terms so that ClearDB can continue.

15. Click the check mark to complete the setup process. The process of creating and provisioning the web app is fairly quick.

16. After the process is complete, you must finish the process of configuring the website. Click the URL, as shown in Figure 10-6. A new browser tab to your site opens.

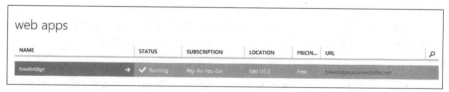

FIGURE 10-6 The Trawbridge web app has been created and is running.

17. Select the language you want to use, as shown in Figure 10-7, and click Continue.

18. On the next page, give your site a title, give yourself a user name and password, and provide your email address (see Figure 10-8). You can choose whether to have your site indexed. Click the Install WordPress button. Installation will only take a moment.

FIGURE 10-7 Select a language for the site.

Welcome

Welcome to the famous five-minute WordPress installation process! Just fill in the information below and you'll be on your way to using the most extendable and powerful personal publishing platform in the world.

Information needed

Please provide the following information. Don't worry, you can always change these settings later.

Site Title

Username

Usernames can have only alphanumeric characters, spaces, underscores, hyphens, periods, and the @ symbol.

Password, twice

A password will be automatically generated for you if you leave this blank.

Strength indicator

Hint: The password should be at least seven characters long. To make it stronger, use upper and lower case letters, numbers, and symbols like ! " ? $ % ^ &).

Your E-mail

Double-check your email address before continuing.

Privacy ☑ Allow search engines to index this site.

Install WordPress

FIGURE 10-8 Fill in the required information for the new site.

19. If everything has completed properly, you can now log on to your site (see Figure 10-9). Click the Log In button.

FIGURE 10-9 The WordPress site has been successfully created.

20. On the sign-in page, enter your user name and password (see Figure 10-10). Then click the Log In button.

FIGURE 10-10 Enter your user name and password on the sign-in page for WordPress.

Customize your website

Technically speaking, your website is up and running. But you have yet to add any content—text, images, video, or whatever else you want. You also haven't established the look and feel you want.

First, you'll familiarize yourself with the WordPress Dashboard page. This page, which is displayed by default when you sign in to your WordPress site, allows easy access to all of your

website's content. Information about your website is organized into modules or widgets in the main part of the page. In addition, the toolbar at the top of the page includes links to various administrative functions. You access all other WordPress settings, customizations, user content, and other administrative functions from the options in the navigation pane, located on the left side of the page.

> **NOTE** If you have signed out of your site, you can sign back in from the home page of your website or by using the following URL: yoursite.*azurewebsites.net/wp-login.php* (where *yoursite* is the name of your website).

> **TIP** This section covers some very basic features in WordPress. You will probably want to explore the platform's various tools and options to build a full-featured site.

Explore WordPress settings

Before you begin customizing your website, take a moment to explore WordPress's settings. Click Settings in the navigation pane to view the following options:

- **General Settings** The General Settings page is the default Settings page. It includes some of the most basic configuration settings for your website. These include your website's title and location, who can register for an account at your site, and how dates and times are calculated and displayed (see Figure 10-11).

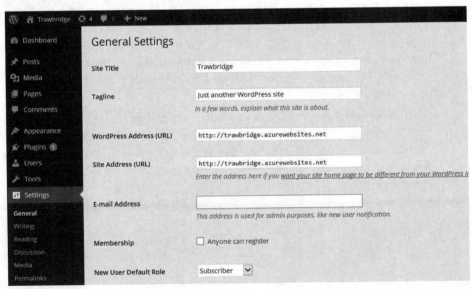

FIGURE 10-11 The General Settings page includes some of the most basic configuration settings for your website.

- **Writing Settings**   On the Writing Settings page, shown in Figure 10-12, you can control the interface you use to enter new blog posts (if you plan to include a blog on your website). Here you control the default post category, link category, and post format. You can also set up the Post Via Email option if you want to be able to submit posts via email.

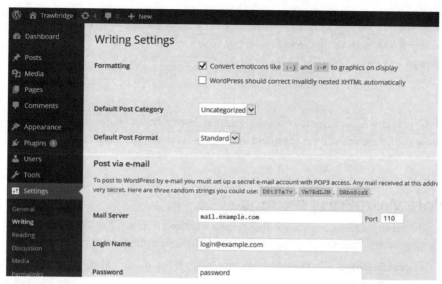

FIGURE 10-12 You use the Writing Settings page to set up the interface to use when creating new blog posts.

- **Reading Settings**   On this page (see Figure 10-13), you can specify whether you want your latest blog posts to appear on your website's main (or front) page or whether you want that page to be static. If you opt to display posts, you can indicate how many should appear. In addition, you can adjust syndication feed features to determine how the information from your website is sent to a reader's web browser or other applications.

- **Discussion Settings**   The Discussion Settings page (see Figure 10-14) is where you control settings that pertain to comments, pingbacks, and trackbacks. You can also control the circumstances under which your website will send you email notifications. Finally, you can specify whether your website should show the avatars and ratings of commenters.

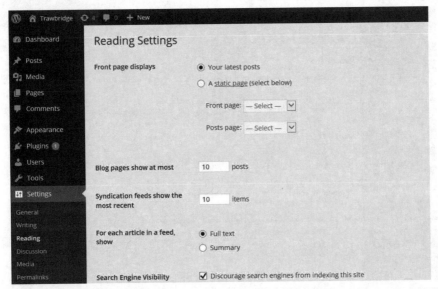

FIGURE 10-13 Use the settings on the Reading Settings page to determine how visitors will see your written content.

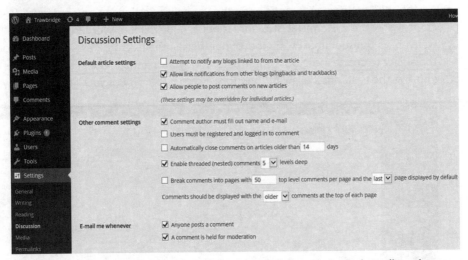

FIGURE 10-14 The Discussion Settings page has control settings that pertain to discussions on your website.

- **Media Settings** On the Media Settings page, you can specify how images, documents, and other media files will be organized when they are uploaded. You can also specify the maximum dimensions in pixels to use when inserting an image into the body of a blog post (see Figure 10-15).

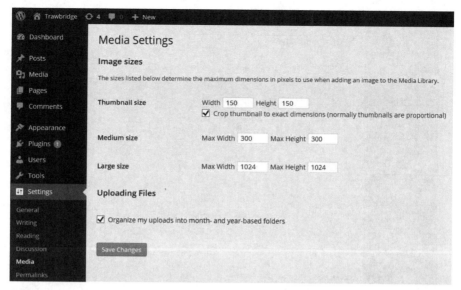

FIGURE 10-15 Choose the default settings for media, such as image sizes and how media files will be organized.

- **Permalink Settings** The options on the Permalink Settings page (see Figure 10-16) control how the custom URL structure is defined. By default, WordPress uses web URLs, which have question marks and lots of numbers in them. WordPress also offers you the ability to create a custom URL structure for your permalinks and archives. This can improve the aesthetics, usability, and forward compatibility of your links.

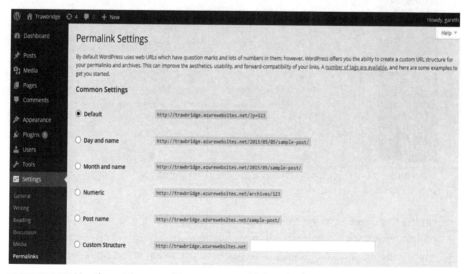

FIGURE 10-16 Use the settings on this page to establish how URLs will be structured on your site.

TIP To learn more about the various settings and options available in WordPress, read the WordPress Help documentation.

Add content to your site

What use would a website be without content? None. Fortunately, WordPress makes it easy to add content to your website.

Perhaps the easiest way to add content is by adding blog posts. These posts are usually displayed in reverse order, with the most recent post appearing first. They can appear on the main page of your website or on a page that you have designated as your blog.

TIP As mentioned in the preceding section, you can specify whether WordPress places your posts on the main page (the default) or on a separate page by changing the setting on the Reading Settings page.

To add a post, follow these steps:

1. In the navigation pane on the left side of the WordPress screen, click Posts. The Posts page opens (see Figure 10-17). From this page, you can add new posts and edit or delete existing ones.

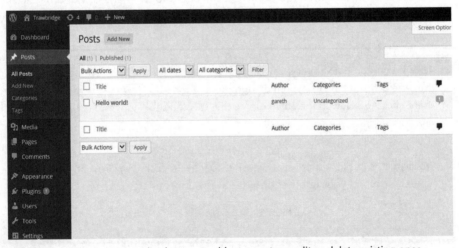

FIGURE 10-17 The Posts page is where you add new posts or edit or delete existing ones.

2. Click the Add New button in the upper-left area of the Posts page. Alternatively, you can click Add New under Posts in the navigation pane. The Add New Post page opens (see Figure 10-18).

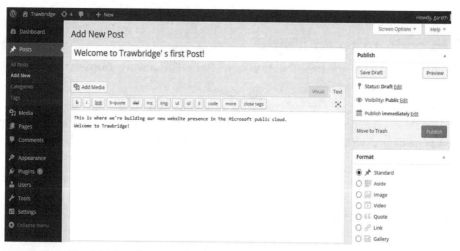

FIGURE 10-18 The Add New Post page is where you enter your new post.

3. Enter a title for the post in the box at the top. Then enter the body of your post in the larger box below. Optionally, use the formatting buttons to format your text, applying bold, italics, or whatever you want. You can also add an image or video by clicking the Add Media button and following the prompts. When you're finished, click the Publish button.

> **TIP** If you don't have time to finish your post, you can save it as a draft. To do so, click the Save Draft button in the upper-right area of the Add New Post page. To access the draft, click Add New in the navigation pane, then on the Add New Post page, click Edit next to the draft.

4. Your post is published on your website. To view it, click View Post at the top of the screen or direct your Internet browser to the appropriate page on your website (see Figure 10-19).

> **TIP** For more information about features and options for writing a post, visit the following pages:
> - *codex.wordpress.org/Posts_Screen*
> - *codex.wordpress.org/Writing_Posts*

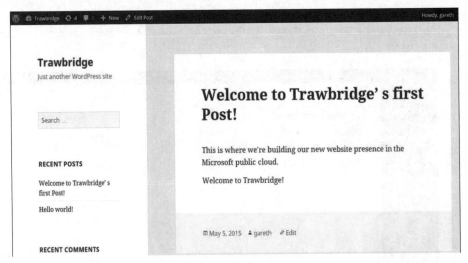

FIGURE 10-19 Your post is published on your website.

Add pages to your site

Most likely, you'll want your website to have more than one page. In fact, your site might have several pages. For example, your main page might feature general information about your company, whereas a second page could outline the products and services you offer, and a third page could include information about where you are located and how to contact you. Other pages could contain information about your company's key people or links to articles about your company on other websites. And, of course, one page could feature a blog.

To add a page to your site, follow these steps:

1. Click Pages in the navigation pane on the left side of the screen. The Pages page opens (see Figure 10-20.) From here, you can add new pages or edit or delete existing ones.

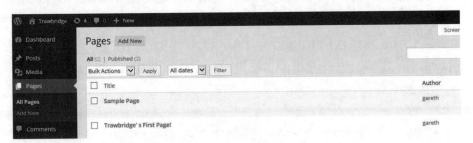

FIGURE 10-20 You can easily add pages to your website.

2. Click the Add New button in the upper-left area of the Pages page. Alternatively, click Add New under Pages in the navigation pane. The Add New Page page opens (see Figure 10-21).

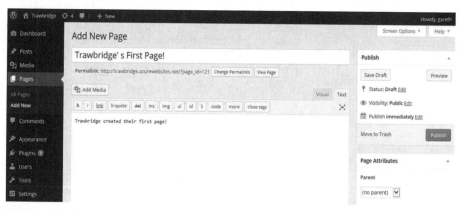

FIGURE 10-21 You can add a new page to the site from the Add New Page page.

3. Adding a page is very similar to adding a new blog post. Enter a title for the page in the box at the top. Then add any other content you want in the larger box below. Optionally, use the formatting buttons to format your text, applying bold, italics, or whatever you want. You can also add an image or video by clicking the Add Media button and following the prompts. When you're finished, click the Publish button.

> **TIP** As with blog posts, you can save a page as a draft if you don't have time to finish it. To do so, click the Save Draft button in the upper-right area of the Add New Page page. To access the draft, click Pages in the navigation pane, and then on the Add New Post page, click Edit next to the draft.

4. Your page is published on your website. To view it, click View Page at the top of the screen or direct your Internet browser to the appropriate page on your website (see Figure 10-22).

> **TIP** For more information about features and options for creating a page, visit the following pages:
> - *codex.wordpress.org/Pages*
> - *https://make.wordpress.org/support/user-manual/content/posts-vs-pages/*

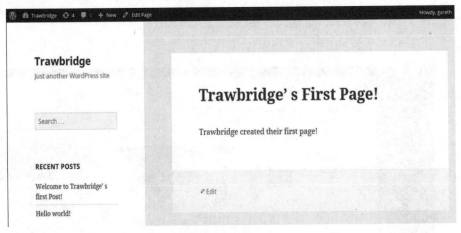

FIGURE 10-22 Your page is published on your website.

Apply a WordPress theme to your site

You might have noticed that the site you've created so far is, well, a little dull. Fortunately, WordPress offers numerous themes. You can apply a theme to your website to quickly and easily change its look and feel.

Changing your website's theme is as easy as publishing a post or a page. Here's how it's done:

1. Click Appearance in the navigation pane on the left side of the WordPress screen.

2. The Themes page opens (see Figure 10-23). Click the Add New button in the upper-left area of the page.

FIGURE 10-23 From the Themes page, you can apply a theme to your website.

3. The Add Themes page opens (see Figure 10-24). Themes are organized into three categories: Featured, Popular, and Latest. Click a category to view its themes, or enter a keyword in the Search Themes box and press Enter to search for a theme.

TIP To view information about a theme, point to it.

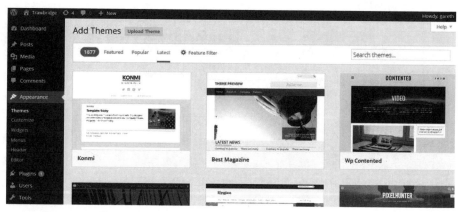

FIGURE 10-24 Choose a theme from the Add Themes page.

4. When you find a theme you like, click it to select it.

5. You'll get a preview of your site with the theme applied. Click Install.

6. WordPress installs the theme on your website. When prompted, click Activate to activate the theme.

7. Go to your website to view the new theme. (Note that you may need to refresh your web browser.) Figure 10-25 shows the Influence theme applied to the example website.

FIGURE 10-25 The Influence theme is applied to the example website.

NOTE Depending on which theme you choose, you might need to change certain WordPress settings to accommodate it.

TIP In addition to the free themes, plug-ins, and widgets available from the WordPress site, there are many paid options and features available online. For example, ThemeForest (*www.themeforest.com*) offers many professionally developed WordPress themes, plug-ins, widgets, and more.

Summary

- By using Azure, you can deploy a scalable site that uses the programming language you choose. It does not restrict you to a particular programming platform but offers a wide choice of today's modern web technologies and source control providers. With Azure's easy-to-use management portal, you can select the type of site you want to deploy, such as .NET, Java, PHP, Node.js, or Python. You can also choose from many content management systems (CMSs) like WordPress, Drupal, Joomla!, DukeNetNuke (DNN), and many more—all from the cloud.

- Within Microsoft Azure you can build websites, web apps, mobile apps, and API apps. Before you use WordPress in Azure to create your website, you'll want to do some planning. Specifically, you need to decide what the purpose of your website will be, what your website will contain, and how you want to present the site content.

- A popular CMS, WordPress is an open-source project that offers a lot of enhancements, such as plug-ins, themes, and services. Most of these enhancements are free, and others are available for purchase. Although many WordPress sites are blogs, the highly customizable nature of WordPress makes it a popular choice as the core web platform for many large companies and educational institutions.

- After you create your website, you must define a resource group for it. A resource group is a container that helps you manage a collection of Azure resources.

- So that the WordPress software can run, you must set up a ClearDB MySQL database to work alongside it.

- The Dashboard page allows easy access to all of your website's content. Information about your website is organized into modules or widgets in the main part of the page. In addition, the toolbar at the top of the page includes links to various administrative functions. You access all other WordPress settings, customizations, user content, and other administrative functions from the options in the navigation pane, located on the left side of the page.

- Perhaps the easiest way to add content is by adding blog posts. These posts are usually displayed in reverse order. They can appear on the main page of your website or on a page that you have designated as your blog.

- Most likely, you'll want your website to have more than one page. In fact, your site might have several pages. For example, your main page might feature general information about your company, whereas a second page could outline the products and services you offer, and a third page could include information about where you are located and how to contact you. Other pages could contain information about your company's key people or links to articles about your company on other websites. And, of course, one page could feature a blog.

- WordPress offers numerous themes. You can apply a theme to your website to quickly and easily change its look and feel.

CHAPTER 11

Build a Windows app by using Windows App Studio

Why build a mobile app?

These days, just about everyone carries a mobile device. In fact, many of us carry multiple devices—including smartphones, tablets, and phablets—everywhere we go, often sneaking a peek every few minutes. We have become almost inseparable from our mobile devices. Email, Twitter, Facebook, Instagram...the many ways of staying connected through technology have become completely integrated into our lives.

As a business owner, how can you take advantage of this trend to boost your business? Building a website is a good first step, but a website alone is no longer enough. Today's users want mobile apps. A mobile app acts as a supplement to your website and a powerful tool in its own right. This chapter explains why and how to build a mobile app.

Prepare to build your mobile app

Before you start building your app, you must answer two simple questions:

- **What kind of app do you want to make?**   Maybe you want to make a game, or perhaps an app that offers useful information. The type of app you want to make

will determine the technologies you will want to use. For example, if you are building a game, you might use Construct 2, a drag-and-drop game creator from a company called Scirra Ltd. (*scirra.com*).

■ **What mobile platforms do you want to target?**   Currently, the top three mobile platforms are Windows Phone, Android, and iOS. Windows 8 is also a viable mobile platform. Depending on the resources you have available to you, you can build your app for any or all of these platforms.

Use the Lean Startup approach

Both your website and your app must represent your company well. They must be attractive enough to draw in customers and visitors and informative enough to keep them coming back.

The audience for your app is your customer. Your primary focus in building your mobile app is to fill a void for your customer and enhance his or her experience with your company. After you've gotten the attention of your customer, you can build a relationship by learning from him or her and enhancing your app based on what you learn.

As you develop your mobile app, consider using the Lean Startup[1] approach, espoused by Eric Ries. The Lean Startup approach involves shortened product cycles to get your technology (in this case, your app) in the hands of the customer as quickly as possible. Instead of investing a lot of time trying to create the perfect app, with this approach you release your minimum viable product (MVP) to the customer as quickly as possible, and then you continually improve it to meet customer needs. The MVP might not have all the features that you ultimately want, but the sooner you get your MVP to market, the sooner you can get the feedback from your customers and make improvements.

The typical steps in the Lean Startup life cycle are building, measuring, and learning. Starting with your MVP, you will release your app and then focus your next update on what your customers are looking for. Pay attention to the ratings and feedback that you receive so you can determine what you might need to change or improve. The point of this approach is to continually learn from your customers and to use that information to improve the app and, with it, your relationship with your customer.

---

[1]   *The Lean Startup: How Today's Entrepreneurs Use Continuous Innovation to Create Radically Successful Businesses* by Eric Ries (Crown Business, 2011)

Tools for building mobile apps

Building an app for the three major mobile device platforms typically means using at least three different programming languages to cover all platforms:

- **Windows Phone** C#, XAML (Extensible Application Markup Language), and HTML and JavaScript are used to build apps for Windows Phone.
- **Android** Java and AXML (Active XML) are used to build apps for Android devices.
- **iOS** Objective C and UIKit are used to build apps for iOS devices.

If you want to develop an app for all three platforms, you will likely need a team of developers, with different members dedicated to each platform to build and then maintain each version of the app.

TIP If you don't have a team of developers available to you, you might still be able to develop your app for all three platforms by using tools like the following:

- **Xamarin (xamarin.com/)** With Xamarin, you can use C# and XAML to write cross-platform applications that are considered to be native to those platforms. This is a great opportunity for programmers who have experience developing in C#, because they can use that same skill set to cross over into mobile app development.
- **PhoneGap (phonegap.com/)** By using PhoneGap, you can create mobile web apps with HTML and JavaScript. These mobile web apps can run on any mobile platform because they only need a browser to run.

These tools make it easier to target multiple platforms, but the person using them still needs to know how to program in one of the relevant languages.

What if you have no dedicated team to build your app, and no programming experience yourself? In that case, you can use Windows App Studio. Windows App Studio is a free, browser-based program that you can use to build Windows Phone and Windows 8 mobile apps—no programming knowledge needed.

TIP Windows App Studio can generate source code for your project. This means that if you *do* have programming knowledge, you can edit the source code to add any features you want. App Studio has a lot of built-in capabilities, but when you combine them with the ability to edit the source code, your options are limitless!

To get started, you need two things:

- A Microsoft account to build the app. This can be a Hotmail account, a Microsoft Outlook account, or another account.

- A Microsoft Developer account to publish the app. To sign up for a Microsoft Developer account, go to *aka.ms/devsignup*. You must pay to obtain a Microsoft Developer account unless you have a BizSpark subscription, in which case you can obtain a Microsoft Developer account free of charge.

With those two accounts, you can quickly and easily create a mobile app for your company without the costly investment of a development team.

What is Microsoft BizSpark?

BizSpark is a Microsoft program that provides free Microsoft products, including software design and development tools, to qualifying startups for three years. Since its inception in 2008, more than 50,000 companies in more than 100 countries have joined BizSpark. To qualify for BizSpark, the startup company must develop software, be privately owned, be less than five years old, and generate less than $1 million in revenue. Find out more about BizSpark at *aka.ms/bizsparkeast*.

Create an empty app

As mentioned, in this chapter you will use Windows App Studio to build an informational app for your business. By using this app, your customers will be able to access data about your business from their mobile devices so they can connect with your business at any time.

To get started, you must open App Studio and create an empty app. Here's how:

1. In your web browser, go to *appstudio.windows.com* to view the Windows App Studio home page, shown in Figure 11-1.

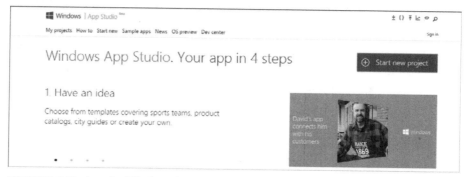

FIGURE 11-1 Start on the Windows App Studio home page.

2. In the upper-right corner of the Windows App Studio home page, click Sign In.

3. On the Sign In page, enter your Microsoft account user name and password.

4. Click My Projects. The My Projects page opens, as shown in Figure 11-2.

FIGURE 11-2 You can start creating your app on the My Projects page in Windows App Studio.

5. Click Start New Project.

> **NOTE** When you start a new project, you can either create a new empty project or create a project from a template. Although you won't be using a template in this example, templates are worth considering for the future. In general, well-made templates are a great resource for getting started. If something has already been done, why re-create it?

6. Click Empty App (see Figure 11-3), and then click Create.

FIGURE 11-3 Click Empty App, and then click Create.

7. In the App Title box (see Figure 11-4), enter a name for your app. Then click Save.

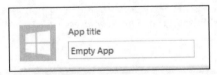

FIGURE 11-4 Name your app.

After you create your empty project, you can access it by clicking My Project and then clicking the name of your app.

Add data sources

App Studio projects are made up of two key components:

- **Data sources**   Any information you want to include in your app.
- **Application sections**   Pages in your app that contain data sources. You can have up to six application sections in your app.

Each application section is linked to one data source. There are several types of data sources:

- RSS feed
- HTML
- YouTube
- Flickr
- Bing
- Facebook
- Instagram
- Collection
- Menu

You'll learn how to add these different types of data sources to your app in the following sections.

Add an RSS feed

An RSS feed is a way of syndicating content. Adding an RSS feed to your app is a great idea if you want to make your app users aware of any new content on your website. When you add an RSS feed, you can set it up to automatically pull blog posts and other new content on your website directly into your app.

To add an RSS feed to your app, all you need is your RSS URL. App Studio takes care of the rest. To find that URL, search your website for a reference to RSS.

> **NOTE**   You can find more information about RSS feeds at *aka.ms/wordpressfeeds*.

After you find the URL, follow these steps:

1. Click the Content tab at the top of the App Studio screen.

2. Click Rss (see Figure 11-5).

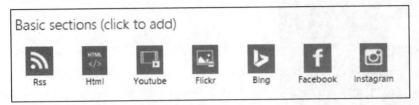

FIGURE 11-5 Click Rss to add an RSS feed to your app.

3. The Add Rss Section dialog box opens (see Figure 11-6). In the Section Name box, enter a name for the section that will contain this data source.

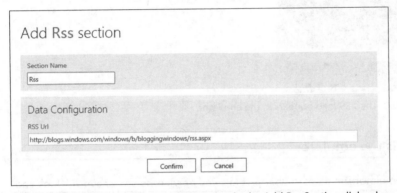

FIGURE 11-6 Enter a name for your RSS section in the Add Rss Section dialog box.

4. In the RSS URL field, enter the RSS URL you identified earlier. Then click Confirm. The section you added appears in the emulator on the left side of the screen (see Figure 11-7).

FIGURE 11-7 The RSS feed appears in the emulator.

What is the emulator?

The emulator simulates your app. It lets you preview how your app will look and work. As you design, develop, debug, and test your app, you'll find the emulator to be a useful tool!

Add a static HTML page

You use the HTML data source to enter a very limited form of raw HTML. HTML is a language used to create the layout of webpages. One use of HTML is to display static text, or text that doesn't change. A good example of this is the text that appears on an About page in your app. To add an HTML data source, follow these steps:

1. Click Html (see Figure 11-5, shown earlier in this chapter).
2. The Add Html Section dialog box opens (see Figure 11-8). In the Section Name box, enter a name for the section that will contain this data source.

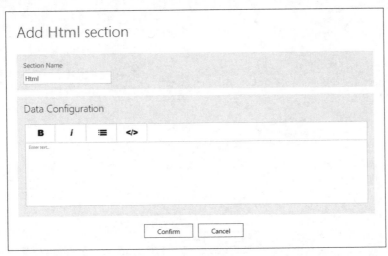

FIGURE 11-8 Enter a name for your HTML section in the Add Html Section dialog box.

3. In the Data Configuration box, enter the static text that you want to appear in your app—for example, **This is my app**. If you want, apply bold or italic formatting to the text, or format it as a list.

4. Click Confirm. The section you added appears in the emulator on the left side of the screen.

> **NOTE** Although you can create an About page with the HTML data source, you will soon discover that App Studio has a better solution to this.

Add a YouTube video page

You use the YouTube data source to incorporate YouTube videos into your app. If you have a YouTube channel for your business, you can use this data source to share videos from that channel in your mobile app. It's just another way to keep your customers up to date with what is going on in your business. Follow these steps:

1. Click Youtube (see Figure 11-5, shown earlier in this chapter).

2. The Add YouTube Section dialog box opens (see Figure 11-9). In the Section Name box, enter a name for the section that will contain this data source.

FIGURE 11-9 Enter a name for your YouTube section in the Add YouTube Section dialog box.

3. In the Data Configuration section, enter a YouTube channel name or search term.

4. Go to *aka.ms/youtubedatasource* and follow the steps to get an API key.

5. Click Confirm. The section you added appears in the emulator on the left side of the screen.

Add a Flickr photo stream

In addition to videos, you can share pictures on your app. If your company has a Flickr stream—for example, with pictures of customers engaging with your business—you can add it as a data source. Follow these steps:

1. Click Flickr (see Figure 11-5, shown earlier in this chapter).

2. The Add Flickr Section dialog box opens (see Figure 11-10). In the Section Name box, enter a name for the section that will contain this data source.

FIGURE 11-10 Enter a name for your Flickr section in the Add Flickr Section dialog box.

3. In the Data Configuration section, enter a user ID or search term and click Confirm. The section you added appears in the emulator on the left side of the screen.

Add a Bing news page

You can use a Bing data source in your app so that users can quickly view recent news about your information, as if they had searched for your company by using Bing in a regular web browser. All you need to do is tell App Studio what to search for. To add Bing as a data source, follow these steps:

1. Click Bing (see Figure 11-5, shown earlier in this chapter).

2. The Add Bing Section dialog box opens (see Figure 11-11). In the Section Name box, enter a name for the section that will contain this data source.

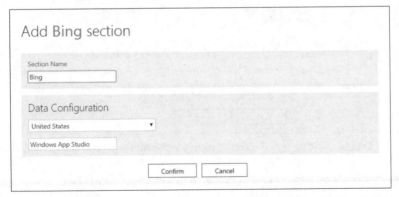

FIGURE 11-11 Enter a name for your Bing section in the Add Bing Section dialog box.

3. In the Data Configuration section, choose the geographic area where your company is located, and enter a search term. Then click Confirm. The section you added appears in the emulator on the left side of the screen.

> **NOTE** Depending on how well-known your business is, you might have to be more specific with your search terms to get relevant results. Play around to discover which search terms return the best results.

Add your Facebook page

Instead of requiring users to manually open their browsers or Facebook mobile apps to view your Facebook page, you can display it right inside your app. If you keep your Facebook page updated and relevant, this data source, similar to the RSS data source, is a great way to create an immediate connection with your customers. Here's how it's done:

1. Click Facebook (see Figure 11-5, shown earlier in this chapter).

2. The Add Facebook Section dialog box opens (see Figure 11-12). In the Section Name box, enter a name for the section that will contain this data source.

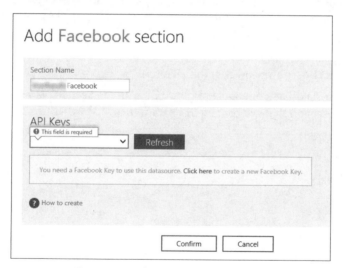

FIGURE 11-12 Enter a name for your Facebook section in the Add Facebook Section dialog box.

3. Go to *aka.ms/facebookdatasource* and follow the steps to get an API key.

4. Click Confirm. The section you added appears in the emulator on the left side of the screen.

Add your Instagram feed

Just as you can set up your app so that users can view your Facebook page from within the app, you can also set it up so that they can view your Instagram feed. Follow these steps:

1. Click Instagram (see Figure 11-5, shown earlier in this chapter).

2. The Add Instagram Section dialog box opens (see Figure 11-13). In the Section Name box, enter a name for the section that will contain this data source.

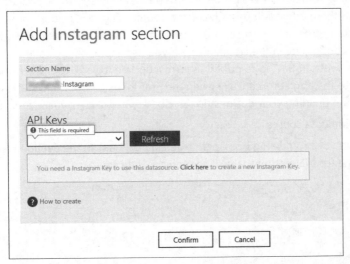

FIGURE 11-13 Enter a name for your Instagram section in the Add Instagram Section dialog box.

3. Go to *aka.ms/instagramdatasource* and follow the steps to get an API key.

4. Click Confirm. The section you added appears in the emulator on the left side of the screen.

Add a collection

You use a *collection* to upload data that you choose. This is content you create rather than content you bring in from a website. A collection is much like a database. A simple example is an Excel document in which you store a list of movies, including title, rating, and year released. A more practical example might be a list of employees, highlighting their experience and including contact information. Or you could display a list of your products with a name, image, description, and cost for each.

You can use several types of columns, including string (text), int (number), image, email, and phone number. These last two—email and phone number—are especially useful because when the user taps them, the appropriate email app or call function opens. (Note that the call function only works on Windows Phone. It does not work in Windows 8.1.)

When you use a collection, it's important to understand the difference between static resources and dynamic resources.

- **Static resources**   These resources do not change. They are stored and packaged within your app.

- **Dynamic resources**   These resources can be updated at any time. They are actually stored in the cloud.

The advantage of using static resources is that your user does not need to be connected to the Internet to access them. Although this advantage is something to consider, your users will likely be connected to Wi-Fi or cellular service most of the time. The advantage of using dynamic resources, or storing data in the cloud, is that if you need to update a collection, you can do so in App Studio without having to publish a formal update to your app. The updated data will be brought into the app automatically when the user loads it from the cloud. In this example, because you are building your business in the cloud, you will use dynamic resources:

1. Click the Collection data source.

2. The Add Collection Section dialog box opens (see Figure 11-14). In the Section Name box, enter a name for the section that will contain this data source.

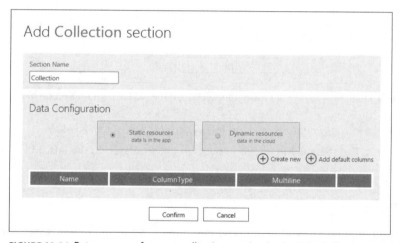

FIGURE 11-14 Enter a name for your collection section in the Add Collection Section dialog box.

3. In the Data Configuration section, click Dynamic Resources. Then click Add Default Columns.

4. Depending on the type of data you want to include, add the appropriate information to each column. You can specify the following:

- **Name** The name of your column
- **ColumnType** The type of data to be stored in the column (text or number, for instance)
- **Multiline** A true or false value for whether that piece of data can have multiple lines

5. Click Confirm. The collection you added appears in the emulator on the left side of the screen.

Add a menu

A menu is not exactly a data source, but it fits best in this category. A *menu* is an individual page that contains a list of items—either links to other application sections or *actions*. You use an *action* to instruct your device to perform a task, such as calling a phone number, emailing a specified email address, getting directions to a particular location, or navigating to a webpage. To add a menu, follow these steps:

> **TIP** You can use a menu to list a set of links to other sections for a nice workaround of the six-section limit. If you use a menu as one of your sections, you can then point to an additional six sections. For more information, go to *aka.ms/appbarwinphone*.

1. Click the Menu data source.

2. The Add Menu Section dialog box opens (see Figure 11-15). In the Section Name box, enter a name for the section that will contain this data source.

FIGURE 11-15 Enter a name for your menu section in the Add Menu Section dialog box.

3. Click Confirm. The Data Source page opens (see Figure 11-16). To add an application section to the menu, click its icon. To add a menu action, click the MenuAction button (white chevron). A blank application section appears. Add what you want the menu to do. When you're finished, click Save. The menu you added appears in the emulator on the left side of the screen.

FIGURE 11-16 Add application sections to your menu on the Data Source page.

Create a visually rich app

Your app could contain a lot of useful information and countless ways to improve your customers' lives. But if it's not pretty to look at, your users won't use it. You must create an app that is visually appealing. In this section, you'll learn how.

Apply a theme

App Studio offers several themes. A theme is a set of graphic elements that you can use to change the look and feel of your app. Specifically, when you choose a theme, you apply a color scheme that affects the color of the text, background, foreground, and application bar along the bottom of the screen. You can also set a background image for your app, either one of your own or one provided for you by App Studio. These might seem like small things, but they go a long way toward customizing the look and feel of your app to fit your business.

> **TIP** If you have a logo, consider using it for your background image. Then change the theme to one that fits with your logo.

To apply a theme, follow these steps:

1. Click the Themes tab at the top of the App Studio screen.

2. The Edit Your Theme page opens (see Figure 11-17). In this example, you'll apply a custom theme. Click the Background list and click the background color you want.

FIGURE 11-17 Apply a theme on the Edit Your Theme page.

3. Click the Box Foreground list and click the foreground color you want.

4. Click the Appbar Background list and click the color you want to use for the application bar.

5. Click the Background arrow.

6. The Select The Image Source dialog box opens (see Figure 11-18). Click the image source—your computer, your OneDrive, or App Studio resources. (In this example, My Computer is selected.)

FIGURE 11-18 Click an image source in the Select The Image Source dialog box.

7. Locate and select the image you want to use, and then click Open. Click Finish to apply the theme and background image. Your changes appear in the emulator on the left side of the screen.

Set the tile

In addition to applying a theme to your application, you can change its tile. The *tile* is the icon that represents your app on the user's Start screen.

Every app has a default tile. However, you can change the default tile and add tiles. There are three tile options to choose from:

- **Flip template** With this option, you can apply a front and back image to your tile. The tile will repeatedly flip between the two images. Both images should be aligned with your app and brand.

- **Cycle template** With this option, you can create a slide show of up to nine images in a collection. (You must create the collection containing the images before choosing this option.)

- **Iconic template** This is a static tile that constantly displays the image you choose.

To change the tile, follow these steps:

1. Click the Tiles tab at the top of the App Studio screen. The Select Your Tiles page opens.

2. If necessary, click Tiles.

3. In this example, you'll set a static tile. Click Iconic Template on the left. A series of options appears on the right (see Figure 11-19).

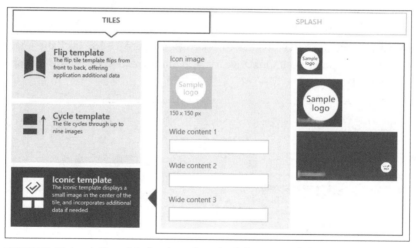

FIGURE 11-19 Iconic Template is selected on the Select Your Tiles page.

4. Click Icon Image and browse to an image or logo.

5. Click Save. Your changes appear in the emulator on the left side of the screen.

Choose the splash screen

A *splash screen* is a screen that is displayed while an app is loading. You can set a splash screen for use with your app. Here's how:

1. On the Tiles tab, click Splash.

2. The Splash page opens (see Figure 11-20). Click the Edit button under the Windows Phone Splash Screen background image.

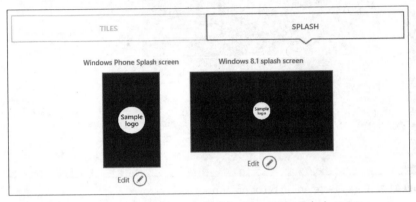

FIGURE 11-20 You can set a splash screen for your app on the Splash page.

3. The Choose File To Upload dialog box opens. Locate and select the image you want to use, click Open, and then click Crop. The image appears on the Splash page and will serve as the splash screen for your app.

4. Repeat steps 2 and 3 for the Windows 8.1 Splash Screen image.

Enable ads

Many companies choose to monetize their apps by including ads in them. This helps them to offset the costs associated with the app, so that they can offer their apps to users free of charge.

Before you can set up your app to handle ads, you must register it and obtain an app ID and an ad unit ID from Microsoft pubCenter.

NOTE App developers can use pubCenter to place ads in apps and earn money from them. Joining pubCenter is free.

To obtain your app ID and ad unit ID, follow these steps:

1. In your web browser, enter **https://pubcenter.microsoft.com/**.

2. The Microsoft pubCenter sign-in page opens. Sign in by using your Microsoft account credentials.

3. The page shown in Figure 11-21 opens. Click Create Ad Units For An App.

FIGURE 11-21 Click Create Ad Units For An App.

4. The Monetize New App page opens (see Figure 11-22). Click Windows Phone.

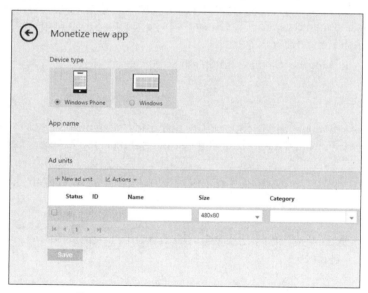

FIGURE 11-22 Choose Windows Phone as the device type on the Monetize New App page.

5. Enter your app's name in the App Name box.

6. In the Ad Units section, enter a name, size, and category for your app and then click Save.

7. The Ad Unit Details page opens (see Figure 11-23). Write down the app ID and ad unit ID, found at the bottom of the page.

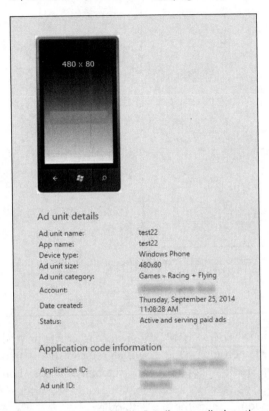

FIGURE 11-23 The Ad Units Details page displays the app ID and ad unit ID.

8. Repeat steps 3 through 7. This time, however, choose Windows as the device type. This will give you the app ID and ad unit ID for the Windows 8 version of your app.

9. Navigate to your App Studio project in your web browser and click the Publish Info tab.

10. Click Enable Ad Client to turn the option on (see Figure 11-24).

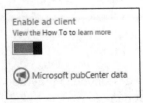

FIGURE 11-24 Turn on the Enable Ad Client option.

11. Click Microsoft pubCenter Data.

12. The Microsoft pubCenter Data dialog box opens (see Figure 11-25). Enter the app ID and ad unit ID for the Windows Phone and Windows 8.1 versions of your app. Then click Confirm.

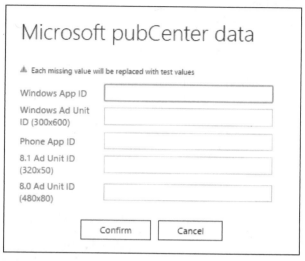

FIGURE 11-25 Enter the app ID and ad unit ID in the Microsoft pubCenter Data dialog box.

Create an About page

As mentioned earlier in this chapter, you can use an HTML data source to create an About page for your app. There's an easier way to accomplish this, however. You can specify that you want to include an About page, and App Studio will generate one automatically based on the information it has about your app. When you take this approach, App Studio also adds some nifty features, like giving the user the option to share the app with others.

To generate an About page automatically, follow these steps:

1. Click the Publish Info tab in App Studio.

2. Turn on the Include About Page option (see Figure 11-26).

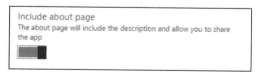

FIGURE 11-26 Turn on the Include About Page option.

3. Enter your app's name in the App Title box and enter a description in the App Description box. Then click Save to generate the About page.

Test and export your app

You've built a complete app to represent your business! Before you submit it to the Windows Store and Windows Phone Store, you must first test it and export it.

Test your app

Before you release your app, it's critical that you test it on an actual Windows Phone device. App Studio makes this easy: you can install the app on your device by scanning a QR code. You can then test all the sections of your app to make sure everything works as expected.

> **NOTE** You'll need to have a QR scanner app installed on your device for this to work. For more information about how to do this for Windows Phone 8.1, visit *windowscentral.com/top-qr-and-barcode-apps-windows-phone*.

To install the app on your phone in order to test it, you must first generate a package containing the app. Follow these steps:

1. On the Finish page in App Studio, click Generate (see Figure 11-27).

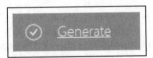

FIGURE 11-27 Click Generate on the Finish page.

2. The Generate App dialog box opens. Under Generation Type, turn on the Publish Packages and Installable Packages options, as shown in Figure 11-28. Finally, click Generate.

FIGURE 11-28 Click Generate in the Generate App dialog box.

3. App Studio opens a page that includes options to download the package for both Windows Phone 8.1 and Windows 8.1. Click Install Windows Phone 8.1 Certificate.

4. Use the QR scanner on your Windows Phone to scan the QR code on the Packages And Source Code page, shown in Figure 11-29. The app will be installed on your phone.

FIGURE 11-29 Scan the QR code on the Packages And Source Code page.

After the app is installed on your phone, take a few minutes to play around with it. Make sure everything looks as you expect it to. If you find any problems with the app, return to your project in App Studio, make the necessary changes, and then repeat the steps in this section to generate the app again.

> **TIP** App Studio provides a How To link for information about testing your app on a device. To access it, click How To under the appropriate package in the Packages And Source Code page. The documentation is very useful, so take some time to look through it.

> **TIP** If you have some programming experience, you can download your app's source code to review it. This gives you the ability to quickly create an app and then add more functionality to it in the source code. To access the source code, click Download Source Code on the Packages And Source Code page.

Export the package

Your next step is to export, or *publish*, the package containing your app. This generates the file that you'll submit to the Windows Store or Windows Phone Store, as described in the next section.

To export your app, follow these steps:

1. On the Packages And Source Code page click the Download Package button under the Windows Phone 8.1 option (see Figure 11-30).

FIGURE 11-30 Click the Download Package button under the Windows Phone 8.1 option.

2. In the same section of the Packages And Source Code page, click the Download Package button under the Windows 8.1 option.

3. Navigate to the two files you just downloaded (AppStudio.WindowsPhone_1.0.0._AnyCPU.appx and StoreApp.zip). These will be in your Downloads folder by default.

4. Right-click the StoreApp.zip file and click Extract All to extract the files.

5. Open the StoreApp folder to view its contents. There should be four files in the folder.

Submit your app to the Windows Store and Windows Phone Store

Your last step is to submit your app to the Windows Store and Windows Phone Store. After you do, your customers will be able to download your app to their computers or mobile devices.

> **NOTE**   Your app won't be available to customers immediately after you submit it. First, it must undergo testing by Windows Store testers. You'll be notified when the app is available for download by customers.

The steps for submitting to the Windows Store and Windows Phone Store are slightly different. To submit your app to the Windows Store, do the following:

1. In your web browser, enter **http://www.dev.windows.com** to open the Windows Dev Center page (see Figure 11-31).

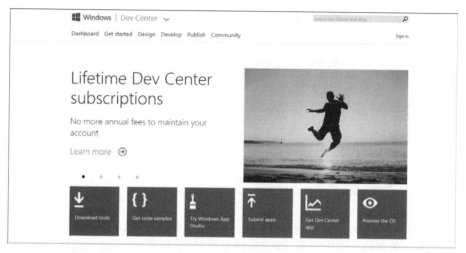

FIGURE 11-31 Start by going to the Dev Center page.

2. Click Sign In and enter your Microsoft account credentials.

3. Click Dashboard. Under Choose Your Dashboard, click Windows Store (see Figure 11-32).

FIGURE 11-32 Choose the Windows Store dashboard.

4. The My Apps page opens (see Figure 11-33). Under Dashboard, click Submit An App.

5. The Submit An App page opens (see Figure 11-34). Click App Name.

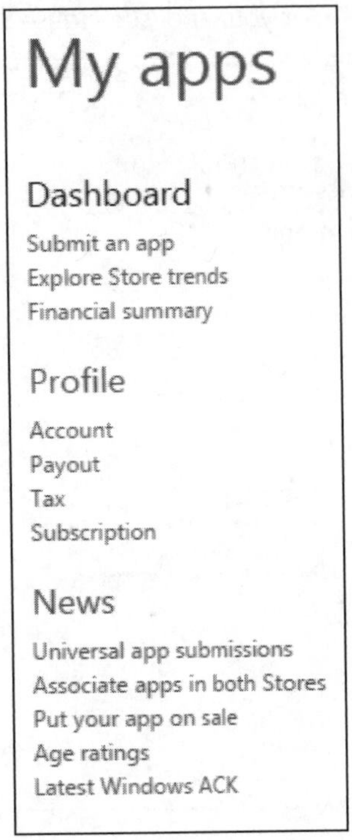

My apps

Dashboard

Submit an app
Explore Store trends
Financial summary

Profile

Account
Payout
Tax
Subscription

News

Universal app submissions
Associate apps in both Stores
Put your app on sale
Age ratings
Latest Windows ACK

FIGURE 11-33 Click Submit An App on the My Apps page.

FIGURE 11-34 Click App Name on the Submit An App page.

6. In the App Name box, enter the name you want to use for your app (see Figure 11-35). This is the name under which the app will be listed in the Windows Store. Then click Reserve App Name.

> **NOTE** The app name you enter must be unique. If there's already an app with the name you entered, you'll be prompted to enter a different one.

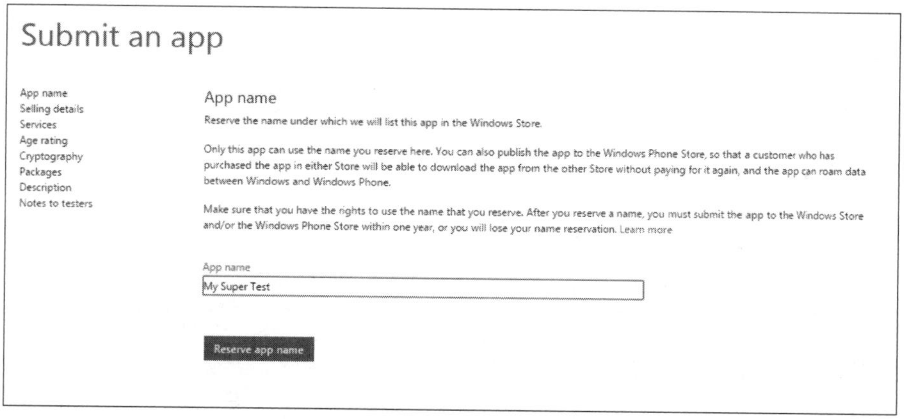

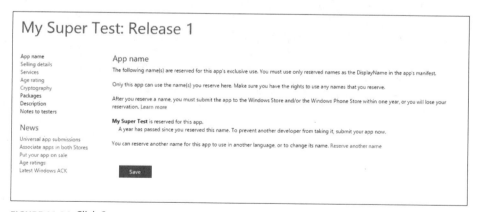

FIGURE 11-35 Enter your app's name in the App Name box.

7. A page showing your app name (in this example, My Super Test) and release number (in this case, Release 1) opens, as shown in Figure 11-36. Click Save.

FIGURE 11-36 Click Save to save your app name.

8. The Submit An App page opens. In this example, the page is now titled My Super Test Release 1 App. Click Selling Details.

9. The Selling Details page opens. Enter a price for your app, choose a category and sub-category, and select the markets for your app. Then click Save.

TIP For more information about choosing your markets, visit *aka.ms/choosingmarkets*.

10. Back on the My Super Test Release 1 App page, click Services.

11. The Services page opens. Click Live Services Site, as shown in Figure 11-37.

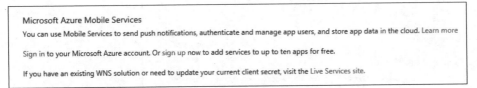

Microsoft Azure Mobile Services

You can use Mobile Services to send push notifications, authenticate and manage app users, and store app data in the cloud. Learn more

Sign in to your Microsoft Azure account. Or sign up now to add services to up to ten apps for free.

If you have an existing WNS solution or need to update your current client secret, visit the Live Services site.

FIGURE 11-37 Click Live Services Site.

12. The App Settings page opens. Notice that it includes an application ID and a publisher ID, as shown in Figure 11-38. Keeping this tab open in your browser, open a new tab, navigate to App Studio, and click the Publish Info tab.

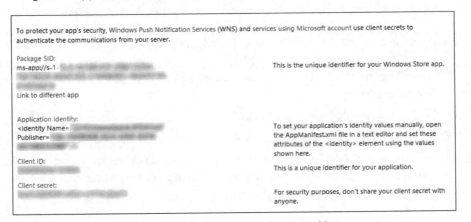

To protect your app's security, Windows Push Notification Services (WNS) and services using Microsoft account use client secrets to authenticate the communications from your server.

Package SID:
ms-app://s-1-

Link to different app

This is the unique identifier for your Windows Store app.

Application identity:
<Identity Name=
Publisher=

To set your application's identity values manually, open the AppManifest.xml file in a text editor and set these attributes of the <identity> element using the values shown here.

Client ID:

This is a unique identifier for your application.

Client secret:

For security purposes, don't share your client secret with anyone.

FIGURE 11-38 The application ID and publisher ID are shown on this page.

13. On the Publish Info page, click Associate App With The Store.

14. The Associate App With The Store dialog box opens (see Figure 11-39). Copy the app ID from the other tab and paste it into the App Identity box. Then enter the app's name in the App Display Name box.

Associate App with the Store

Check the How To to see where you can obtain this values.

App Identity:

Example: 0000AppStudio

App Display Name

Example: AppStudio

Publisher ID

Example: CN=00000000-0000-0000-0000-000000000000

Publisher Name

Example: AppStudio

Confirm   Cancel

FIGURE 11-39 Provide the requested information in the Associate App With The Store dialog box.

15. Copy the publisher ID from the other tab and paste it into the Publisher ID box. Then enter the publisher name in the Publisher Name box. When you're finished, click Confirm. (Remember that the publisher name is the name you created for your Windows Store developer account.)

16. On the Publish Info page, click Save.

17. Back on the My Super Test Release 1 App page, click Age Ratings.

18. The Age Ratings And Ratings Certificate page opens. Click the age rating you want. (You won't be uploading any age certificates in this example.) Then click Save.

19. Back on the My Super Test Release 1 App page, click Cryptography.

20. The Cryptography page opens. Click No, and then click Save.

> **NOTE** For more information about cryptography, go to *aka.ms/exportcrypto.*

21. Back on the My Super Test Release 1 App page, click Packages.

22. The Packages page opens. Click Browse To Files, upload the .appx file that you exported from App Studio, and click Save.

23. Back on the My Super Test Release 1 App page, click Description.

24. The Description page opens. Enter a description for the app. Then upload the screen shots in the WinPublishPackage folder. Finally, click Save.

25. Back on the My Super Test Release 1 App page, click Notes To Testers.

26. The Notes To Testers page opens. If you have information you want to share with the Windows Store testers, enter it here. Then click Save.

27. Back on the My Super Test Release 1 App page, click the Submit For Certification button. Your app is submitted to the Windows Store.

As mentioned, the steps for submitting to the Windows Store and Windows Phone Store are slightly different. Here's what you need to do to submit your app to the Windows Phone Store:

1. Navigate to the Windows Phone dashboard (see Figure 11-32, shown earlier in this chapter).

2. On the Dashboard page (see Figure 11-40), click Submit App.

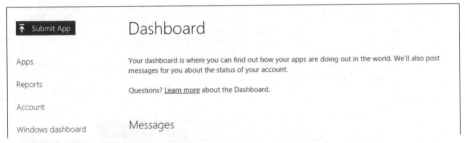

FIGURE 11-40 Click Submit App on the Windows Phone Store Dashboard page.

3. The Submit App page opens (see Figure 11-41). Click App Info.

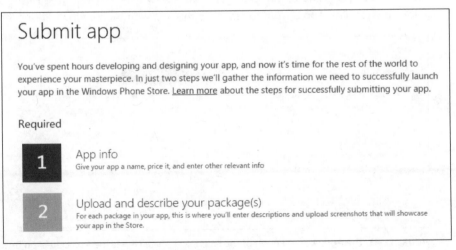

FIGURE 11-41 Click App Info on the Submit App page.

4. The App Info page opens. In the App Name section of the page (see Figure 11-42), click the Name list and choose the app you submitted in the previous steps to the Windows Store.

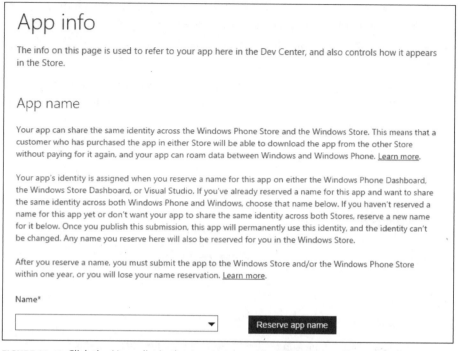

FIGURE 11-42 Click the Name list in the App Name section of the App Info page.

5. The Reserve App Name button changes to an Associate App button (see Figure 11-43). Click the Associate App button to associate this app with the Windows Phone Store.

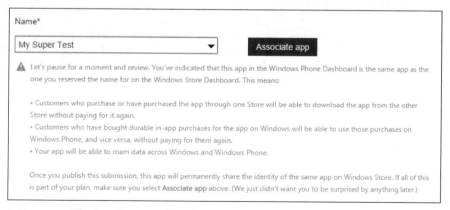

FIGURE 11-43 The App Name section of the App Info page includes the Associate App button.

6. In the App Category section of the App Info page (see Figure 11-44), click the Category list and then click the category that best describes your app. Do the same in the Subcategory list.

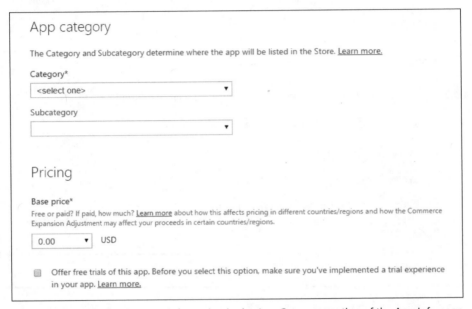

FIGURE 11-44 Enter the category information in the App Category section of the App Info page.

7. In the Pricing section of the App Info page (also shown in Figure 11-44), enter a price that is appropriate for your app. (This app will be free.)

8. In the Market Distribution section of the App Info page (see Figure 11-45), click Distribute To All Available Markets At The Base Price Tier. This will make your app available in as many markets as possible. Click Save.

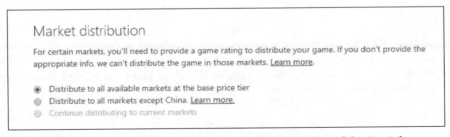

FIGURE 11-45 Click the first option in the Market Distribution section of the App Info page.

9. On the Submit App page, click Upload And Describe Your Package(s).

10. The Packages page opens (see Figure 11-46). Click Add New.

Packages

This is an important page, because in addition to uploading your package, you're also creating your customer's first impression of your app. The info you provide will be part of the Store's listing of your app. If you're updating an existing app, this page will also include packages that you've already uploaded. All these packages will be available in the Store after you've published your submission.

Add new

FIGURE 11-46 Click Add New on the Packages page.

11. Upload your Windows Phone app package (see Figure 11-47).

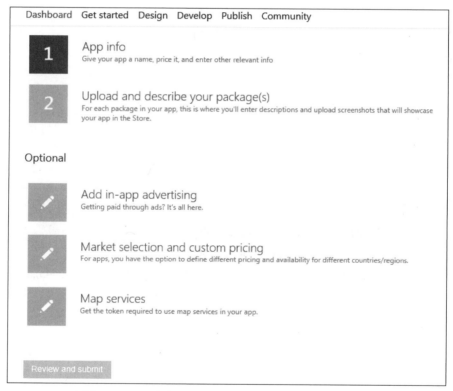

Dashboard   Get started   Design   Develop   Publish   Community

1   App info
Give your app a name, price it, and enter other relevant info

2   Upload and describe your package(s)
For each package in your app, this is where you'll enter descriptions and upload screenshots that will showcase your app in the Store.

Optional

Add in-app advertising
Getting paid through ads? It's all here.

Market selection and custom pricing
For apps, you have the option to define different pricing and availability for different countries/regions.

Map services
Get the token required to use map services in your app.

Review and submit

FIGURE 11-47 Adding your app information is the first step to the process; then you can upload and describe your package or packages.

12. Add a description, keywords, app, and screen shots (exported from App Studio) and click Save.

13. Click Review and Submit. Your Windows Phone app is submitted to the Windows Phone Store.

Summary

- Although building a website is important, it is no longer enough. Today's users want mobile apps. A mobile app acts as a supplement to your website and a powerful tool in its own right.

- Before you start building your app, you must answer two simple questions: What kind of app do you want to make, and what mobile platforms do you want to target?

- Building an app for the three major mobile device platforms typically means using at least three different programming languages. If you want to develop an app for all three platforms, you will likely need a team of developers, with different members dedicated to each platform to build and then maintain each version of the app. If you have no dedicated team to build your app, you can use Windows App Studio. Windows App Studio is a free, browser-based program that you can use to build Windows Phone and Windows 8 mobile apps—no programming knowledge needed.

- App Studio projects are made up of two key components: data sources and application sections. A data source is any information you want to include in your app. An application section is a page in your app that contains a data source.

- Your app could contain a lot of useful information and countless ways to improve your customers' lives. But if it's not pretty to look at, your customers probably won't use it. You must create an app that is visually appealing. You can do this by applying themes, changing the app's tile, and implementing a splash screen.

- App Studio offers several themes. A *theme* is a set of graphic elements that you can use to change the look and feel of your app. When you choose a theme, you apply a color scheme that affects the color of the text, background, foreground, and application bar along the bottom of the screen. You can also set a background image for your app, either one of your own or one provided for you by App Studio.

- In addition to applying a theme to your app, you can change its tile. The tile is the icon that represents your app on the user's Start screen.

- A splash screen is a screen that is displayed while an app is loading.

- Many companies choose to monetize their apps by including ads in them. This helps them to offset the costs associated with the app, so that they can offer their apps to users free of charge.

- Before you submit your complete mobile app to the Windows Store and Windows Phone Store, you must first test it and export it.

- Before you release your app, it's critical that you test it on an actual Windows Phone device. App Studio makes this easy: you can install the app on your device by scanning a QR code. You can then test all the sections of your app to make sure everything works as expected.

- Exporting, or publishing, the package containing your app generates the file that you'll submit to the Windows Store or Windows Phone Store.

- Your last step is to submit your app to the Windows Store and Windows Phone Store. After you do, your customers will be able to download your app to their computers or mobile devices. (Note that your app won't be available to customers immediately after you submit it. First, it must undergo testing by Windows Store testers. You'll be notified when the app is available for download by customers.)

Index

A

A/B testing 80
Access 8
Access Panel Extension 213–215
Account Portal, Microsoft Intune 88–93
accounts
    associating 65, 66
    creating 63, 72
    Microsoft Dynamics CRM Online 63–65
    Microsoft Intune, managing 88
    Office 365, adding 22–26
    searching 65
actions 255
Active Directory Domain Services (AD DS)
    See also security
    ADSIEdit tool 149
    described 148
    role 176
    virtual machines, installing on 148
Active Directory Users and Computers tool 153
activities
    adding 72, 74–76, 78
    editing 78
    logging calls 75
    viewing 78, 79
AD DS (Active Directory Domain Services)
  See Active Directory Domain Services (AD DS)
ad unit ID 259
Add-WindowsFeature cmdlet 185
Admin Center
    adding users 22–26
    app tiles 14
    dashboard 14
    editing user accounts 26

    managing domains 21
    Office 365 14, 33
    SharePoint 29, 30
Admin Console, Microsoft Intune 94, 95
ads, enabling on apps 259–262
ADSIEdit tool 149
alerts
    Microsoft Intune 95, 98–100
    public cloud services 155–157
Android
    Company Portal app 121
    email 32
    Microsoft Dynamics CRM Online app 82
    Office Mobile 32
    OneDrive app 50
    policy-managed apps 117
    programming languages 243
    RemoteApp, setting up 199–203
APNs (Apple Push Notification service) certificate
    110–116
app ID 259
App Studio *See* Windows App Studio
Apple Push Notification service (APNs) certificate
    110–116
applications
    Office 365 7–9
    Office Mobile 11, 33
    Office Online 11
Application Server role 176
apps
    See also mobile apps; third-party apps
    Microsoft Dynamics CRM Online 82
    publishing 196, 197
    remote access 189
    RemoteApp 189

H

history, files 45, 46
hosting providers 16
HTML pages, adding to apps 248, 249
hybrid cloud 2 *See also* private cloud; public cloud
hybrid deployment 189

I

IaaS (infrastructure as a service) 2, 3, 130 *See also* Azure
iconic template, tiles 258
IDs, ad unit and app 259
IIS role *See* Web Server (IIS) role
importing contacts 58–61
infrastructure as a service (IaaS) 2, 3
Instagram feed, adding to apps 253
instant messaging, Skype for Business 4, 9
in-store excellence business process 77
Internet browser, accessing OneDrive 47
Internet Information Services *See* Web Server (IIS) role
Internet Protocol (IP) addresses 137
Intune *See* Microsoft Intune
iOS
    Apple Push Notification service (APNs) certificate 110–116
    Company Portal app 121
    email 32
    Microsoft Dynamics CRM Online app 82
    Office Mobile 32
    OneDrive app 50
    policy-managed apps 117
    programming languages 243
    RemoteApp, setting up 199–203
iPad
    Microsoft Dynamics CRM Online app 82
    Microsoft Office for iPad 31
IP addresses 137
iPhone, Microsoft Dynamics CRM Online app 82

K

Key Influencers Report 81

L

Languages Report 81
leads
    converting to opportunities 68
    Microsoft Dynamics CRM Online 66–68
    searching 67
Lean Startup 242
licensing
    See also subscriptions
    available subscriptions 25
    Microsoft Intune 95
    Office 365 26
    subscription model 2
logging calls 75
Lync *See* Skype for Business

M

malware 95, 98
marketing *See* Microsoft Dynamics Marketing
marketing list builder business process 77
marketing messages 80
marketing reports 80
markets for mobile apps 269
menus, adding to apps 255
Microsoft Access 8
Microsoft Azure *See* Azure
Microsoft Azure Backup 164, 165
Microsoft Azure For Businesses, free trial xiv
Microsoft Azure RemoteApp *See* RemoteApp
Microsoft BizSpark 244
Microsoft Developer account 244
Microsoft Dynamics CRM Online
    See also CRM (customer relationship management)
    accounts data type 58, 63–66
    activities, adding 78
    activities, tracking 74–80
    Android app 82
    business processes, automated 76, 77
    Buzz Report 81
    case data types 58, 70–74
    contacts, creating 61
    contacts data type 58–62
    contacts, editing 62
    contacts, importing 58–61
    contacts, viewing 62

P

S

X

Y

About the author

Raised in Spokane, Washington, Blain Barton has been with Microsoft for more than 22 years and has held many diverse positions, starting in 1988 as a Team Leader in Manufacturing and Distribution, then progressing to Team Manager for Microsoft Visual Basic within Microsoft Product Support, Product Consultant for the Microsoft Word Division, and OEM Systems Engineer. He currently serves as a Senior Technical Evangelist within the US Developer Experience and Evangelism - DX Team working with IT Professionals and startup companies.

Blain has organized and delivered a wide array of technical events. He has presented more than 2,000 live events and has received several "top-presenter" speaking awards. He has traveled around the world, delivering OEM training sessions about pre-installing Windows on new PCs.

In 2010, Blain co-founded IT Pro Camp, Inc., a 501(c)(3) charity in Tampa, Florida, raising sponsorship support for delivering IT pro events within his local communities. He attended Washington State University, graduating with a bachelor's degree in English and business, with a minor in computer science. After college, Blain was a professional snow skiing instructor in the Cascade Mountains before starting his career with Microsoft. When Blain is not working in the IT field, he enjoys biking, boating, fishing, and drumming. In addition to his hobbies, he runs a 10-acre palm tree silviculture operation in Homosassa, Florida, and currently resides outside of Tampa, Florida. You can find Blain on Facebook and LinkedIn, read his blog (*aka.ms/blainbarton*), and follow him on Twitter @blainbar.

About the contributors

Adnan Cartwright   The CEO of Integrity Solutions, Inc., Adnan has worked with many companies to help them secure, expand, and maintain their networks by using the most up-to-date technology available. He is a recipient of the Microsoft Most Valuable Professional (MVP) award in Software Packaging, Deployment, and Servicing. A graduate from the ITT Technical Institute with degrees in Information Technology and Computer Networking Systems and Information Systems Security, Adnan is actively involved within the technical community and presents at numerous events. He is also the founder of the Florida IT Server Group, which is located both in South Florida and Jacksonville, Florida. Adnan has a passion for teaching and sharing technical knowledge with both young adults and IT professionals. Adnan is one of the organizers of the IT Pro Camp and a volunteer for the I Center Community Foundation, which teaches IT skills to at-risk kids.

Yung Chou   Yung Chou is a Senior Technical Evangelist within the Microsoft US Developer Experience and Evangelism - DX team. Within the company, he has had opportunities on serving customers in the areas of support account management, technical support, technical sales, and evangelism. Prior to Microsoft, he established capacities in system programming, application development, consulting services, and IT management. His technical focuses have been on virtualization and cloud computing with strong interests in hybrid cloud, Windows Azure Infrastructure Services, and emerging enterprise computing architecture. He has been a frequent speaker in technical conferences, roadshow, and Microsoft events.

Jennelle Crothers   Before joining Microsoft, Jennelle spent 15 years as a systems administrator "jack of all trades" overseeing Windows domains, Microsoft Exchange Server, desktops, and other IT infrastructure systems, where she struck fear into the hearts of end users with complex password policies and email retention tags. When not reading something related to technology, Jennelle helps raise puppies for Guide Dogs for the Blind and enjoys reading dystopian novels. One of these days, she'll finish that quilt she started in 2011. Jennelle currently works on the US Developer Experience and Evangelism - DX Team as a Technical Evangelist. Follow her on Twitter @jkc137 or visit her blog at *www.techbunny.com.*

Joe Homnick   A Florida CPA, Joe has more than 30 years of IT experience and is a principal owner of Homnick Systems (HSI), an IT company located in Boca Raton, Florida. A Microsoft Certified Partner, HSI delivers services in the areas of system development and implementation through the practices of software consulting, development, training, and mentoring. They hold competencies in cloud implementation, business intelligence, software development, application life cycle

management, and portals and collaboration. Joe enjoys speaking and can be found presenting at conferences like Microsoft Tech Ed, the Microsoft Professional Developers Conference (PDC), and the SQL PASS Summit. Joe founded the Gold Coast Users Group (*GCUsersGroup.org*), which serves the South Florida area, delivering Microsoft SQL Server, operating systems, and developer knowledge to the community for more than 20 years. His previous professional experience includes being an adjunct professor at Florida Atlantic University and a computer audit specialist for KPMG. Check out his blog at *JoeBlog.Homnick.com* and network with him on Facebook, Twitter, and LinkedIn.

Alex Melching Alex works as a Senior Technical Specialist at TechHouse IT Consulting Solutions based in Sarasota, Florida, specializing in facilitating small businesses in the cloud with Microsoft Online Services, including Office 365, Microsoft Dynamics CRM Online, and Microsoft Azure. He is a member and speaker of the IT Pro Camp, a non-profit organization delivering free IT learning to local tech communities around Florida. Alex is an avid blogger for Alex's Cloud (*alexs-cloud.com*) on the Microsoft Office 365 and Azure platforms. Alex is heavily involved in the local tech community around the Tampa Bay area of Florida and actively speaks and demos at colleges, universities, tech events, and conferences.

Jeff Mitchell Jeff Mitchell is an IT Pro and problem solver who brings passion, expertise, and finesse to his work with both people and technology. During his 14 years in the field, Jeff has identified and implemented IT solutions ranging from geographically dispersed systems for small and medium clients to enterprise deployments of private and hybrid cloud integrated solutions. Heavily tied into the community of Northwest Florida, Jeff has worked as Infrastructure Admin, Chief Technology Officer, Office 365 Practice Manager, and Director of IT and Cloud Infrastructure. Jeff has been a member of the Pensacola ITT Tech's Program Advisory Committee, contributing to the school's degree programs in Information Systems and Cybersecurity and Network Systems Administration. He has also spoken at IT Gulf Coast, IT Pro Camps, SQL Saturdays, and other events throughout the southeastern United States. Jeff lives in Fort Walton Beach, Florida, where Bit-Wizards' corporate office is located. He knows more about Batman than you and enjoys New Orleans Saints football and playing the guitar. You can reach him on Twitter @JeffMitchellFL or at the following:

- **Speaker Blog URL:** *bitwizards.com/Blogs/Jeff-Mitchell*
- **Podcast: Full Frontal Nerdity – @ffntech ffntech.com** *https://itunes.apple.com/us/podcast/full-frontal-nerdity/id946699904?mt=2*
- **LinkedIn:** *linkedin.com/in/jeffmitchellfl/*

Tommy Patterson   Tommy began his virtualization adventure during the launch of VMware's ESX Server's initial release. At a time when most admins were adopting virtualization as a lab-only solution, he pushed through the performance hurdles to quickly bring production applications into virtualization. Since the early 2000s, Tommy has spent most of his career in a consulting role, providing assessments, engineering, planning, and implementation assistance to many members of the Fortune 500. Troubleshooting complicated scenarios and incorporating best practices into customers' production virtualization systems has been his passion for many years. Now he shares his knowledge of virtualization and cloud computing as a Senior Technical Evangelist in the US Developer Experience and Evangelism - DX Team in Atlanta Georgia. You can follow Tommy at *virtuallycloud9.com/*.

James Quick   After graduating from Vanderbilt University with a double major in computer science and Spanish, James joined Microsoft as a Technical Evangelist in South Florida, focusing on mobile application development for Windows 8 and Windows Phone. Since joining Microsoft, he has worked with various Meetup groups, organizations, and schools, giving professional development training for Miami Dade High School teachers and college professors, leading numerous workshops in the community, and speaking at local events such as ITPalooza and South Florida Code Camp. James currently works as a Technical Evangelist on the US Developer Experience and Evangelism - DX Team.

Kevin Remde   A Senior Technical Evangelist at Microsoft and a highly sought-after speaker and IT community organizer, Kevin is also a prolific blogger. He shares his thoughts, ideas, and tips on his "Full of I.T." blog (*aka.ms/FullOfIT*). Before joining Microsoft, Kevin held positions such as software engineer, information systems professional, and information systems manager. He loves sharing helpful new solutions and technologies with his IT professional peers. Kevin currently works on the US Developer Experience and Evangelism - DX Team.

Dan Stolts   Also known as the "ITProGuru," Dan is a technology expert in systems management and security. He is a Senior Technical Evangelist at Microsoft and also owns a hosting and consulting firm (*BayStateTechnology.com*). He is proficient in many enterprise technologies, especially in the server area (Windows Server, System Center, Virtualization, and Azure) and holds many certifications, including MCT, MCITP, MCSE, and TS. Dan currently specializes in system management, virtualization, and cloud technologies. He is an enthusiastic advocate of technology and is passionate about helping others. Dan currently works on the US Developer Experience and Evangelism - DX Team in Boston, Massachusetts. You can reach him on his primary blog at *itproguru.com* or on Twitter *@ITProGuru*.

Ed Wilson   Ed Wilson is the Microsoft Scripting Guy and a well-known scripting expert. He writes the daily Hey, Scripting Guy! blog at *blogs.technet.com/b /heyscriptingguy/*. He has also spoken at TechEd and at the Microsoft internal TechReady conferences. He has written more than a dozen books, including nine on Windows scripting that were published by Microsoft Press. He has also contributed to nearly a dozen other books. His newest book by Microsoft Press is *Windows PowerShell Best Practices*. Ed holds more than 20 industry certifications, including Microsoft Certified Systems Engineer (MCSE) and Certified Information Systems Security Professional (CISSP). Prior to coming to work for Microsoft, he was a senior consultant for a Microsoft Gold Certified Partner, where he specialized in Active Directory design and Exchange implementation. In his spare time, he is writing a mystery novel. For more about Ed you can go to *ewblog.edwilson.com /ewblog/*.

About the technical reviewer

Randall Galloway is the technical editor for numerous computer-related books covering Microsoft Exchange, SharePoint, Windows Server, Windows, SQL Server, Hyper-V, Windows PowerShell, Office, Microsoft Intune, System Center, Windows Server Update Services, and Azure Active Directory. He also has experience in creating content for Microsoft Certified Professional exams, Microsoft Press *Training Kits*, and Microsoft Official Curriculum courseware.

Randall currently works as a trusted business advisor, aligning Microsoft services to customer priorities, with responsibility for service delivery and satisfaction with key stakeholders. He has been working in the computer industry for 21 years and is a 15-year Microsoft veteran.

From technical overviews to drilldowns on special topics, get *free* ebooks from Microsoft Press at:

www.microsoftvirtualacademy.com/ebooks

Download your free ebooks in PDF, EPUB, and/or Mobi for Kindle formats.

Look for other great resources at Microsoft Virtual Academy, where you can learn new skills and help advance your career with free Microsoft training delivered by experts.

Microsoft Press

Now that you've read the book...

Tell us what you think!

Was it useful?
Did it teach you what you wanted to learn?
Was there room for improvement?

Let us know at http://aka.ms/tellpress

Your feedback goes directly to the staff at Microsoft Press,
and we read every one of your responses. Thanks in advance!

 Microsoft